ABSOLUTE BEGINNER'S GUIDE

TO

eBay®

Third Edition

Michael Miller

800 East 96th Street
Indianapolis, Indiana 46240

Absolute Beginner's Guide to eBay, Third Edition

Copyright © 2005 by Que Publishing

International Standard Book Number: 0-7897-3431-1

Library of Congress Catalog Card Number: 2005924989

Printed in the United States of America

First Printing: June 2005

08 07 06 05   4 3 2 1

Trademarks

All terms mentioned in this book that are known to be trademarks or service marks have been appropriately capitalized. Que Publishing cannot attest to the accuracy of this information. Use of a term in this book should not be regarded as affecting the validity of any trademark or service mark.

eBay is a registered trademark of eBay, Inc.

Warning and Disclaimer

Every effort has been made to make this book as complete and as accurate as possible, but no warranty or fitness is implied. The information provided is on an "as is" basis. The author and the publisher shall have neither liability nor responsibility to any person or entity with respect to any loss or damages arising from the information contained in this book.

Bulk Sales

Que Publishing offers excellent discounts on this book when ordered in quantity for bulk purchases or special sales. For more information, please contact

U.S. Corporate and Government Sales
1-800-382-3419
corpsales@pearsontechgroup.com

For sales outside of the U.S., please contact

International Sales
international@pearsoned.com

Associate Publisher
Greg Wiegand

Acquisitions Editor
Michelle Newcomb

Development Editor
Kevin Howard

Managing Editor
Charlotte Clapp

Project Editor
Dan Knott

Copy Editor
Cheri Clark

Indexer
Ken Johnson

Proofreader
Suzanne Thomas

Technical Editor
Jenna Lloyd

Publishing Coordinator
Sharry Lee Gregory

Interior Designer
Ann Jones

Cover Designer
Dan Armstrong

Page Layout
Susan Geiselman
Michelle Mitchell

Contents at a Glance

Table of Contents

About the Author

Michael Miller is a top eBay seller and a successful and prolific author. He has a reputation for practical, real-world advice and an unerring empathy for the needs of his readers.

Mr. Miller has written more than 60 nonfiction books over the past 15 years, for Que and other major publishers. His books for Que include *Tricks of the eBay Masters*, *Making a Living from Your eBay Business*, *Bad Pics Fixed Quick*, and *Absolute Beginner's Guide to Computer Basics*. He is known for his casual, easy-to-read writing style and his ability to explain a wide variety of complex topics to an everyday audience.

Mr. Miller is also president of The Molehill Group, a strategic consulting and authoring firm based in Carmel, Indiana. As a consultant, he specializes in providing strategic advice to and writing business plans for Internet- and technology-based businesses.

You can email Mr. Miller directly at abg-ebay@molehillgroup.com. His website is located at www.molehillgroup.com, and his eBay user ID is trapperjohn2000.

Dedication

To my mother and father—who spend too much time and money on eBay auctions!

Acknowledgments

Thanks to the usual suspects at Que, including but not limited to Greg Wiegand, Michelle Newcomb, Cheri Clark, Stephanie McComb, Kevin Howard, Dan Knott, Jenna Lloyd, Ken Johnson, and Suzanne Thomas.

We Want to Hear from You!

As the reader of this book, *you* are our most important critic and commentator. We value your opinion and want to know what we're doing right, what we could do better, what areas you'd like to see us publish in, and any other words of wisdom you're willing to pass our way.

As an associate publisher for Que Publishing, I welcome your comments. You can email or write me directly to let me know what you did or didn't like about this book—as well as what we can do to make our books better.

Please note that I cannot help you with technical problems related to the topic of this book. We do have a User Services group, however, where I will forward specific technical questions related to the book.

When you write, please be sure to include this book's title and author as well as your name, email address, and phone number. I will carefully review your comments and share them with the author and editors who worked on the book.

Email: feedback@quepublishing.com

Mail: Greg Wiegand
            Associate Publisher
            Que Publishing
            800 East 96th Street
            Indianapolis, IN 46240 USA

For more information about this book or another Que Publishing title, visit our Web site at www.quepublishing.com. Type the ISBN (excluding hyphens) or the title of a book in the Search field to find the page you're looking for.

INTRODUCTION

eBay is a true phenomenon.

In 2004, eBay transactions defined a new economy worth more than $34 billion. Read that number again; it's not a misprint. *Thirty-four billion dollars.* That's $34 billion in sales that didn't exist before eBay. Thirty-four billion dollars of transactions that appeared seemingly out of thin air. Thirty-four billion dollars in merchandise that wouldn't have been sold otherwise.

Where did that $34 billion come from? It came from you and from me and from 135 million other people around the world who log on to the eBay site to buy and to sell all manner of merchandise. Before eBay, there was no global marketplace for the 135 million of us; there was no way to buy and to sell that $34 billion of merchandise, except for small local garage sales and flea markets.

eBay made that $34 billion happen. eBay brought 135 million of us together.

In doing so, eBay became one of the first—and maybe the only—of the online businesses to make a profit from day one of its existence. eBay kept its costs low by not actually handling any of the merchandise traded on its site, and generated revenue by charging listing fees and sales commissions on every transaction.

Smart people, with a smart concept.

And here's somebody else who's smart about eBay:

You.

You're smart because you bought this book to help you learn how to buy and sell merchandise on the eBay site. You know that you need to learn how eBay works before you can start buying and selling, and you also know that a little extra knowledge can give you the edge you need to be a real auction winner.

Absolute Beginner's Guide to eBay, 3rd Edition, will help you get started with eBay auctions—even if you've never bought anything online in your life. Read this book and you'll learn how to bid and how to sell, and what to do when the auction ends.

More important, you'll learn how to maximize your chances of winning important eBay auctions—without paying through the nose. And if you're a seller, you'll learn how to stand out from the crowd and generate more bids—and higher selling prices.

You'll also learn that buying and selling on eBay isn't that hard, and that it can be a lot of fun. You'll even discover that you can actually make a living from your eBay activities, if you don't mind a little hard work.

Really!

How This Book Is Organized

This book is organized into five main parts:

- **Part I, "Essential eBay,"** shows you how online auctions work, as well as how to sign up for eBay membership and find your way around the eBay site.

- **Part II, "eBay for Bidders,"** tells you everything you need to know about bidding for items in eBay auctions. You'll take the Bidding 101 tutorial, learn how to search for specific types of items, discover the best ways to pay for those auctions you win, and find out how to avoid getting ripped off by unscrupulous sellers.

- **Part III, "eBay for Sellers,"** is the flip side of the coin. This section tells you everything you need to know about selling on eBay; you'll take the Selling 101 tutorial, figure out what to sell and for how much, determine what payment methods to accept, learn how to create more effective item listings, find out how to pack and ship your merchandise, and discover how to best manage your current auctions.

- **Part IV, "Using eBay's Advanced Features,"** is all about the little extras you can find on the eBay site. You'll discover how to track your auctions in My eBay, learn how to create a personal About Me page, and find out how to use post-auction feedback.

- **Part V, "Becoming a Power Seller,"** is for the really ambitious eBay user. You'll learn how to manage your auctions with third-party software and services, how to sell and ship internationally, and how to turn your hobby into a full-time profession—and make a real living from your eBay auctions.

Taken together, the 30 chapters in this book will help you get the most from your eBay experience. By the time you get to the end of the final chapter, you'll be buying and selling online just like a pro!

Conventions Used in This Book

I hope that this book is easy enough to figure out on its own, without requiring its own instruction manual. As you read through the pages, however, it helps to know precisely how I've presented specific types of information.

Web Page Addresses

There are a lot of Web page addresses in this book—including addresses for specific pages on the eBay site. They're noted as such:

www.molehillgroup.com

Technically, a Web page address is supposed to start with http:// (as in http://www.molehillgroup.com). Because Internet Explorer and other Web browsers automatically insert this piece of the address, however, you don't have to type it—and I haven't included it in any of the addresses in this book.

Special Elements

This book also includes a few special elements that provide additional information not included in the basic text. These elements are designed to supplement the text to make your learning faster, easier, and more efficient.

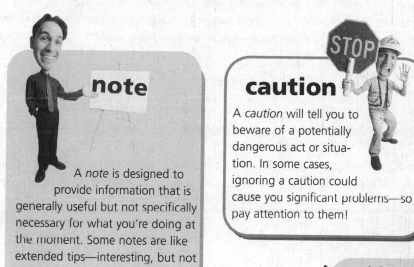

note

A *note* is designed to provide information that is generally useful but not specifically necessary for what you're doing at the moment. Some notes are like extended tips—interesting, but not essential.

caution

A *caution* will tell you to beware of a potentially dangerous act or situation. In some cases, ignoring a caution could cause you significant problems—so pay attention to them!

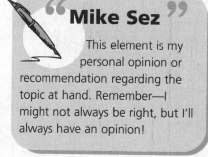

"Mike Sez"

This element is my personal opinion or recommendation regarding the topic at hand. Remember—I might not always be right, but I'll always have an opinion!

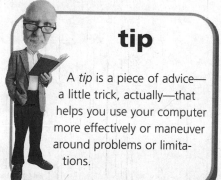

tip

A *tip* is a piece of advice—a little trick, actually—that helps you use your computer more effectively or maneuver around problems or limitations.

Finally, in various parts of this book you'll find big *checklists*. Use these checklists to prepare for the upcoming task—just check off the items on the list, and you'll be ready to go.

Further Reading

I'd be somewhat remiss if I didn't point you to further reading on the subject of
eBay—in particular, books you can read after this one to help you be even more successful with your eBay auctions. To this end, I draw your attention to two other
books I've written that you might find useful:

- *Tricks of the eBay Masters* (Que, 2004), which assembles 600 tricks and tips
  from almost 200 successful eBay buyers and sellers—great advice that any
  eBayer can use.

- *Making a Living from Your eBay Business* (Que, 2005), which shows you how to
  turn your eBay hobby into a profitable business. (This one's more of a business book than an eBay book—just what you need to turn pro!)

Let Me Know What You Think

I always love to hear from readers. If you want to contact me, feel free to email me
at abg-ebay@molehillgroup.com. I can't promise that I'll answer every message, but
I will promise that I'll read each one!

If you want to learn more about me and any new books I have cooking, check out
my Molehill Group website at www.molehillgroup.com. Who knows—you might find
some other books there that you'd like to read.

PART

i

ESSENTIAL EBAY

1

Introducing eBay, the World's Largest Online Auction

What is it you need?

A new hard drive for your computer? A vintage German military helmet? An authentic prop from your favorite movie? A specific trading card or comic book or Barbie doll? How about some jewelry, or an antique desk, or a new DVD recorder for your home theater system? Or, perhaps, you have one of these items that you would like to sell?

Whatever you're buying or selling, there's an increasingly popular way to trade merchandise over the Internet, called an *online auction*. And the biggest online auction is *eBay*.

What Is eBay—And How Did It Come to Be?

What is eBay? I think the site's official mission statement does a good job of summing up what eBay is all about:

> eBay's mission is to provide a global trading platform where practically anyone can trade practically anything.

What eBay does is simple: It facilitates the buying and selling of merchandise between users, over the Internet, in an auction format. This makes eBay a person-to-person auction site. eBay itself doesn't buy or sell anything; it carries no inventory and collects no payments. eBay is just the middleman in the auction process, hooking up buyers and sellers around the world—and collecting fees for doing so.

The eBay Story

eBay was one of the first auction sites on the Internet, launched way back on Labor Day of 1995. It almost single-handedly pioneered the concept of online auctions and, in doing so, carved out the dominant market share. (It also made a lot of money for those who invested in the firm—especially in the early years.)

As the official story goes, founder Pierre Omidyar launched eBay as the result of a conversation with his then-girlfriend, an avid collector of PEZ dispensers. She supposedly commented to Pierre about how great it would be if she were able to collect PEZ dispensers using the Internet. Pierre did her a favor and developed a small PEZ-dispenser trading site, originally called Auction Web.

This small site quickly became a big site. Pierre started charging users a small fee to list items, to help pay his expenses. The day that Pierre opened his mailbox and saw $10,000 worth of fees was the day he quit his day job and made eBay a full-time proposition.

Because of its fee-based model, eBay is that rare website that made money from day one. That made eBay an attractive candidate for venture capital investment and eventual IPO; the company did, in fact, go public in 1998, and it made a lot of people (including Pierre) a lot of money.

Today eBay is one of the most successful Internet businesses in the world, having weathered the storms of the dot-com implosion quite nicely,

note

Although this book focuses on eBay, there are some other online auction sites you might want to check out, including Amazon.com Auctions (auctions.amazon.com), Bidville (www.bidville.com), Overstock.com Auction (www.auctions. overstock.com), and Yahoo! Auctions (auctions.yahoo.com)—although none of these sites is nearly as big as eBay.

thank you. It also survived (and thrived) as dozens of smaller online auction sites closed their doors. The result is that eBay, under the leadership of current CEO Meg Whitman, is the dominant online auction site, with no real competition. It truly is the number-one place to buy and sell any type of item online.

How Big Is eBay?

How big is eBay? Just look at these statistics:

- On any given day eBay has close to *28 million items* listed for auction.
- As of the end of 2004, eBay had more than *135 million registered users*—56 million of which are "active" users.
- During the entire year of 2004, *$34 billion worth of merchandise*, in more than *1.4 billion individual transactions*, was traded over eBay.

All this activity makes eBay not only the biggest shopping site on the Internet, but also the largest online community of any type—bigger even than Yahoo! or America Online.

And that's not small potatoes.

How Does an eBay Auction Work?

If you've never used eBay before, you might be a little anxious about what might be involved. Never fear; participating in an online auction is a piece of cake, something tens of millions of other users have done before you. That means you don't have to reinvent any wheels; the procedures you have to follow are well established and well documented.

An online auction is an Internet-based version of a traditional auction—you know, the type where a fast-talking auctioneer stands in the front of the room, trying to coax potential buyers into bidding *just a little bit more* for the piece of merchandise up for bid. The only difference is that there's no fast-talking auctioneer online (the bidding process is executed by special auction software on the auction site), and your fellow bidders aren't in the same room with you—in fact, they might be located anywhere in the world. Anyone can be a bidder, as long as they have Internet access.

note

Before you can list an item for sale or place a bid on an item, you first have to register with eBay. There's no fee to register, although eBay does charge the seller a small *listing fee* to list an item for sale, and another small *transaction fee* when the item is sold. eBay doesn't charge any fees to buyers.

We'll get into the detailed steps involved with buying and selling later in this book; for now, let's walk through the general operation of a typical eBay auction:

1. You begin (as either a buyer or a seller) by registering with eBay.

2. The seller creates an ad for an item and lists the item on the auction site. (eBay charges anywhere from $0.25 to $4.80 to list an item.) In the item listing, the seller specifies the length of the auction (1, 3, 5, 7, or 10 days) and the minimum bid he or she will accept for that item.

3. A potential buyer searching for a particular type of item (or just browsing through all the merchandise listed in a specific category) reads the item listing and decides to make a bid. The bidder specifies the maximum amount he or she will pay; this amount has to be equal to or above the seller's minimum bid, or higher than any other existing bids.

4. eBay's built-in bidding software automatically places a bid for the bidder that bests the current bid by a specified amount—but doesn't reveal the bidder's maximum bid. For example, the current bid on an item might be $25. A bidder is willing to pay up to $40 for the item, and enters a maximum bid of $40. eBay's "proxy" software places a bid for the new bidder in the amount of $26—higher than the current bid, but less than the specified maximum bid. If there are no other bids, this bidder will win the auction with a $26 bid. Other potential buyers, however, can place additional bids; unless their maximum bids are more than the current bidder's $40 maximum, they are informed (by email) that they have been outbid—and the first bidder's current bid is automatically raised to match the new bids (up to the specified maximum bid price).

5. At the conclusion of an auction, eBay informs the high bidder of his or her winning bid. The seller is responsible for contacting the high bidder and arranging payment. When the seller receives the buyer's payment (by check, money order, or credit card), the seller then ships the merchandise directly to the buyer.

6. Concurrent with the close of the auction, eBay bills the seller for a small percentage (starting at 5.25%) of the final bid price. This selling fee is directly billed to the seller's credit card.

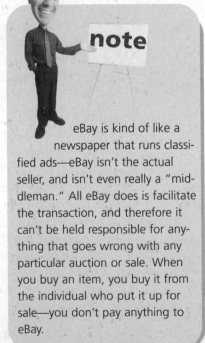

note

eBay is kind of like a newspaper that runs classified ads—eBay isn't the actual seller, and isn't even really a "middleman." All eBay does is facilitate the transaction, and therefore it can't be held responsible for anything that goes wrong with any particular auction or sale. When you buy an item, you buy it from the individual who put it up for sale—you don't pay anything to eBay.

That's how it works, in general. For more detailed instructions on how to bid in an eBay auction, see Chapter 3, "Bidding 101: A Tutorial for Beginning Bidders." For more detailed instructions on how to place an item for sale on eBay, see Chapter 10, "Selling 101: A Tutorial for Beginning Sellers."

What You Can—And What You Can't—Trade on eBay

As you can tell from eBay's mission statement, you should be able to trade practically anything you can think of on the eBay site. You can't trade literally everything, of course; there are some types of items that eBay refuses to deal with. Read on to learn more.

> **note**
>
> eBay management is constantly reevaluating its category listings—introducing new categories, subdividing crowded existing categories, or eliminating little-used categories.

Major Categories

To give you an idea of what you'll find up for auction, here's a list of eBay's major item categories:

- Antiques
- Art
- Books
- Business and industrial
- Cars, parts, and vehicles (eBay Motors)
- Cameras and photo
- Cell phones
- Clothing, shoes, and accessories
- Coins
- Collectibles
- Computers and networking
- Consumer electronics
- Crafts
- Dolls and bears
- DVDs and movies
- Entertainment memorabilia

- Gift certificates
- Health and beauty
- Home and garden
- Jewelry and watches
- Music
- Musical instruments
- Pottery and glass
- Real estate
- Specialty services
- Sporting goods
- Sports cards and memorabilia
- Stamps
- Tickets
- Toys and hobbies
- Travel
- Video games
- Everything else...

Most of these major categories include dozens—or hundreds—of subcategories for specific types of items. For example, the Collectibles category has more than three dozen subcategories (from Advertising to Vintage Sewing), and most of these subcategories have subcategories of their own. The result is that eBay is divided into literally thousands of separate categories and subcategories—with more being added every day.

What You *Can't* Trade on eBay

Of course, you can't sell just *anything* on eBay—there are some items that eBay prohibits you from selling. This list of what you *can't* buy or sell on eBay makes a lot of sense; most of these items are illegal, are controversial, or could expose eBay to various legal actions.

eBay's list of prohibited items includes the following:

- Alcohol
- Animals (except for tropical fish and snails) and wildlife products
- Catalog sales
- Counterfeit CDs, videos, computer software, or other items that infringe on someone else's copyright or trademark
- Counterfeit currency and stamps
- Credit cards
- Drugs and drug paraphernalia
- Embargoed goods and goods from prohibited countries
- Firearms and ammunition
- Fireworks
- Government IDs and licenses
- Human body parts and remains
- Lock-picking devices
- Lottery tickets
- Mailing lists and personal information
- Multi-level marketing, pyramid, and matrix programs
- Postage meters
- Prescription drugs and devices
- Recalled items
- Satellite and cable TV descramblers
- Stocks and other securities
- Stolen property

- Surveillance equipment
- Tobacco
- Weapons and knives

Other items, such as artifacts and adult items, fall into the questionable category. If you're in doubt about a particular item, check out eBay's Questionable Items page at pages.ebay.com/help/sell/questions/prohibited-items.html.

What's What (and What's Where) on eBay

Not even counting the millions of individual auction listings, eBay has a ton of content and community on its site—if you know where to find it. (And the home page isn't always the best place to find what you're looking for!)

eBay's Home Page—For New Users

On your first visit to the eBay site (www.ebay.com), you'll be prompted to register as a new user. The Welcome to eBay page, shown in Figure 1.1, provides some general overview information on using the site, and also provides a shortcut to registration. Just click the Register Now button, and then follow the onscreen instructions. (Learn more about eBay registration in Chapter 2, "Joining Up and Getting Started.")

FIGURE 1.1
Welcome to eBay—for new users.

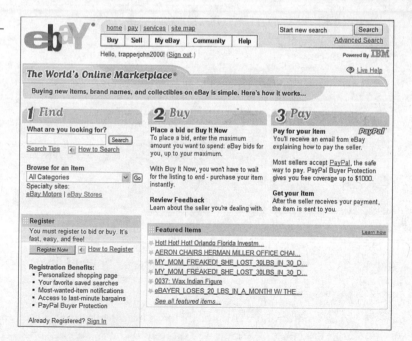

eBay's Home Page—For Registered Users

After you've registered with eBay, you see the site's normal home page, shown in Figure 1.2. From here, you can access eBay's most important features and services—as well as sign in to your eBay account, if you've already registered. (Learn more about eBay registration in Chapter 2, "Joining Up and Getting Started.")

note

There are also several links *above* the Navigation Bar—Home, Pay, Services, and Site Map. Like the Navigation Bar, these links appear at the top of most eBay pages.

FIGURE 1.2

Access the most important parts of eBay from the home page (www.ebay.com).

The big chunk of space in the middle of the page is probably best ignored; it's nothing more than a big advertisement for the category or items du jour. Better to focus on the links along the top and left side of the page.

Across the top of the home page—across virtually every eBay page, as a matter of fact—is the Navigation Bar. This bar includes links to the major sections of the eBay site: Buy, Sell, My eBay, Community, and Help. When you click one of these links, you go to the main page for that section.

To the right of the Navigation Bar is the Search box. This is what you use to search for items you might want to buy; enter your query into the box and then click the Search button. More advanced search options are available by clicking the Advanced Search link. (Learn more about searching eBay in Chapter 4, "Searching for Items to Buy.")

Along the left side of the home page is a collection of links to specific eBay item categories and specialty sites. When you want to find an item to bid on, it's easy to click through the categories listed on the left of the home page—or to search for items using the Search box.

For other key activities, refer to the information in Table 1.1, which shows you which links to click.

TABLE 1.1   Key Home Page Operations

To Do This	Click This Link
Sign up for eBay membership	Register
Sign into the eBay site (for buying and selling)	Sign In
Browse items for sale	Buy
Sell an item	Sell
Access your My eBay page	My eBay
Access message boards	Community
Read help files	Help
Get "live" help via instant messaging	Live Help
Pay for items you've purchased	Pay
Access various eBay services	Services
Access other parts of eBay via the Site Map	Site Map

Where to Find Everything Else: eBay's Site Map

Unfortunately, there's just so much stuff on the eBay site—and it's so haphazardly organized—that most users never find some of eBay's most interesting and useful features. In fact, you simply can't access many features from the home page. To really dig down into the eBay site, you need a little help—which you can get from eBay's Site Map page.

You can access the Site Map page by clicking the Site Map link above the Navigation Bar. This page, shown in Figure 1.3, serves as the true access point to eBay's numerous and diverse features.

If you've never visited the Site Map page, I guarantee you'll be surprised at everything you'll find there. The Site Map offers direct links to a bunch of features and services that you probably didn't even know existed!

FIGURE 1.3

Use the Site Map
to quickly access
all the different
parts of the eBay
site.

You can also use the links on the Site Map page to keep up with all the new features of the site—and keep up on the daily events and happenings. For example, if you're new to eBay, you might want to check out the discussion boards, community help, and chat rooms links in the Community section. If you want to learn how to use various site features, try the Buyer Guide and Seller Guide links in the Help section. To find out about any technical system updates (or planned outages), click the System Announcements link (in the News section).

Contacting eBay

Although you *could* use eBay's various discussion boards to try to contact eBay (as eBay suggests), you'll quickly discover that this method of communication often leaves something to be desired—like a fast response! Instead, try contacting eBay staff *directly* through the Web form support system. Start at the Contact Customer Support page (shown in Figure 1.4), located at pages.ebay.com/help/contact_inline/. Select a topic, subtopic, and specific issue, and then click Continue. The following "instant help" page includes links that answer the most common questions. To continue through to contact eBay, click the Email link to display the Contact Us form. Enter your message or question and then click the Send button.

You can also contact eBay by phone (800-322-9266 or 408-558-7400) or by snail mail, at

> eBay Inc.
>
> 2145 Hamilton Avenue
>
> San Jose, CA 95125

FIGURE 1.4

Contact eBay by using the form on the Contact Customer Support page.

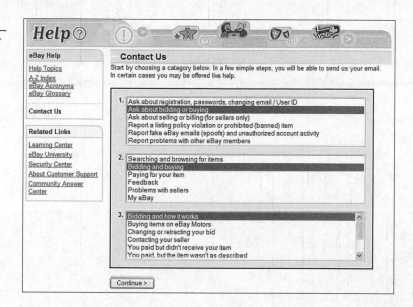

THE ABSOLUTE MINIMUM

Here are the key points to remember from this chapter:

■ eBay was founded in 1995 as a site for trading PEZ dispensers; today eBay is the world's largest online auction community, facilitating the trading of all sorts of items between buyers and sellers around the world.

■ An eBay online auction is similar to a traditional auction, except that automated bidding software replaces the role of the human auctioneer.

■ eBay's home page (www.ebay.com) lets you access the most important operations—although the Site Map page is better for finding all of eBay's features and services.

2

JOINING UP AND GETTING STARTED

You can browse through eBay's millions of listings anonymously (and without registering), but if you want to buy or sell something, you have to register with the eBay site. Registration involves telling eBay who you are, where you live, and how to contact you. If you're interested in selling on eBay, you'll also need to give eBay a valid credit card number—which won't be charged. (At least, not yet!)

Although eBay registration is free, selling an item isn't. You have to pay eBay a fee for every item you list for sale, and for every item you actually sell. You *don't* have to pay eBay when you buy an item; fees are charged exclusively to sellers.

Read on to learn more about eBay's registration process—and its fee structure.

Everybody Does It: Filling Out eBay's Registration Form

Registration is free, easy, and relatively quick. But before you register, you need to be prepared to enter some key information, as detailed in the following checklist:

Checklist: Before You Register

- ☐ Your name
- ☐ Your street address
- ☐ Your email address
- ☐ Your phone number
- ☐ Your date of birth
- ☐ Your credit card number (optional if you're only going to be bidding on items; mandatory if you're going to be selling items on auction)
- ☐ Your checking account number (not necessary if you're only going to be bidding on items; mandatory if you're going to be selling items on auction)

Signing Up for Basic Membership

With this information at hand, you register as an eBay user by following these steps:

1. From the Welcome to eBay page, click the Register Now button—or, from the eBay home page, click the Register link above the Navigation Bar.

note

eBay asks all members to supply a valid physical address and telephone number. They don't disclose this info to any third parties outside the eBay site, although they will supply appropriate personal data to other eBay users on their request. (It's how they try to contact deadbeat bidders and sellers.) You can get more details from eBay's Privacy Policy, found at pages.ebay.com/help/policies/privacy-policy.html.

Your eBay user ID must be at least two characters long, and can contain letters, numbers, and/or certain symbols. It cannot contain spaces, Web page URLs, or the following symbols: @, $, &, %, ', <, or >—and you can't use your email address as your user ID.

If you ever move, you'll need to change the address and phone number information eBay has on file. Just go to your My eBay page, click the My Account link, click the Personal Information link, and then click the item you want to change: User ID, Password, Registration Information, Email Address, and so on.

2. When the Registration page appears (as shown in Figure 2.1), enter the following information, and then click the Continue button:

- First name and last name
- Street address (including city, state, ZIP Code, and country)
- Telephone numbers—primary (required) and secondary (optional)
- Date of birth
- Email address

> **note**
>
> You'll also have to provide a credit card number if you're a bidder using a free web-based email account, such as Hotmail, Yahoo! Mail, or Gmail.

3. When the Choose User ID and Password page appears (as shown in Figure 2.2), select one of the user names that eBay suggests for you, or create and enter your own user ID into the Create Your Own ID box.

4. Still on the same page, create and enter a password (at least six characters long, with no spaces) into the Create Password box. Enter the password again into the Re-Enter Password box.

FIGURE 2.1

Enter your name, address, phone number, and email address.

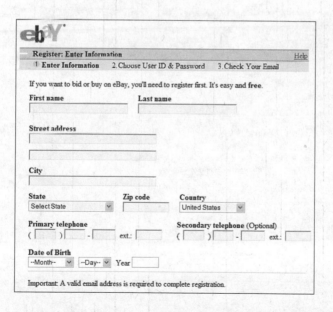

5. Still on the same page, select a question from the Secret Question list, and then enter your answer in the Secret Answer box. (This is used if you ever forget your password.) Click Continue when done.

FIGURE 2.2

Select a user
name and pass-
word.

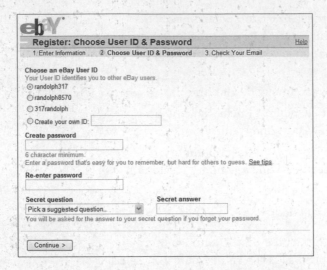

6. eBay now verifies your email address and sends you a confirmation message. When you receive the email (like the one shown in Figure 2.3), click
   the Complete eBay Registration button in the email message to finalize your
   registration.

FIGURE 2.3

eBay's confirma-
tion email.

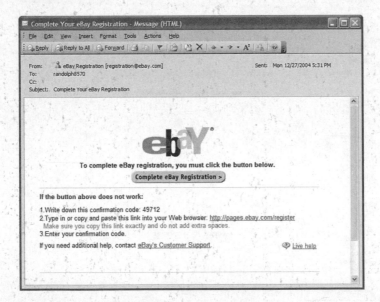

Creating a Seller's Account

If you intend to sell items on eBay, you'll need to provide a little bit more information to eBay—in particular, your checking account number and either a credit or

debit card number. The credit/debit card number is for billing purposes; your card is billed for
all seller's fees you incur. (You can also choose
to pay via checking account withdrawal; eBay
bills your account once a month.) The checking
account information is used to confirm that you
are who you say you are, in an attempt to weed
out fraudulent sellers from the system.

To set up your eBay account for selling, follow
these steps:

1. After you've completed your normal registration, click the Create a Seller's
   Account link and when the next page
   appears, click the Create Seller's Account
   button. (Alternately, you'll be prompted to
   create a seller's account the first time you try to sell something on eBay.)

2. When the Enter Credit or Debit Card page appears (as shown in Figure 2.4),
   enter your credit card number, expiration date, and card identification number,
   and then click the Continue button.

> **tip**
>
> Even if you're just a buyer,
> you still might want to enter
> your credit card informa-
> tion—not that eBay requires
> it, or will charge anything
> against it. Registering your
> card allows you to access
> eBay's adult areas and sets every-
> thing in place in case you do want
> to list items for sale in the future.

FIGURE 2.4

Enter your credit
card number to
pay your eBay
fees.

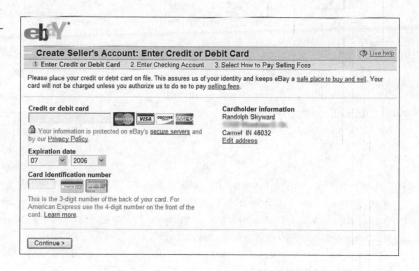

3. When the Enter Checking Account page appears (as shown in Figure 2.5), enter
   your name, your bank's name, your bank routing number, and your checking
   account number. Click the Continue button.

FIGURE 2.5

Enter your
checking
account number
to create a
seller's account.

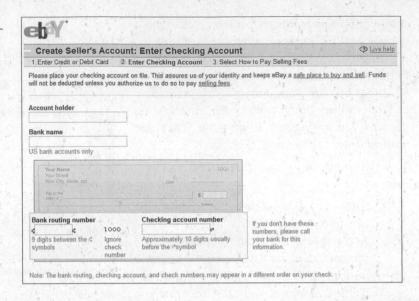

4. When the Select How to Pay Selling Fees page appears, select how you want to pay your eBay fees—as a debit from your checking account or via credit card. Click the Submit button when done.

Your credit card information will be applied to your eBay account within 12 to 24 hours—at which time you'll be able to participate fully in everything eBay has to offer.

The Costs of Using eBay

You don't have to pay eBay anything to browse through items on its site. You don't have to pay eBay anything to bid on an item. You don't even have to pay eBay anything if you actually buy an item (although you will be paying the seller directly, of course). But if you're listing an item for sale, you gotta pay.

eBay charges two main types of fees:

- **Insertion fees** (I prefer to call them *listing* fees) are what you pay every time you list an item for sale on eBay. These fees are based on the minimum bid or reserve price of the item listed. These fees are nonrefundable.

> **" Mike Sez "**
>
> While you have the option of using an automatic checking account withdrawal to pay your fees, I recommend that you go with credit card billing instead. I don't like the idea of eBay (or any other company) having automatic access to my checking account; who knows whether I'll have enough funds on tap the day they decide to make the automatic withdrawal? Credit card payment is easy and just as automatic, with few (if any) hassles.

■ **Final value fees** (I prefer to call them *selling* fees, or *commissions*) are what you pay when an item is actually sold to a buyer. These fees are based on the item's final selling price (the highest bid). If your item doesn't sell, you aren't charged a final value fee.

eBay also charges various fees for different types of listing enhancements. Table 2.1 lists all the fees eBay charges, current as of March 2005. (Fees for items listed in the eBay Real Estate and eBay Motors categories are typically higher.)

View eBay's current fee structure at pages.ebay.com/help/sell/fees.html. These fees apply to its primary auction site; other specialty sites, such as eBay Stores and Half.com, have different fee structures.

TABLE 2.1 eBay Fees

Type of Fee	Explanation	Fee
Insertion fee	In a regular auction, based on the opening value or minimum bid amount. In a fixed-price auction, based on the Buy It Now price. In a reserve price auction, based on the reserve price. In a Dutch auction, based on the opening value or minimum bid—multiplied by t he number of items offered, up to a maximum of $4.80.	Items priced $0.01–$0.99: $0.25 Items priced $1.00–$9.99: $0.35 Items priced $10.00–$24.99: $0.60 Items priced $25.00–$49.99: $1.20 Items priced $50.00–$199.99: $2.40 Items priced $200.00–$499.99: $3.60 Items priced $500 and up: $4.80
Final value fee	In regular auctions, fixed-price auctions, and successful reserve price auctions, based on the closing bid. In Dutch auctions, based on the lowest successful bid—multiplied by the number of items sold.	5.25% of the amount of the high bid to $25.00, *plus* 2.75% of that part of the high bid from $25.01 up to $1,000, *plus* 1.5% of the remaining amount of the high bid that is greater than $1,000. For example, if the item sold for $1,500, you'd pay 5.25% of the first $25 ($1.31) plus 2.75% of the next $975 ($26.81) plus 1.5% of the remaining $500 ($7.50), for a total fee of $35.62.
Scheduled listings	Schedules your item to be listed at a specific date and time, up to three weeks in advance.	$0.10

TABLE 2.1   (continued)

Type of Fee	Explanation	Fee
List in two categories	Enables you to list your item in two separate categories.	Double listing and upgrade fees
Reserve price auction	Additional fee for holding a reserve price auction.	Items priced $0.01–$49.99: $1.00 Items priced $50.00–$199.99: $2.00 Items priced $200 and up: 1% of the reserve price (maximum $100)
Buy It Now	Fee to use the Buy It Now instant purchase option in an auction listing (doesn't apply to fixed price auctions)	Items priced $0.01–$9.99: $0.05 Items priced $10.00–$24.99: $0.10 Items priced $25.00–$49.99: $0.20 Items priced $50.00 and up: $0.25
10-day auction	Additional fee for longer auctions.	$0.40
Featured Plus!	Puts your listing at the top of the listing pages for that category, and also displays your listing (randomly) in the Featured Items section of the related category home page.	$19.95
Gallery	Displays a thumbnail picture of your item in the Gallery section.	$0.35
Gallery Featured	Randomly displays your Gallery listing at the top of the category, at a larger size.	$19.95
Gift Services	Adds a Gift icon to your listing and lets you offer gift wrap, express shipping, and shipping to the gift's recipient.	$0.25
Bold	Boldfaces the title of your item on the listing pages.	$1.00
Border	Puts a color border around your item on the listing page.	$3.00
Highlight	Puts a color shading behind your item on the listing pages.	$5.00
Home Page Featured	Displays your listing (randomly) in the Featured area on eBay's home page and on the Featured Items section of the related category page.	$39.95
Item Subtitle	Adds a subtitle to your item listing.	$0.50
Listing Designer	Applies fancy templates to your listings.	$0.10

There's all manner of fine print associated with these fees. Here are some of the more important points to keep in mind:

- Insertion fees are nonrefundable. (Although if a buyer ends up not paying for an item, you can relist the item and request a credit for the second insertion fee.)

- You will not be charged a final value fee if there were no bids on your item or (in a reserve price auction) if there were no bids that met the reserve price—that is, if your item didn't sell.

- It doesn't matter whether the buyer actually pays you (or how much he or she actually pays); you still owe eBay the full final value fee. (You can, however, request a refund of this fee if the buyer punks out on you; see Chapter 22, "Dealing with Deadbeat Bidders," for more info.)

Invoicing on your account occurs once a month for the previous month's activity. You'll get an invoice by email detailing your charges for the month; if you've set up your account for automatic credit card billing, bank account withdrawal, or PayPal billing, your account will be charged at that time. (If you prefer to pay by check, now's the time to get out the old checkbook.)

Protecting Yourself from Phishing Scams

There's one last thing worth mentioning about your eBay account. eBay will never send you emails asking your to update your account and then provide a link in the email for you to click for that purpose. While eBay will send you emails (and lots of them—either informational or promotional in nature), they don't send out the type of "instant account management" email shown in Figure 2.6.

If you receive this type of email, for either your eBay or PayPal account, you can be sure it's a scam—in particular, a "phishing" scam. If you click the link in the email (which looks like a real, honest-to-goodness eBay URL), you won't be taken to eBay. Instead, that fake URL will take you to another site, run by the scammer, which will be tricked up to look like the eBay site. If you enter your personal information, as requested, you're actually delivering it to the scammer, and you're now a victim of identity theft. The scammer can use the information you provided to hack into your eBay account, make unauthorized charges on your credit card, and maybe even drain your banking account.

caution

Phishing emails come in all shapes and sizes, many of which look extremely official. If you receive one of these phony emails, you can report it to spoof@ebay.com.

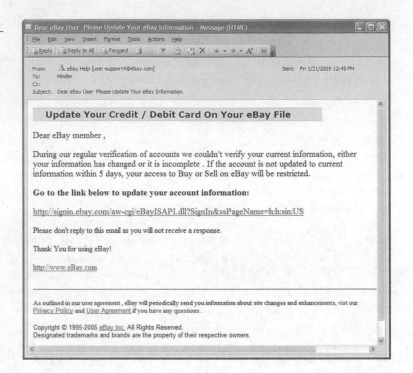

It goes without saying that you should never respond to this type of email, no matter how official-looking it appears. If you want to make changes to your eBay or PayPal account, never do so from an email link. Instead, use your web browser to go directly to the official site, and make your changes there. No one from eBay or PayPal will ever ask you for this information via email. Be warned!

Getting Started

Now that you're all signed up (and aware of eBay's fee structure), you're ready to start bidding—and selling. The bidding process is fee-free; all you have to do is find something you want to buy, and start bidding. (This process is detailed in Chapter 3, "Bidding 101: A Tutorial for Beginning Bidders.") The selling process is a little more involved and costs a little money. (This process is detailed in Chapter 10, "Selling 101: A Tutorial for Beginning Sellers.") Whichever you choose, get ready for lots of action—and fun!

THE ABSOLUTE MINIMUM

Here are the key points to remember from this chapter:

- Before you can bid or sell on eBay, you need to create an eBay user account; registration is free.

- If you want to sell items on eBay, you'll have to leave a checking account and credit card or debit card number on file.

- Buyers are never charged any fees by eBay.

- eBay charges sellers various fees, including listing fees (nonrefundable) and final value fees (if your item actually sells).

- eBay will never send you emails asking you to click a link to update your account; if you get one of these emails, it's a scam!

PART

eBay for Bidders

3

BIDDING 101: A TUTORIAL FOR BEGINNING BIDDERS

After you've browsed through or searched the item listings and actually found something you're interested in, it's time to pony up and make a bid.

How does bidding work? In a nutshell, it's as simple as telling eBay how much you'd be willing to pay for an item—and then finding out whether anyone else is willing to pay more than you. If you've made the highest bid, you win the auction—and you have to buy the item.

It's important to remember that it doesn't cost you anything to bid. You only have to pay if you win—and even then, you don't have to pay any fees to eBay. (All eBay fees are charged to the seller.) You'll have to pay the seller the amount of your winning bid, plus any necessary shipping and handling costs to get the item to you.

Sounds easy enough, doesn't it?

Understanding the Bidding Process

It's important that you know all about the item you want to buy before you place your bid. It's also important that you know how eBay's bidding process works—or you could end up paying too much, or (even worse) not enough to win the auction!

Deciding How Much to Bid

Determining how much to bid on an item on eBay is no more complex than determining how much you'd pay for an item at a flea market or garage sale. You should bid an amount no higher and no lower than what the item is worth for you—and what you can afford. It doesn't matter what the current bid level is; you should make your bid in the amount of what you're willing to pay.

That doesn't mean you'll actually have to pay that amount, of course. Thanks to eBay's automated bidding software (discussed in the next section, "Understanding Proxy Bidding"), registered bids will only be as high as necessary to beat out the next-highest bidder. If you bid $40 but the next highest bidder bid only $20, you'll win the auction with a $20.50 bid.

And you should make that $40 bid even if, at the time, the current bid is only $1. Now, you might think that if the bidding is at the $1 level, you should bid no more than $2 or so. This isn't the case, again thanks to eBay's automated bidding software. If the item is worth $40 to you, bid the $40—and let eBay's proxy software handle the mechanics of the bidding process.

How, then, do you determine that an item is worth $40—or $4 or $400? The key thing is to never bid blind; always make sure you know the true value of an item before you offer a bid.

note

Learn more about browsing and searching the item listings in Chapter 4, "Searching for Items to Buy."

" Mike Sez "

If you remember nothing else from this book, remember this: Always enter the highest amount that you're willing to pay for an item, no matter what the current bid level is. If you think an item is worth $40, enter $40 as your maximum bid—and don't worry if the current bid is half that amount. You also shouldn't get upset if the bidding goes higher than your specified maximum; have the discipline to bid only as high as you initially thought the item was worth. If you're bidding on a collectible, invest in an up-to-date price guide (or reference one online). Whatever you're bidding on, search eBay for completed auctions on similar items, and determine a reasonable price range. Make it a point to shop around, and make your bid accordingly.

This means that you need to do a little research before you make a bid. If you're bidding on a piece of new merchandise, check the price in a catalog, at your local retailer, or with an online retailer.

Understanding Proxy Bidding

The automated bidding software used by eBay is called *proxy* (or "robot") software. If you're a bidder, eBay's proxy software can save you time and help ensure that you get the items you want. (If you're a seller, it doesn't really matter, because all you're interested in is the highest price at the end of the auction—no matter how it got there!)

On eBay, proxy software operates automatically as an *agent* that is authorized to act in your place—but with some predefined bidding parameters. You define the maximum amount you are willing to bid, and then the proxy software takes over and does your bidding for you.

The proxy software bids as little as possible to outbid new competition, up to the maximum bid you specified. If it needs to up your bid $1, it does. If it needs to up your bid $5, it does—until it hits your bid ceiling, when it stops and bows out of the bidding.

The proxy software bids in the official bid increments used by eBay. If the next bid is $0.50 higher than the current bid, the software ups your bid $0.50. In no instance does the software place a bid *over* the next bid increment. (It's pretty smart software!)

Of course, because all bidders are using eBay's proxy software, what happens when you have two users bidding against each other? Simple—you get a proxy bidding war! In this instance, each proxy automatically ups its bid in response to the last bid by the other proxy, which rapidly (seemingly instantaneously) increases the bid price until one of the proxies reaches its maximum bid level.

Let's say one proxy has been programmed with a maximum bid of $25, and another with a maximum bid of $26. Even though the initial bid might be $10, the bids rapidly increase from $10 to $11 to $12 and on to $26, at which point the first proxy drops out and the second proxy holds the high bid.

Bid Increments

To better understand proxy bidding, it helps to know eBay's bid increments. The bid increment is automatically calculated by eBay based on the current price of the item—the higher the price, the higher the bid increment, as shown in Table 3.1.

TABLE 3.1   eBay Bid Increments

Current Price	Bid Increment
$0.01–$0.99	$0.05
$1.00–$4.99	$0.25
$5.00–$24.99	$0.50
$25.00–$99.99	$1.00

TABLE 3.1   (continued)

Current Price	Bid Increment
$100.00–$249.99	$2.50
$250.00–$499.99	$5.00
$500.00–$999.99	$10.00
$1,000.00–$2,499.99	$25.00
$2,500.00–$4,999.99	$50.00
$5,000.00 and up	$100.00

Proxy Bidding, by Example

Let's walk through a detailed example of proxy bidding. The process is totally auto-mated, and goes something like this:

1. You see an item that has a current bid of $100, and you tell eBay that you're willing to pay $115 for it. The $115 becomes your maximum bid.

2. The bid increment on this item is $2.50, so eBay's bidding software—your proxy—bids $102.50 in your name. This becomes the current high bid.

3. Another bidder sees this item, and bids the next bid increment (as specified on the item listing page), $105.

4. Your proxy sees the new bid, and ups its bid automatically to $107.50.

5. A third bidder sees the item, and enters a maximum bid of $150. In accor-dance with the current bid increment, his proxy enters a bid of 110.

6. Your proxy responds with a bid of $112.50.

7. The third bidder's proxy responds with a bid of $115.

8. Since the next bid increment would be $117.50—which is over your maximum bid amount—your proxy drops out of the bidding, and eBay notifies you (by email) that your bid has been surpassed. (If the auction were to end right then, the third bidder would win the auction with a bid of $115. Even though he spec-ified a $150 maximum bid, the bidding never got that high.)

9. At this point, you can place a new maxi-mum bid for the item, or you can throw in the towel and let the new bidder have the item.

note

When you view the bid history for an item, only actual bids—not automatically generated proxy bids—are dis-played.

Proxy Bidding Advice

The nice thing about proxy bidding is that you can engage in a fierce bidding war—and never get your hands dirty! The proxy software does all the dirty work for you, and just notifies you of the results.

When you're placing your bid, realize that just because you set a maximum bid price doesn't mean you'll have to actually pay that price. The proxy software works in your favor to keep your final price as low as possible; don't assume that just because you specified a price, the bidding will always rise to that level.

Also feel comfortable that the proxy software will never exceed your maximum bid price. It just won't happen; the software is smart enough to know your limits. And by bidding your maximum right away, you guarantee that you won't get carried away and pay too much at the end of a heated competition. Remember, if you lose an auction because the bidding goes higher than your maximum, you didn't want to pay that much for the merchandise anyway. Get comfortable with that—and be glad the proxy software helped you stay within your limits.

Of course, some bidders don't like proxy bidding. It is true that if two or more people are bidding for the same item, the bids can automatically (and quickly) rocket up until they max out. For this reason, some bidders prefer to bid the bare minimum on every single one of their bids—effectively defeating the purpose of the proxy software. Of course, if you choose to operate this way, you have to be a lot more hands-on with your bidding, essentially checking back on all your bids as frequently as necessary to ensure that you always end up on top.

How to Read an Item Listing

Before we do any bidding, let's take a look at a typical eBay item listing to see what you can find out about the item and its seller.

Each listing page includes several distinct sections, each of which is equally important—which means that you need to take your time and read through the *entire* item listing before you place your bid. Don't skim; read carefully and pay attention to the details. If the seller mentions a known fault with the merchandise (in the Description section) but you gloss over it, don't even think about complaining when you receive the item after the auction, fault and all. It's your responsibility to read—and agree to—all the information in the listing.

Let's look at each of these sections in detail.

Title, Number, and Your Information

The very top of the item listing, shown in Figure 3.1, displays the listing title (on the left) and the item number (on the right). The item number is important; you use this number to reference the auction in all correspondence, and when paying by PayPal or other payment services.

FIGURE 3.1
FIGURE 3.1

The title and number of the current auction— along with details of your bid.

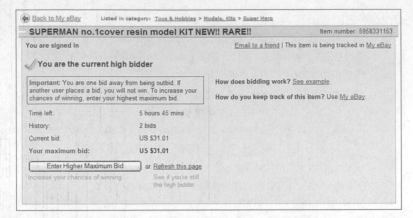

Just below the title is a section that displays your personal information regarding the current auction. If you haven't yet bid, this section is fairly empty; it will tell you if you're signed in, or if you're tracking this item in My eBay.

If you've placed a bid, this section will grow to display the status of your bid—whether you're the high bidder (as in Figure 3.1) or you've been outbid. If you're the *seller* of an item, this section will display the current bid price.

Auction Details

The Auction Details section is next, as shown in Figure 3.2. This section tells you about the status of the current auction. In particular, you will see the current bid price, the time left in the auction, the number of bids placed (history), the ID of the current high bidder, and the location of the item.

tip

Directly above the item number is the category that the item is listed in. Click the category link to view other auctions in this category.

___

If you're not tracking this item, you'll see a Watch This Item link on the right side of this section. When you click this link, this auction is added to the Items I'm Watching section of your My eBay page; you can then use your My eBay page to track the high bids in this auction. (Learn more about My eBay in Chapter 25, "Creating a Home Base with My eBay.")

___

There's also an Add to Calendar link at the very bottom of the page, under the "What else can you do?" heading. Click this link to add a note about this auction to your Microsoft Outlook calendar.

FIGURE 3.2

The Auction Details and Seller Information sections.

There's one more important item in the Auction Details section—a Place Bid button. Although there's a whole bidding section at the bottom of the page, if you like what you see so far, you can place your bid right from the top of the page by clicking this button.

Seller Information

On the right side of the Auction Details section (also shown in Figure 3.2) is a shaded box that lists important seller information. Most important is the seller's eBay ID and current feedback rating. There are also a handful of useful seller-related links, including these:

- *Read feedback comments*—to learn more about the seller's eBay history
- *Add to Favorite Sellers*—to track all future auctions by this seller
- *Ask seller a question*—to send a question via email to the seller
- *View seller's other items*—to see what else the seller currently has for auction

tip

To see who else has bid on this item, you can click the history link.

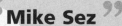

"Mike Sez"

If I find an item I'm interested in, I like to take a look at that seller's other items. I've often found other items worth buying from a particular seller. (And some sellers will combine items for lower shipping costs if you buy more than one item.)

Description

The Description section, shown in Figure 3.3, offers a description of the item for sale, as written by the seller. Because the main item description is written completely by the seller, the amount of detail varies from auction to auction. Some sellers provide a wealth of detail; some write terse one-line descriptions. If the seller doesn't include enough detail in the description, you can always email for more information—or decide that if this wasn't important enough for the seller to spend more time on, it's not important enough for you to bid on, either.

FIGURE 3.3

A typical eBay item description.

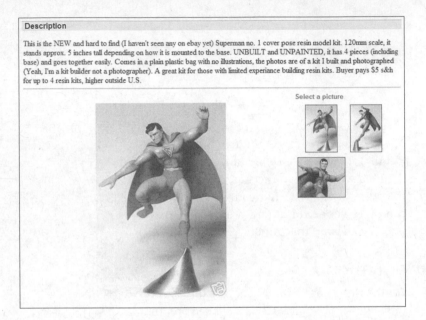

Description

This is the NEW and hard to find (I haven't seen any on ebay yet) Superman no. 1 cover pose resin model kit. 120mm scale, it stands approx. 5 inches tall depending on how it is mounted to the base. UNBUILT and UNPAINTED, it has 4 pieces (including base) and goes together easily. Comes in a plain plastic bag with no illustrations, the photos are of a kit I built and photographed (Yeah, I'm a kit builder not a photographer). A great kit for those with limited experiance building resin kits. Buyer pays $5 s&h for up to 4 resin kits, higher outside U.S.

Select a picture

Depending on the type of item, the Description section might also include some stock details about the item, provided by eBay; for example, a listing for a CD (like the one in Figure 3.4) might include artist, format, release date, and label information, along with the CD cover art. Additional information, such as a track listing or editorial review, might also be provided under the main item description.

FIGURE 3.4

Stock item details as provided by eBay for certain types of items.

Description

Blue Roses From The Moons

Item Specifics - Music: CDs

Artist:	Nanci Griffith	Release Date:	Mar 25, 1997
Format:	CD	Record Label:	Elektra Entertainment
Genre:	Country	UPC:	075596201520
Sub-Genre:	Mainstream	Album Type:	--
		Condition:	--

Stock Photo

Additional information

Often accompanying the text description are one or more pictures of the item. Some of these pictures might appear a tad small; if you see a Supersize Picture link under a thumbnail picture, click the picture to view it at a larger size.

Shipping, Payment Details, and Return Policy

The Shipping and Payment Details section, shown in Figure 3.5, lists the shipping/handling charge for the item, if the seller has stated a flat fee. In some auctions, this section will include a Shipping Calculator; enter your ZIP Code to calculate your specific shipping charge.

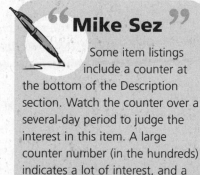

" Mike Sez "

Some item listings include a counter at the bottom of the Description section. Watch the counter over a several-day period to judge the interest in this item. A large counter number (in the hundreds) indicates a lot of interest, and a lot of potential last-minute bidders. A small counter number (in the single digits or the teens) indicates less interest—which means you may be able to win this item without bidding too high.

FIGURE 3.5

The Shipping and Payment Details section.

Shipping, payment details and return policy		
Shipping Cost	**Services Available**	**Available to**
US $5.00	Standard Flat Rate Shipping Service	United States Only
Will ship to Worldwide.		
Shipping insurance		
US $1.25 Optional		
Seller's payment instructions		
You will be sent an invoice by e-mail. Read carefully and follow the instructions. If you have not received an invoice within 3 days, please e-mail.		

Also listed here are details on whether the seller offers shipping insurance, where the seller will ship to (U.S. only or internationally), and the seller's payment instructions and return policy.

Payment Methods Accepted

Next up is another short section, shown in Figure 3.6, listing the payment methods accepted by the seller. Most sellers accept personal check and money orders; many accept credit cards via the PayPal service.

FIGURE 3.6

The Payment Methods Accepted section.

Payment methods accepted
This seller,   prefers PayPal.
• **PayPal** (MasterCard VISA DISCOVER AMEX eCHECK)
• Money order/Cashiers check
Learn about payment methods.

Ready to Bid?

eBay put the main bidding section, shown in Figure 3.7, at the very bottom of the page. All you have to do is enter your bid into the Your Maximum Bid box, and then click the Place Bid button.

Ready to bid?   help

SUPERMAN no.1cover resin model KIT NEW!! RARE!!

Current bid: US $31.01

Your maximum bid: US $ [   ]   (Enter US $32.01 **or more**)

[Place Bid >]   You will confirm in the next step.

eBay automatically bids on your behalf **up to** your maximum bid.
Learn about bidding.

Before You Bid

Although anyone is free to browse on eBay, to place a bid you have to be a registered user. If you haven't registered yet, now's the time. (For information on registering, see Chapter 2, "Joining Up and Getting Started.")

Before you place your bid, be sure to read all the details of the item you're interested in. In particular, look at the following:

■ Is the item you're bidding on new or used? If it's new, what kind of warranty does it come with? If it's used, what's your recourse if you're dissatisfied with the item?

■ What condition is the item in? Is it an original, or a reproduction? Is there any way to verify that condition—through photos of the item, perhaps?

■ Check out the seller's feedback rating —is it positive? (Never deal with a user with a negative total feedback number.) You might even want to click the Read Feedback Comments link in the Seller Information section to view his or her feedback profile; this is where you can read the individual comments about this person left by other users.

■ What methods of payment will the seller accept? Are you comfortable using one of these payment options?

■ How much shipping and handling is the seller charging? Are these fees in line with what you think actual shipping will cost? If you or the seller lives outside the U.S., will the seller ship internationally?

> **"Mike Sez"**
>
> If you have any questions about a particular item, ask 'em! Click the Ask Seller a Question link in the Seller Information section to send the seller an email, and ask whatever questions you want. If the seller doesn't respond, pass this auction by. And if something about the listing sounds too good to be true, it probably is!

In other words, take your time and become knowledgeable about and comfortable with both the item and the seller before you place your bid. If you find anything—anything at all—that makes you uncomfortable, don't bid.

All that said, let's look at a final checklist for buyers; check off each item before you make your bid.

Checklist: Before You Bid

- ☐ Make sure you're an official registered eBay member.
- ☐ Read the item description—thoroughly.
- ☐ Note the payment methods that the seller will accept.
- ☐ Note how the seller intends to ship the item, and the shipping/handling price being charged.
- ☐ Check the seller's feedback rating—and click the feedback rating to browse through comments from other eBay users.
- ☐ Note the current bid level, and the next bid price.
- ☐ Research the value of the item. (That means searching eBay for pricing on completed auctions of similar items, as well as doing your own online and offline research.)
- ☐ Determine the maximum amount you're willing to pay for the item.
- ☐ Subtract the estimated shipping/handling price from the price you're willing to pay; this becomes your maximum bid price.
- ☐ Email the seller if you have any questions about anything.
- ☐ Decide whether you really want to bid; every bid you make should be a serious, binding bid.

note

The seller's feedback rating reflects the number of successful auctions the seller has conducted. The higher the rating, the more reliable the seller. (Learn more about feedback in Chapter 27, "Understanding and Using Feedback.")

" Mike Sez "

It's okay for shipping/handling to be a little higher than actual shipping; the seller has to pay for packing materials and so forth. But if the charge runs more than 10%–15% (up to a buck or so) higher, the seller is viewing shipping/handling as a profit center, at your expense.

Just Do It—Placing a Bid

You've waited long enough. Now it's time to finally place your bid!

Here's what you do:

1. Scroll down to the Ready to Bid? section of the listing page, and enter your maximum bid amount.

2. If you're bidding in a Dutch auction (in which the quantity is more than one), enter the number of items you want to bid on.

3. Click the Place Bid button.

4. When the Submit Your Bid page appears, enter your user information (if prompted), confirm your bid, and then click the Submit button.

5. Your bid is officially entered and the item listing page is redisplayed. At the top of the page, in the blue shaded box, is your bidder status; this is where you learn whether you're the current high bidder or whether you've already been outbid.

Remember, eBay's proxy bidding system will automatically place your bids for you, up to but not exceeding your specified maximum bid amount. If the minimum bid is currently $10, and you entered a maximum bid of $20, eBay enters your bid as $10. Your bid will get raised automatically if and when other bidders enter higher bids.

Bidding in Other Types of Auctions

The preceding section covered the typical eBay auction, one without a lot of bells and whistles. eBay offers a lot of different auction options, however (as you'll learn in Chapter 13, "Choosing the Right Listing Options"), and the bidding procedure is slightly different depending on the type of auction being held.

Dutch Auctions

A Dutch auction is an auction in which the seller has more than one of an item for sale. An example might be a seller with a half-dozen T-shirts (all identical), or a gross of inkjet cartridges. Although most sellers on Dutch auctions are small businesses that want to unload multiple quantities of an item, you'll also find some individuals with several like items to sell.

In a Dutch auction, the seller specifies both the minimum bid and the number of items available in the auction, as shown in Figure 3.8. As in a normal auction, bidders bid at or above that minimum for the item—although, in a Dutch auction, bidders can specify a specific *quantity* that they're interested in purchasing.

FIGURE 3.8

An example of a
Dutch auction—
note the quantity
available.

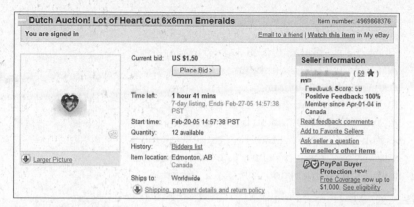

When you're bidding in a Dutch auction, you not only have to place your bid, but
also have to indicate how many of the item you'd like to buy. You enter the desired
amount in the Quantity box in the Ready to Bid? section of the listing page. (This
box—shown in Figure 3.9—appears only in Dutch auctions, not in regular auctions.)

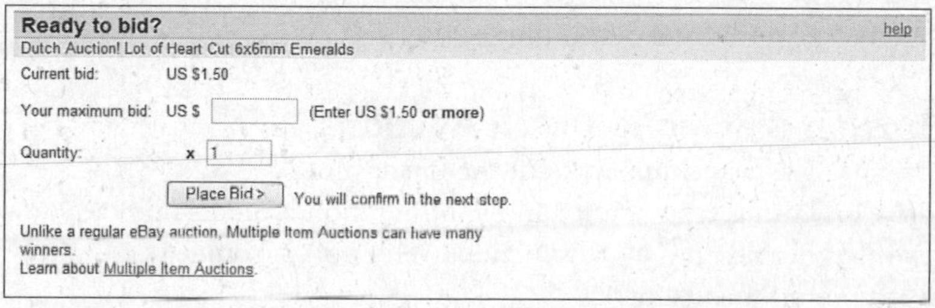

FIGURE 3.9

Enter the quan-
tity you want for
a Dutch auction
item.

Determining who "wins" a Dutch auction is a little different from determining who
wins a normal auction. In a Dutch auction, the highest bidders purchase the items,
but all buyers pay only the amount that matches the lowest successful bid.

Dutch Auctions, by Example

Let's work through an example. Say a seller has 10 identical copies of a particular *Lord
of the Rings* T-shirt. The seller indicates the number of items available (10) and the
minimum bid (let's say $5). Potential buyers enter their bids, which must be equal to
or higher than the minimum bid of $5; each buyer also indicates the quantity (from 1
to 10) that he or she is interested in purchasing.

If 11 people bid $5 each (for one shirt apiece), the first 10 bidders will win the auction,
each paying $5 for their items, and the last bidder will be out of luck. But if the 11th
person had placed a higher bid—$6, let's say—then that 11th bidder would be listed as
the #1 bidder, and the last $5 bidder (chronologically) would be knocked from the list.
All 10 winning bidders, however—including the person who bid $6—would have to
pay only $5 for the item. (Highest bidders, lowest bids—get it?)

In a Dutch auction, the minimum price ends up being raised only if enough bidders place bids above the minimum bid. In our example, if 9 bidders bid over the minimum, but the 10th bidder bid $5, all bidders would still pay $5. But if the lowest bid was $6 (and the other bidders bid from $6 to $10), all 10 bidders would pay $6 (the lowest current bid). So posting a higher bid increases a buyer's chances of winning an item at a Dutch auction, but it also increases the risk of raising the price for everybody.

When a potential buyer bids on multiple copies of the item, those toward the end of the list may not get the quantity they desire. Still using our T-shirt example, if the top bidder wants three shirts, the remaining shirts are distributed among the next seven bidders—leaving the last or lowest two bidders out in the cold.

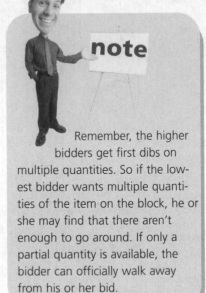

note

Remember, the higher bidders get first dibs on multiple quantities. So if the lowest bidder wants multiple quantities of the item on the block, he or she may find that there aren't enough to go around. If only a partial quantity is available, the bidder can officially walk away from his or her bid.

Tips on Bidding in Dutch Auctions

Dutch auctions actually benefit the buyer more than any other type of auction by letting higher bidders pay the lowest bid price. Should you bid on a Dutch auction? Why not? If someone is selling something you want, by all means, bid!

How much should you bid? Ah, there's the issue. I actually like bidding on Dutch auctions later in the game so that I can get a handle on how many other bidders I'm competing with. The number of bidders versus the quantity of items available determines my strategy:

- If the seller has a large quantity of items and a small number of bidders, bid the minimum. In this scenario, everybody wins because there's more than enough merchandise to go around.

- If the seller has a small quantity of items and a large number of bidders, you probably should bid higher than the minimum. In fact, in this scenario, treat it like a normal auction and bid the highest amount you're willing to pay. The worst thing that could happen is you lose the auction; the second worst is that you're a winning bidder and you have to pay your maximum bid; the best scenario is that you're a winning bidder but get to pay a lower amount (because of a lower bid entered by another winning bidder).

Reserve Price Auctions

In a *reserve price* auction, the seller has reserved the option to set a second price (the *reserve price*) that is higher than the opening bid. At the end of an auction, if the high bid does not meet or exceed the seller's reserve price, the auction is unsuccessful and the seller does *not* sell the item to the high bidder. Sellers sometimes use a reserve price on high-end items if they want to make sure that the market does not undervalue what they are selling.

In other words, the reserve price is the lowest price at which a seller is willing to sell an item (unrelated to the opening bid price). The seller specifies the reserve price when the item is initially listed (naturally, the reserve price should be above the minimum bid price). The reserve price is known only to the seller (and to eBay) and is never disclosed to bidders.

A reserve price auction begins just like any other auction, at the minimum bid price. The only difference is the reserve price indication in the listing's auction details, as shown in Figure 3.10. You place your bid as you would in a normal auction, and the auction proceeds pretty much as normal.

Reserve price auctions are not available for Dutch auctions. In a Dutch auction, the minimum price is the minimum price.

FIGURE 3.10

An example of a reserve auction in which the reserve price hasn't yet been met.

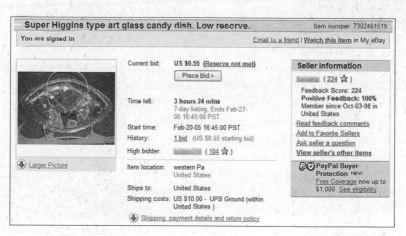

If your maximum bid is equal to or greater than the reserve price, the item's current price is raised to the reserve price, and the reserve price has officially been met. If, through the course of the auction, the reserve price is *not* met, the auction ends with the item unsold.

Reserve Price Auctions, by Example

Let's look at a brief example of a reserve price auction. Suppose a seller has a leather jacket to sell that she feels is worth $50—but she wants to set a lower initial bid, to get the bidding going early. So the seller sets $25 as the initial bid, and $50 as the reserve price.

The first bidder on this item sees the $25 initial bid (the reserve price isn't displayed, of course) and bids $25. The bidder is notified that he has the current high bid, but that the reserve price has not been met. If the auction were to end right now, the item would *not* be sold—the seller is obligated to sell only if the reserve price is met.

The bidding continues, and the bid price increases until it hits $50. At that point, the last bidder is notified both that he is the high bidder and that the reserve price has been met. If the auction ends now—or at any point afterward—the seller *is* obligated to sell, because the reserve price ($50) has been met.

So, in this example, any bids under $50 don't win the auction; any bids $50 and over can be winning bids.

Tips for Bidding in Reserve Price Auctions

If you want to bid in a reserve price auction, what should your strategy be? It depends on how badly you want the item.

If you really, really, really want the item, you should place your first bid and see whether you hit the reserve price. If you didn't, place a new, higher bid, and see whether it hits the reserve price. If you still didn't, repeat until your bid is high enough to guarantee a win.

For most bidders, however, this is simply a strategy to ensure writing a large check. In most cases, play a reserve price auction as you would a normal auction, and let the high bid be the high bid. If you have the high bid and the reserve price isn't met, it's no skin off your nose; it simply means that the seller set an unreasonable reserve price. You always have the option of contacting the seller post-auction to see whether he or she is willing to sell at the current bid price, even though the reserve hasn't been met, using eBay's Second Chance Offer feature. The seller isn't obligated to do so, of course, but some might be willing to let the merchandise go to forgo starting a whole new auction (and paying another listing fee)—or they may be willing to negotiate a selling price somewhere in between your bid and the reserve. You never know until you ask!

tip

If you don't like the whole bidding process, there are other ways to buy things on eBay, including the popular Buy It Now option. Learn more in Chapter 8, "Other Ways to Buy on eBay."

What to Do After You've Bid

Let's forget about all those special types of auctions and fixed-priced items for a minute, and get back to the normal auction process. Let's assume that you've found an item you want and you've placed a bid. What happens next?

The answer to this question is a four-letter word: *wait*. And, as Tom Petty says, the waiting is the hardest part.

That's certainly true with online auctions.

Immediately after you place a high bid, eBay automatically sends you an email notifying you of your bid status. You'll also receive an email once a day from eBay, notifying you of your status in any and all auctions in which you're the highest bidder. In addition, if you get outbid on an item, eBay sends you an immediate email informing you of such.

Otherwise, feel free to check in on all of your auctions in progress, just to see how things are proceeding. Remember that a watched kettle never boils—and constantly tracking your auctions doesn't make the time go any faster, either.

Keeping Track of Your Bids

The easiest way to keep track of your bids is with the All Buying view on your My eBay page. Just click the My eBay link in the eBay Navigation Bar to view all the items on which you're currently bidding. (Learn more about My eBay in Chapter 25, "Creating a Home Base with My eBay.")

Increasing Your Bid Amount

As you get further along in a particular auction, you might suddenly realize that your maximum bid isn't going to hold, and you want to ensure a large enough bid to win a long, hard-fought auction. How can you increase your bid—even though you're currently the high bidder?

It's really easy. Just return to the item listing page and place a new bid, making sure that your new maximum bid is higher than your old maximum bid. (You can't decrease your maximum bid!) When you enter this new bid, it replaces your previous bid.

Pretty easy, isn't it?

caution

Know that increasing your maximum bid while you're the current high bidder can inadvertently increase your existing bid. That's because eBay's proxy bidding software will increase the bid to the next bid increment even if the new bid is placed by the current high bidder. This might only affect your bid by a few pennies (or dollars, depending on how far away you are from the next bid increment), but it's something to be aware of.

Oh, No! You've Been Outbid!

It happens. Your auction is progressing, and then you get that dreaded email from eBay informing you that you've been outbid.

What do you do?

First, you have to decide whether you want to continue to play in this auction. If you decided up front that an item was only worth, let's say, $10, and the bidding has progressed to $15, you might want to let this one go.

On the other hand, if you hedged your bets with the earlier bid, you might want to jump back into the fray with a new bid. If so, return to the item's listing page and make a new bid. Maybe your new bid will be higher than the current high bidder's maximum bid.

Or maybe not. You don't know until you try!

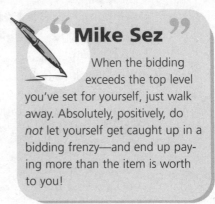

Mike Sez

When the bidding exceeds the top level you've set for yourself, just walk away. Absolutely, positively, do *not* let yourself get caught up in a bidding frenzy—and end up paying more than the item is worth to you!

Retracting a Bad Bid

Everybody makes mistakes. What happens if you place a bid in an auction that you shouldn't have placed?

Fortunately—but reluctantly—eBay lets you retract bids under certain circumstances.

When does eBay allow you to retract your bid? Well, if the seller has substantially changed the description of the item after you bid, you're free to change your mind, too. You can also retract your bid if you made a "clear error" in the amount of your bid. What's a "clear error?" Well, bidding $100 when you meant to bid $10 is clearly an error; other circumstances are left up to your judgment.

The thing is, you can always retract a bid (because you can always claim a "clear error"), but you won't win any friends doing so. In fact, if you retract too many bids, eBay will come after you and possibly kick you off the site. So retract a bid if you have to, but don't make a habit of it.

How do you retract a bid? It's actually fairly easy; just follow these steps:

1. Click the Services link above the Navigation Bar.

2. When the Services page appears, scroll down to the Bidding and Buying Services section and click the Retract Your Bid link.

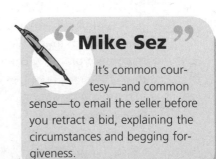

Mike Sez

It's common courtesy—and common sense—to email the seller before you retract a bid, explaining the circumstances and begging forgiveness.

3. When the Bid Retractions page appears, enter the item number of the auction and then choose an explanation for your retraction from the pull-down list.

4. Click the Retract Bid button; your bid is now deleted from the auction in process.

Bidding in the Final Moments

It's during the last hour of most auctions that the bidding really heats up. If you wait for an email to inform you when you've been outbid during an auction's final minutes, you might not have enough time to log on to eBay and make a new bid. For that reason, many bidders will log on to eBay (and on to the individual auction about to end) and manually monitor the auction's closing minutes. Just remember to hit the Refresh or Reload button on your browser frequently, to keep the item listing page up-to-date with the latest bids!

note

The reason for all this last-minute bidding activity is the use of a technique called *sniping*. Learn more about how to win auctions with sniping in Chapter 9, "Secrets of Successful Bidders."

Five Common Bidding Mistakes

You'll learn some tips on how to be a better bidder in Chapter 9. But let's take a moment and examine some of the things you can do *wrong*—actions that can either keep you from winning or cause you to pay too much.

Mistake #1: Bidding Too Early

When you're interested in a particular item, it's tempting to place your bid as soon as you read the item description. The problem with this is that as soon as that bid is entered, you've announced your intentions to other bidders—who might then react by placing even higher bids. So, right away, you've started a bidding war—which you could lose.

There's really no benefit to bidding early in a long auction. So what if you place your bid on day one of a seven-day auction? The only bid that really counts is the one that's in as the auction closes. Besides, when you bid early, the bidding price goes up faster. It's better to hold off and place a later bid, one that other bidders won't have as much time to respond to. Bid early, and you're likely to either lose to a higher bidder or unnecessarily drive the price higher; bid later, and you're more likely to win—with a lower bid.

Mistake #2: Bidding Too Low

If you really, really, really want to win a particular auction, there's no point in being cheap. You think you can get by with a low-ball bid, so that's what you offer. The problem is, if the item is really worth a higher price, someone else will bid that amount—and you'll lose the auction.

It's especially tempting to bid low when the seller sets an unrealistically low starting price. Don't get suckered in by a low price early in the auction. If you think an item is really worth a particular price, bid that full amount. Remember, eBay's bidding software automatically sets the current bid level for you, so you'll never pay more than you have to—and if there's not much bidding, you might actually end up paying a lower amount. But if you want to win, you have to bid high enough to beat all other bidders. Don't be cheap!

Mistake #3: Bidding Too High

On the other hand, don't be a dummy and bid an unrealistically high amount for something that isn't worth that much. You'd be shocked at how many items sell for *more* than their fair value on eBay; a lot of buyers just don't know what things are worth when they place their bids, and end up overpaying. Do your homework ahead of time, and find out what that item is really worth. Then place an appropriate bid—and don't bid more than that. If you get outbid, tough; the item wasn't worth that much, anyway!

Mistake #4: Getting Caught Up in a Bidding Frenzy

One reason that many items sell for too high a price is that it's easy to get caught up in a bidding frenzy. If an item is popular and several bidders are interested, you'll see the current bid price keep going up and up and up as each bidder tries to stay in the game. I know the feeling; when bidding starts to heat up, you don't want to lose. So you keep placing higher bids, trying to stay a few dollars ahead of the other bidders—and end up bidding up the price way too high.

The solution to this problem is simple—don't lose your head in the heat of the moment! Set a maximum amount you'll pay for the item, and do not—repeat, *do not*—bid any higher than that amount, no matter how hot and heavy the bidding. It's okay to lose one every now and then!

Mistake #5: Not Reading the Fine Print

You've found an item you want. The bid price is reasonable. You think you can win the auction, and get a pretty good deal, besides.

But when the auction ends, you get an email from the seller telling you that the final price is several dollars higher than what you expected. That's because the seller added a shipping and handling fee to the selling price. Now, you should expect to pay shipping/handling; that's your responsibility as the buyer, and you should factor that into your total cost of the auction. But many inexperienced bidders get surprised by this charge and end up with an unsatisfactory auction experience.

So make sure you know what the shipping and handling fee is before you place your bid. If the seller doesn't include this fee in the item listing, email him with your ZIP code and ask him to estimate the fees to your location. And always be on the lookout for higher-than-normal shipping/handling fees, or other unexpected charges. You probably don't want to pay $10 to ship a $2 item—especially if the actual shipping might be only half that. Although it's common for sellers to include a "handling charge" on top of actual shipping charges (to pay for boxes, packing material, and so on), you don't want to pay *too much* over the actual costs. Jacking up the handling charges is one way unscrupulous sellers make a little extra money on each transaction, and you don't want to play along. Bottom line? Be sure to read the fine print before you bid—especially where it concerns shipping and handling charges.

You Won! Now What?

You've somehow waited patiently (or not) throughout the entire process. As the clock ticked down to zero, no other viable competitors entered the arena, and your high bid stood. You won!

Now things *really* start to happen. You'll receive an email from eBay notifying you that you've won the auction. You'll also receive an email from the item's seller, telling you how much you need to pay, and where to send the payment. Then you'll need to reply to the seller, make your payment, and wait for the item to arrive.

To learn about the post-auction process in more detail, turn to Chapter 6, "After the Auction: Taking Care of Business."

THE ABSOLUTE MINIMUM

Here are the key points to remember from this chapter:

- Before you place a bid, you have to be a registered eBay user—and you should check out the feedback rating and comments of the item's seller.

- You place your bid in the Ready to Bid? section of the item listing page; then you enter your user ID, password, and the maximum bid you're willing to make.

- eBay's proxy bidding software manages your bidding, raising your bid as necessary up to but not exceeding your specified maximum bid amount.

- If, at any point during the auction, you get outbid, you have two options: Place another (higher) bid, or walk away free and clear.

- When you win an auction, you'll be notified by eBay; you should then contact the seller to arrange payment and shipping terms.

4

SEARCHING FOR ITEMS TO BUY

Let's get right down to it: eBay is the largest auction site on the Web, no questions asked. It's big. It's bigger than big. It's, like, really incredibly massively big. Think of the biggest thing you've ever seen, and eBay is bigger than that.

If you want to browse through the largest selection of merchandise for sale on the Internet, this is the place to go.

However, eBay's size (it's big, remember?) sometimes makes it difficult to find that *one* item you're looking for. So how do you find that one special item among the 28 million or so items that are up for bid on eBay on any given day?

Browsing or Searching—Which One Is for You?

There are two main ways to locate items to bid on and buy on eBay. You can leisurely browse through eBay's thousands of categories and subcategories, or you can perform a targeted search for specific items.

Table 4.1 shows you what's good and what's bad about both browsing and searching.

TABLE 4.1   Browsing Versus Searching—Strengths and Weaknesses

Question	Browsing	Searching
How easy is it to do?	Easy	Not as easy
How quickly can you find a specific item?	Slow	Fast
How many items will you find?	A lot	Not quite as many
Will you find the specific item you're looking for?	Not always	Yes
Can you isolate items geographically?	Yes	Yes
Can you find other bidders and sellers?	No	Yes

The bottom line: If you're not sure what you're looking for, or if you're looking for all types of items within a general category, you should browse. If you're looking for a specific item or type of item, you should search.

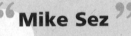

"Mike Sez"

Many eBay categories are so large they're practically unbrowsable. (Do you really want to click through a hundred pages of listings to find the item you want?) I definitely recommend searching over browsing—you'll find what you're looking for a *lot* faster!

Browsing: The Easy Way to Find Things

eBay has an ever-increasing number of categories, listing all sorts of items—antiques, books, coins, collectibles, comics, computers, dolls, electronics, figures, gemstones, glass, jewelry, magazines, music, photography, pottery, sports memorabilia, stamps, toys, and many, many more. To view all the items within a specific category or subcategory, you need to browse through eBay's category listings.

eBay's main categories are listed on its home page. You can also access a complete list of eBay's categories and subcategories by clicking the Buy link on the eBay Navigation bar; this takes you to eBay's Buy hub, shown in Figure 4.1, which displays all the major categories, along with quite a few subcategories.

You see, to make browsing easier, eBay's major categories are divided into a hierarchy of subcategories. For example, if you click the Antiques link on eBay's home page, you'll see Antiquities, Architectural and Garden, Asian Antiques, and a dozen other subcategories. In fact, many of eBay's subcategories have their own subcategories—which makes them sub-subcategories, I guess!

FIGURE 4.1
eBay's Buy hub.

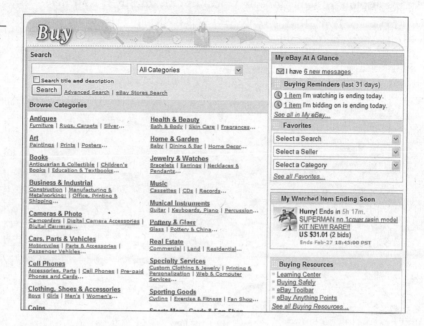

When you access a main category page, like the one in Figure 4.2, you see a list of subcategories. (Some category pages will have a top-level subcategory list at the top of the page, and a detailed list of all subcategories at the bottom.) Click a subcategory link, and you'll see either a list of additional subcategories or a list of available items.

FIGURE 4.2
A typical eBay category page.

When you finally get to the list of items within a category or subcategory, the page looks similar to the one in Figure 4.3. At the top of the page are three tabs; these tabs display All Items for sale, Auctions only, or Buy It Now items only. The first listings on the page are the Featured items (sellers pay extra for this placement); below that (or on the next page, sometimes) are the complete listings, with items ending soonest listed first.

FIGURE 4.3

eBay item listings.

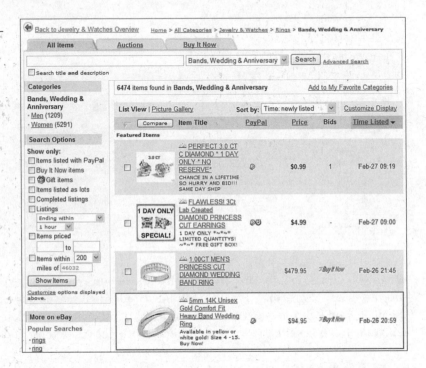

Some listings have pictures or icons either before or after the title. If it's a picture, great; that means the listing has an accompanying photograph. Same thing if you see a green Picture icon.

If you see a yellow Gallery icon, that means the item is listed in eBay's Gallery. (The Gallery lets you browse through listing pictures, rather than listing text; you access the Gallery at pages.ebay.com/buy/gallery.html.) A Gift icon indicates that the seller offers various gift services, such as gift wrap. The New icon indicates that the item has been listed within the past 24 hours. And the Buy It Now icon indicates that the seller has chosen the Buy It Now option for this item.

Table 4.2 shows the various icons you might encounter.

TABLE 4.2   Listing Icons

Feature	Icon
Picture	📷
Gallery	🏠
Gift	⊕
New	✦
Buy It Now	*Buy It Now*

Searching: The Powerful Way to Find Things

You could browse through the merchandise categories listed on eBay's home page, as I just described, but given the huge number of categories, this could take forever—and, besides, you're never quite sure whether all sellers have picked the right categories for their merchandise. (Does a Batman statue belong in the Collectibles: Comics: Figurines category or the Toys & Hobbies: Action Figures: Superhero category?) In most cases, a better solution is to use eBay's built-in search engine.

Using eBay's Basic Search Function

eBay's home page has a simple search box, shown in Figure 4.4, which works fine for simple searches. Just enter your keywords, click the Search button, and view your results. It's pretty easy.

FIGURE 4.4

Simple searching
from eBay's
home page.

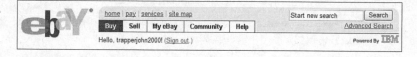

Using the Find It Now Page

More sophisticated searches can be had when you click the Advanced Search link below the home page Search box. This takes you to the Find Items page, shown in Figure 4.5. From here you can

- Search by keyword
- Search by auction item number
- Restrict your search to a specific category
- Search by both title and description
- Search completed listings only

- Sort your results by time, price, distance, or payment method
- Personalize how you want your search results displayed.

Let's look at how you can use eBay's Advanced Search page for some of the more common types of searches.

Using the Advanced Search Page

The Find Items page isn't the last word in eBay searches. When you click the Advanced Search link on the Find Items page (not to be confused with the similar link on eBay's home page), you're taken to eBay's Advanced Search page, shown in Figure 4.6. In addition to the options present on the normal Find It Now page, this page offers the following advanced search functions:

> **tip**
>
> I particularly like searching *completed* auctions only—a great way to get a handle on final selling prices for various types of items. Note that you can also opt to display completed items after you've initiated a search; when the Items Matching page appears, go to the Display section at the left side of the page, and then click the Completed Items link. When you're done looking at the completed items, click the View Active Items link to return to the current auctions.

- Choose to search for all the words in a query, any of the words in a query, an exact phrase, or an exact match for the query
- Exclude specific words from the results of a search
- Narrow your search to items within a specific price range
- Include or exclude items from specific sellers
- Narrow your search to items located in or available to specific countries outside the U.S.
- Limit your results to items listed in a specific currency
- Search for items offered in multiple quantities or lots
- Narrow your search to items offered with the Buy It Now option
- Limit your results to items that can be paid for via PayPal
- Show only those items that display a Gift icon
- Limit your search to items ending within a specified time period
- Narrow your search to items located a specified distance from a given location
- Display only those items that have a specified number of bids
- Display only those items that offer eBay Anything Points
- Limit your search to those items listed by nonprofit organizations

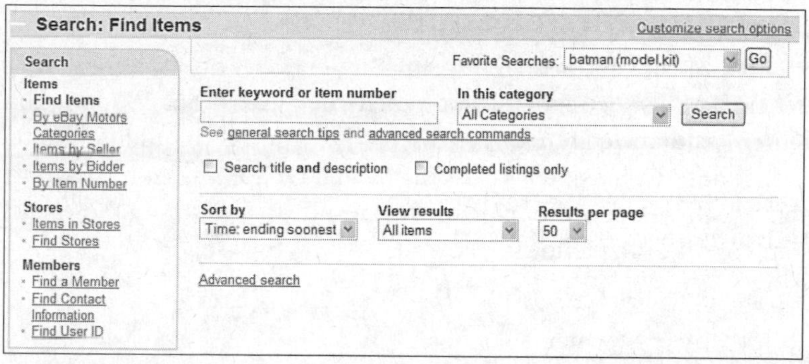

FIGURE 4.5

More sophisti-
cated searching
from the Find
Items page.

FIGURE 4.6

Even more
search options
on the Advanced
Search page.

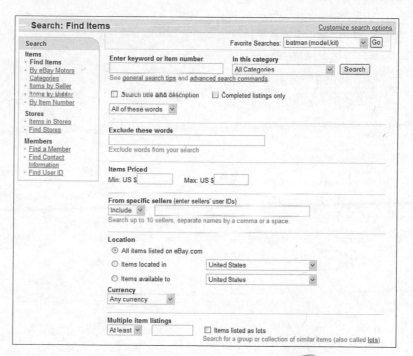

Whew—that's a lot of options! The bottom line
is that you can use the Advanced Search page
to conduct very targeted searches, using just
about any criteria you can think of. Given the
huge number of items listed on eBay on any
given day, this ability to generate more targeted
results is welcome.

tip

If you can't find what you
want in eBay's normal auctions, you can expand your
search to include merchandise offered for sale in eBay
Stores. Learn more in
Chapter 8, "Other Ways to
Buy on eBay."

Fine-Tuning Your Search Results

When you click the Search button, eBay searches all its current auction listings and generates a list of auctions that match your search query. Along the left side of the search results page is a list of matching categories (in addition to the matching individual auctions), as well as the Search Options section shown in Figure 4.7. You can use these options to narrow your results to show only those auctions that match some or all of the following criteria:

- Items listed with PayPal
- Buy It Now items
- Gift items
- Items listed as lots (multiple quantities offered)
- Completed listings
- Listings ending within a specified time period
- Items selling within a specified price range
- Items listed within a specified number of miles from a given location

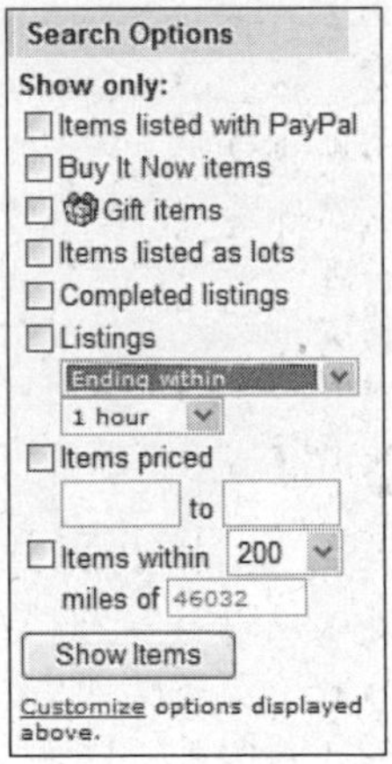

FIGURE 4.7

Narrowing down your search results with Search Options.

Search Options

Show only:
- [ ] Items listed with PayPal
- [ ] Buy It Now items
- [ ] 🌐 Gift items
- [ ] Items listed as lots
- [ ] Completed listings
- [ ] Listings
  - [Ending within ▾]
  - [1 hour ▾]
- [ ] Items priced
  - [____] to [____]
- [ ] Items within [200 ▾]
  - miles of [46032]

[Show Items]

Customize options displayed above.

Select the options you want, and then click the Show Items button. eBay now filters the search results to match the new criteria you selected.

Complex Searches—For Simpler Results

Whichever search page you choose to use, you can generate better results by using special commands and operators in your search queries. Table 4.3 lists the commands you can use when searching on eBay.

TABLE 4.3   eBay Search Commands

To Do This	Use This Command	Example
Search for part of a word	`*`	`bat*`
Search for either word (NOTE: Do not include spaces after the comma.)	`(word1,word2)`	`(batman,robin)`
Search for an exact phrase	`" "`	`"batman pez dispenser"`
Must include a word	`+`	`batman +pez`
Must exclude a word	`-`	`batman -pez`
Must exclude two or more words	`-(word1,word2)`	`-(batman,robin)`

Note that eBay automatically assumes that you want to search for items that match all the words in your query. This is the equivalent of inserting a Boolean AND between all the words in your query; a query for `batman robin` essentially looks for items that match "batman" AND "robin."

Practice Makes Perfect: Some Sample Searches

Let's quickly put together a few sample searches using some of the commands we've discussed.

First, say you want to look for all Batman-related merchandise. The search is simple; enter this query in the search box:

`batman`

That's almost too simple. What if you want to search not only for Batman, but also for Batgirl or Batmobile or Batplane or Bat*anything*? For this task, you apply the * wildcard to create this query:

`bat*`

> **caution**
>
> If you're an experienced searcher, you're probably used to using Boolean operators (AND, OR, NOT, and so on) to fine-tune your query. Well, forget your ANDs and NOTs; eBay doesn't permit the use of Boolean operators in its search function. In fact, if you enter Boolean operators in your query, eBay will treat them as keywords—and search for them!

Good enough. Now, let's make it more complex. You want to search for Bat stuff, but not *all* Bat stuff—just PEZ dispensers or costumes. For this search, enter this query:

`bat* (pez,costume)`

What if you want to look for something by title—such as the title of a movie? This is where you use quotation marks to surround the exact phrase you're searching for. If you want to search for anything associated with the movie *Batman Forever*, you enter this query:

`"batman forever"`

What if you want to search for Batman stuff but don't want anything related to Adam West? In this case, you use the exclude operator, in the form of a - sign, to automatically exclude any listings that include the designated word. The query looks like this:

```
batman -west
```

Conversely, if you want to look only at Batman items that had something to do with George Clooney, you use the include operator, in the form of a + sign, to search only for items which include that specific word.
The query looks like this:

```
batman +clooney
```

Finally, don't be afraid to string several of these commands together to create a more complex query—which will return more targeted results. Let's do a hypothetical search for all *Batman Forever* props and comics featuring George Clooney but not including Jim Carrey. (Whew!) Here's the query:

```
"batman forever" (prop,comic) +clooney
-carrey
```

See how it works? It's a little like constructing an algebraic equation; you just have to think it through logically, and use all the tools you have at hand.

> **tip**
>
> Don't be surprised if you enter that complex sample query into eBay's search engine and end up with zero results. The more targeted the query you enter, the fewer results will be returned—and some queries can be so targeted that nothing matches at all.

Saving Your Searches—and Repeating Them

You've taken the time to create a complex search. You figure you'll want to repeat that search at some point in the future, to keep looking for the items you want. You don't want to reenter the query every time you perform the search.

What do you do?

When it comes to repeating your searches, eBay makes it easy. All Items Matching pages (which display your search results) include an Add to My Favorite Searches link, at the top right of the page. Click this link, and this search is now listed on the Favorites tab of your My eBay page.

You can repeat a saved search by following these steps:

1. From the Navigation Bar, click the My eBay link.
2. On your My eBay Page, click the All Favorites link.

3. On the All Favorites page, shown in Figure 4.8, scroll to the My Favorite Searches section.

4. Identify the search you want to repeat, and click that search's link.

The search is now executed, as originally entered.

FIGURE 4.8

Saved searches on your My eBay page.

All Favorites			
My Favorite Searches (4 searches; 4 emails)		Add new Search ⌃ ⌄	
☐ Name of Search △	Search Criteria	Email Settings	Action
☐ batman (model,kit)	batman (model, kit)	99 days left (Last sent Feb-26-05)	Edit Preferences ⌄
☐ batman animation cells	batman Sort: Ending Soonest	157 days left (Last sent Feb-26-05)	Edit Preferences ⌄
☐ batman original art	batman original art	157 days left (Last sent Feb-26-05)	Edit Preferences ⌄
☐ superman (model,kit)	superman (model, kit)	157 days left (Last sent Feb-26-05)	Edit Preferences ⌄
Delete		Search items will be emailed to ebay@molehillgroup.com	

Get Notification of New Items That Match Your Search

If you want to be automatically notified when new items of a particular type come up for auction, you're in luck. You can instruct eBay to email you when new items appear that match any of your saved searches.

Just follow these instructions:

1. Navigate to the My Favorite Searches section of the All Favorites page in My eBay.

2. Click the Edit Preferences link next to the search you want to be notified of.

3. When the Edit Favorite Search Preferences page appears, select the Email Me Daily Whenever There Are New Items option.

4. Pull down the accompanying list and select a duration.

5. Click the Save Search button when done.

When you've activated this notification service, eBay will send you an email (one a day) when new items that match your search criteria come up for auction. The email contains links for each new item in your search; click a link to open your Web browser and display the matching item.

Mike Sez

eBay's email notification service is a great tool for active eBay bidders or for anyone searching for that elusive item. I love having eBay tell me when it has something for me, rather than having to log on and do a manual search every day. I highly recommend this service!

THE ABSOLUTE MINIMUM

Here are the key points to remember from this chapter:

- Browse through eBay's categories and subcategories when you're not sure of the exact item you're looking for.

- Use eBay's search pages to track down specific items for sale.

- Use wildcards and other search operators to fine-tune your item search.

- Click the Add to My Favorite Searches link to save your search criteria for future use—and then access your saved searches from your My eBay page.

- Activate eBay's email notification service to have eBay notify you when desired items come up for auction.

5

THE BEST WAYS TO PAY

In practically all eBay auctions, the buyer has to pay before the seller ships; that's just the way it is. In effect, this means that the risk of the transaction is on the buyer; the buyer is trusting the seller to actually ship the merchandise (in the agreed-on condition) when the payment is made.

With that in mind, how you pay is every bit as important as how much you pay. Read on to learn more about the payment options available—and to figure out which method of payment you should use.

Different Ways to Pay

How can you pay for your auction item? Well, you might not have too many choices. This is because most experienced sellers specify which methods of payment they'll accept, right up front in the item listing. So even if you want to pay by credit card, if the seller doesn't accept plastic, you're out of luck.

Paying by Cash

Nothing could be simpler than paying by cash. Cram some greenbacks and a few coins into an envelope, stick a stamp on it, and you're done.

Right?

Wrong.

Paying by cash is definitely the least recommended method of payment. There are a few reasons for this, all involving safety.

First, it's hard to hide cash in an envelope. Even if you wrap the bills in several sheets of paper and use a double envelope, there's something about a wad of cash that draws attention.

Second, it's easy to steal. Some disreputable types might see a cash-laden envelope sitting in a mailbox and make a grab for it. Easy to do.

Third, there's nothing to track. If the seller says he never received your payment, there's nothing to trace to prove otherwise. (That's why cash is the preferred method of payment for illegal drug dealers—it's virtually untraceable.)

So, unless the auction item is priced absurdly low (so low you don't care if the money gets ripped off), you should probably avoid paying by cash.

Paying by Check

One popular method of payment is the tried-and-true personal check. It's pretty easy for you as the buyer to pull out the checkbook, write a check, and put it in the mail—although some sellers might not like accepting checks, for several reasons. Checks are too easy for the buyer to cancel, which could leave the seller in the lurch. Plus, it's difficult for a seller to verify that funds actually exist for payment.

In addition, paying by check will probably slow down your item's shipment. That's because smart sellers wait for the check to clear before they ship your item. However, for many buyers, paying by check is still an easy way to go.

Let's face it. Many other methods of payment—especially cashier's checks and money orders—are a bit of a hassle. To draw a money order or cashier's check, you have to make a special trip to the bank or the post office, stand in line, pay a fee, and only *then* can you send your payment. With a personal check, you write the check from the comfort of your own desk, pop it in an envelope, and have the payment in the mail almost immediately.

Know, however, that some sellers will hold items paid for by a personal check for one to two weeks, until the check clears your bank. Other sellers will look at a buyer's feedback rating, and if it's strong, they'll go ahead and ship the merchandise when they receive the check. (That's one good use for eBay's feedback rating, as discussed in Chapter 27, "Understanding and Using Feedback.") But don't expect all sellers to ship immediately if you pay by personal check, especially if they haven't dealt with you before or you're a relatively new user of the auction site. And an increasing number of sellers are no longer accepting personal checks for payment; read the listing description to make sure before you bid.

Paying by Money Order or Cashier's Check

Some sellers state that they prefer cashier's checks or money orders, and try to discourage payment by personal check. This is understandable; to the seller, cashier's checks and money orders are just like cash, but a personal check isn't good until it clears the bank.

To you, the buyer, there are two potential downsides to paying via money order or cashier's check. First, it's a hassle; you have to go to the bank or post office or credit union, wait in line, fill out a form, and then arrange funding. Depending on your local conditions, that's probably a 15- to 30-minute effort.

Second, depending on where you get your money orders, there may be a fee involved. The U.S. Postal Service, for example, charges $0.90 to cut a money order. Your bank may charge less (or more—or, in rare instances, nothing), but it's one more fee to add to what you're paying for the auction item. If you won a relatively low-priced item, the charge might not be worth it.

tip

One of the best places to purchase a money order is your local Wal-Mart, with charges as low as $0.46.

Paying by Credit Card—Via PayPal

Paying via credit card is a pretty good deal for most buyers. Assuming that you pay your credit card bill in full when it arrives, there are no fees involved. Unlike with money orders or cashier's checks, you don't have to leave home to arrange payment. You also have an excellent paper trail for your payment; you know almost immediately if the seller has received payment. And, unlike personal checks, credit cards ensure faster shipment; as soon as you authorize payment, the buyer receives his funds and can ship the item to you.

tip

If you need an item in a hurry—around the holidays, for example—choosing a seller who accepts credit cards can be the key to a successful transaction. (If in doubt, email the seller while the auction is still in progress and ask!)

Unfortunately, most private individuals don't have the capability to accept credit card payment—and most sellers on eBay happen to be individuals. Many small businesses sell items on eBay, however, and most of these firms *do* accept payment by credit card.

There is, however, a way for an individual seller to accept credit card payments: by using PayPal. PayPal serves as the middleman for these transactions; you pay PayPal via credit card, and PayPal handles all the credit card paperwork and sends a check to the seller (or deposits funds in the seller's checking account). From your standpoint, using PayPal is transparent—you don't even have to pay any additional fees (outside of your normal credit card fees, of course). So if you see a PayPal logo in the item listing (like the one in Figure 5.1), you're in luck; that means you can use your credit card to pay, if you win.

FIGURE 5.1
Look for the PayPal logo at the bottom of an auction listing.

Paying via PayPal is relatively easy. When an auction ends (and you're the high bidder, of course!), you should receive an end-of-auction email from eBay. If the seller offers payment via PayPal, there will be a Pay Now button displayed in the email message. (Alternately, if you go to the closed item listing, you'll find a Pay Now button there, as well.) Click the Pay Now button and you'll be transferred to the PayPal site, where you can enter your credit card number and complete payment.

You can also pay for an eBay auction directly from the PayPal site (www.paypal.com). Just make sure you know the seller's eBay ID or email address, the number and title of the auction, and the total amount you owe (including shipping and handling). From the PayPal main page, click the Send Money tab to display the Send Money page. Follow the instructions there to enter the seller's email address and necessary auction information.

Of course, PayPal isn't just for credit card payments. You can make PayPal payments from your debit card, via a checking account withdrawal, or via withdrawal of standing funds in your PayPal account. Just choose the payment method you prefer, when prompted.

No matter how you choose to fund your purchase, one of the nice things about paying via PayPal is the site's Buyer Protection plan. Qualified auction purchases are eligible for up to $1,000 coverage, so if you get stiffed by a negligent seller or receive something significantly different from what you ordered, you're protected. Look for the PayPal Buyer Protection icon in the auction listing's Seller Information box to make sure you're buying from a qualified seller.

note

If you're not yet a PayPal member, you might be prompted to create a Personal account before you can initiate a payment. Personal membership is free.

tip

If you like the idea of a payment service but don't want to deal with PayPal, look for sellers that accept payments via an alternative service, such as BidPay (www.bidpay.com) or CheckFree (www.checkfree.com).

Paying by Credit Card (Without PayPal)

Some of the sellers on eBay are actually traditional retailers selling selected merchandise online. Many of these retailers—as well as some large individual sellers—are set up to receive credit card payments on their own, no PayPal required. Again, paying by credit card is the way to go for most buyers, so these sellers are easy to deal with. Just make sure that when you submit your credit card information, you're doing so on a secure website, and your information will be safe.

Paying Cash on Delivery

You might occasionally have the option of C.O.D. (cash on delivery) payment. Although this is rare when buying from an individual (especially so since eBay doesn't include C.O.D. as one of its default payment methods), it is a good route to take if you can. With C.O.D. payment, you don't actually part with your money until you receive the merchandise—and you can't stiff the seller, either, because if you don't pay the delivery guy, he doesn't give you your stuff.

Using Escrow

A final option, used primarily in higher-priced auctions, is the use of an escrow service. This is a company that acts as a neutral third party between the buyer (you) and the seller, holding your money until you receive the seller's merchandise. If you don't get the goods (or the goods are unacceptable), you get your money back; the seller gets paid only when you're happy.

eBay recommends using escrow for all auctions above $500 for which the seller doesn't accept credit card or PayPal payments.

Here's how a typical escrow transaction works:

1. At the end of an auction, you and the seller contact each other and agree to use an escrow service. The escrow service's fees can be split between the two parties or (more typically) can be paid by you, the buyer. Fees differ widely from service to service.

2. You send payment (by check, money order, cashier's check, or credit card) to the escrow service.

3. After your payment is approved, the escrow service instructs the seller to ship the item.

4. You receive the item, verify its acceptability, and notify the escrow service that all is fine hunky-dory.

5. The escrow service pays the seller.

Although you can use any third-party escrow service, eBay recommends Escrow.com (www.escrow.com). Go there for further information and instructions.

Evaluating Different Methods of Payments

Now you know how you *can* pay; you still want to know how you *should* pay.

Which Method Is Fastest?

When it comes to speed, paying by credit card (either directly or via PayPal) wins hands down. The seller receives his funds a few seconds after you click the Send button on the payment page, which means that shipment can occur almost immediately.

Paying by personal check is definitely the slowest method. Not only do you have to wait for the postal service to deliver your check to the seller, but you also have to wait for the seller to wait—for your check to clear your bank. All this waiting means that the seller probably won't be able to ship your item for at least two weeks after the end of the auction, and maybe longer.

Coming somewhere in the middle are money orders, cashier's checks, and plain old cash. You still have to depend on snail-mail delivery of your payment, but when the seller receives it, he can ship your item immediately. Depending on the speed of the mail, figure anywhere from two days to a week before your item is shipped.

Which Method Is Safest?

Of course, how you pay for an item can increase or decrease your protection during a transaction; some methods of payment are safer for you than others.

The least safe method of payment for a buyer is cash; there's nothing to track, and it's very easy for someone to steal an envelope full of cash. Also considered less safe (although better than cash) are cashier's checks and money orders; like cash, they provide no money trail to trace if you want to track down the seller. Paying by check gives you a minor trail to trace, but when the check is cashed, it's still pretty much a done deal.

A safer way to pay is by credit card. When you pay by credit card, you can always go to the credit card company and dispute your charges if the item you bought never arrived or was misrepresented. The same safety measures typically apply to credit card payments made through PayPal and other bill pay services—although you should check with the bill pay service, just to be sure.

For the ultimate protection when buying an expensive item in a person-to-person option, use an escrow service. Because the escrow service acts as a neutral third party between you and the seller, if you don't receive what you won—or are otherwise dissatisfied with the item—you get your money back, guaranteed.

> **" Mike Sez "**
>
> If you have the choice (and have a credit card), my personal recommendation is to pay by plastic. You'll have a paper trail if anything goes south, as well as protection from your credit card company (above a certain amount). If payment by plastic isn't available, I pay by check if I'm not in a hurry, or by money order if I am.

Which Method Should You Use?

Use Table 5.1 to determine how you want to pay, based on several key conditions.

TABLE 5.1   When to Use Which Payment Method

Situation	Payment Method
Very low-priced item (<$5 total), trusted seller, no time to write a check or get to the bank	Cash
Low-priced item, no hurry for shipment	Check
Low-priced item, need fast shipment, trusted seller, don't want to use credit card	Money order/cashier's check
Higher-priced item *or* need fast shipment *or* desire fraud protection	Credit card/PayPal
High-priced item, desire protection in case item doesn't meet expectations, don't mind paying additional fees	Escrow

THE ABSOLUTE MINIMUM

Here are the key points to remember from this chapter:

- Paying by cash is very unsafe, but it can result in relatively fast shipping.

- Paying by cashier's check or money order can be just as fast as paying by cash, and slightly safer.

- Paying by personal check is safer than cashier's check or money order and provides a nice paper trail—but it can slow down shipment of your item by one to two weeks.

- Paying by credit card is probably the best way to go, when available (typically via PayPal); it's fast and safe.

- For really expensive items, consider using an escrow service. For a fee, the escrow service holds onto your funds until you receive the item—and are 100% satisfied.

IN THIS CHAPTER

- Using the Post-Auction Checklist
- Making Contact—and Paying
- Waiting for Your Doorbell to Ring…
- Receiving the Goods
- Finishing Things Up and Leaving Feedback

AFTER THE AUCTION: TAKING CARE OF BUSINESS

You've somehow waited patiently (or not) throughout the entire auction process. As the clock ticked down to zero, no other viable competitors entered the arena, and your high bid stood. You won!

Now things *really* start to happen.

Using the Post-Auction Checklist

When you're an auction winner, you have a bit of work to do. Work through the tasks in this post-auction checklist to make sure you've covered all the bases.

Checklist: After You've Won .

- ☐ Receive eBay's end-of-auction email
- ☐ Use eBay's Pay Now feature

  or
- ☐ Wait for the seller to contact you and respond to the seller's email

  or
- ☐ Use the Request Total link on the closed listing page to request the total amount due to the seller
- ☐ Choose a shipping method, if a choice is offered
- ☐ Decide whether you want insurance
- ☐ Choose a payment method
- ☐ Send payment
- ☐ Receive the item
- ☐ Examine the item
- ☐ Email the seller that you've received the item
- ☐ Leave feedback for the seller

Making Contact—And Paying

The first thing that happens after an auction ends is that eBay sends you an email notifying you that you've won the aforementioned auction. Depending on what kinds of payments the seller specified, you might be able to pay directly from this email message.

note

Remember, in the world of online auctions, the buyer pays for everything—including shipping. Don't expect the seller to throw in shipping for free! Before placing a bid, remember to mentally add the approximate shipping costs to your bid price so that you're prepared for the total cost when the auction is over.

Calculating the Final Price

In most cases, the price you pay will include your high bid and a reasonable amount of shipping and handling fees. Don't be surprised if the shipping/handling actually runs a little more than what you might know the actual shipping to be; remember, the seller has to cover the costs of packaging supplies and the labor involved to pack and ship the item. If shipping/handling runs a few bucks more than actual shipping, don't sweat it.

You should also think about whether you need insurance on this item. In most cases buyers don't opt for insurance, but if you're buying a high-priced, rare, or very fragile item, you might want to protect yourself against damage in shipment. (That's if the seller offers insurance, of course; not all sellers do.)

Many sellers offer several shipping options (insurance versus no insurance, UPS versus FedEx versus USPS Priority Mail, and so on), at different costs to you. Others ship only one way. If given the choice, pick the best compromise between cost and speed. If not given the choice, live with it.

> **" Mike Sez "**
>
> Insurance might not make sense for lower-priced items. For example, the U.S. Postal Service charges $1.30 for $50 worth of insurance, which isn't necessarily a bargain for lower-priced items. However, if your item is higher-priced—or might be easily damaged—it might be worth it to insure the package.

If you have special shipping concerns (for example, FedEx doesn't deliver to your address), you should raise them *before* you bid on an item. If you can't work out something else, don't bid in this auction.

Paying via Credit Card

If the seller accepts PayPal payments, your end-of-auction notification will look like the one in Figure 6.1. This same Pay Now button also appears in the closed auction listing page on eBay; as shown in Figure 6.2.

FIGURE 6.1

Pay directly from eBay's end-of-auction notification email...

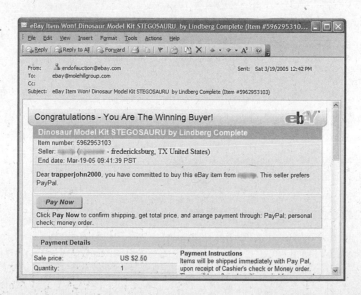

FIGURE 6.2

...or pay from
the closed auc-
tion listing page.

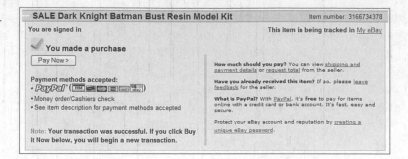

When you click the Pay Now button, you're transferred to a Review Your Purchase page, like the one shown in Figure 6.3. Make sure that all the transaction details are correct, and then scroll to the bottom of the page, select a payment method, and click the Continue button.

FIGURE 6.3

Choose how you
want to pay.

Review Your Purchase ? Need Help?

Please review and confirm this information regarding your purchase. When you are ready to pay, click the **Continue** button below.

Review shipping address

Seller should ship to: **Michael Miller**
11443 Woodview E. Dr.
Carmel, IN, 46032
United States
Change shipping address

Review payment details

Item #	Item Title	Qty.	Price	Subtotal
3166734378	SALE Dark Knight Batman Bust Resin Model Kit	1	US $9.99	US $9.99

Shipping and handling: US $10.50
Shipping insurance: (not offered) --
Other discounts (-) or charges (+): `-0.00`
(seller discounts. services. etc.)

Total: US $20.49
recalculate

Please make sure the amounts above are correct.
Not sure how much to pay? Request total from seller

Select a payment method (seller accepts the following)

For fast, secure online payment with your credit card or bank account, use PayPal – it's free.

⊙ PayPal* (VISA)
PayPal Buyer Protection offered. See coverage and eligibility.

○ Money order/Cashiers check
○ Other

Continue >

If you select to pay via PayPal, you're now taken to a PayPal payment page. Follow the onscreen instructions to make your payment.

Paying via Check or Money Order

If the seller doesn't accept PayPal payments, your end-of-auction notification looks like the one in Figure 6.4. Click the Send Payment Information button and you're taken to the Review Your Purchase page (shown back in Figure 6.3). Select your method of payment and click the Continue button.

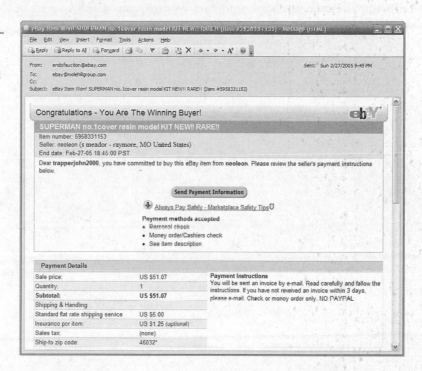

If you opted for a non-PayPal payment method, you'll now see the Send Information to the Seller page, shown in Figure 6.5. Make sure that all the information here is correct, and then click the Send Information to Seller button.

If you're paying by personal check, now is the time to write the check and put it in the mail. If you're paying by cashier's check or money order, head to the bank or post office, cut a payment, and then put it in the mail. Remember to include your name and shipping address, along with the item number and description, with your payment. (Or just include a printout of the Send Information to the Seller email that eBay sent to you.)

Contacting the Seller Directly

In some instances, you might also receive an email message directly from the seller. The seller's email should tell you how much you need to pay (your high bid amount plus shipping and handling) and where to send the payment.

If you don't hear from the seller within 24 hours, you might want to take the initiative and send your own email. (This is especially important if the shipping/handling charges were not specified ahead of time, and you need to know the total charges so you can send the proper payment.) Click the seller's name on the listing page to generate an email message, introduce yourself, and gently inquire about shipping and handling costs and where you should send your payment.

FIGURE 6.5

Sending your payment information to the seller.

Waiting for Your Doorbell to Ring...

Now you wait for the item to arrive. If the wait is too long, you should contact the seller and confirm that the item was actually shipped out on a particular date; if an item appears to be lost in shipment, the two of you can work together to track down the shipment with the shipping service. Just be sure to allow adequate time for your payment to clear and for the item to actually ship from the seller to you. (This might range from a few days for a credit card payment to a few weeks if you pay via personal check.)

This is also the stage of the process where some unlucky buyers discover that they're dealing with deadbeat sellers—frauds who take your money but never ship your item. If you find yourself in this situation, there are options available to you; turn to Chapter 7, "Dealing with Fraudulent Sellers," to learn more.

Receiving the Goods

In most cases the item arrives promptly. Now you should unpack the item and inspect it for any damage. If the item is something that can be tried out, you should make sure that the item actually works. If all is fine, email the seller to say that you received the merchandise and that you're happy. If all isn't fine, email the seller and let him or her know that you have a problem.

If you have a problem—or if you didn't receive the merchandise at all after a reasonable amount of time—you should first try to work out a compromise with the seller. Most sellers will bend over backward to make you happy; some won't.

If you can't work out anything with the seller, turn to eBay for assistance. See Chapter 7 for instructions on what to do when a deal goes bad.

tip

When your item arrives, check it out immediately. Don't wait a month before determining that there's something wrong; find out now whether the item is in good shape and delivers what was promised.

Finishing Things Up and Leaving Feedback

You've made your bid, won the auction, paid the seller, and received the merchandise. Now you're done—right?

Wrong.

The last thing you need to do is leave feedback about the seller. Whether it was a good transaction or a bad one, you need to let your fellow eBay members know how things turned out.

To leave feedback, go to the listing page for the item you just bought, click the Leave Feedback to Seller link, and then fill in the resulting form. You can leave positive, negative, or neutral feedback, as well as a one-line comment about the transaction. Make sure you really want to leave the comments you've written, and then click the Leave Comment button. Your feedback will be registered and added to the seller's other feedback comments.

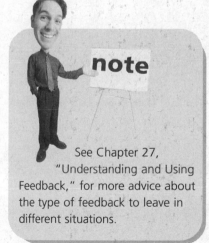

note

See Chapter 27, "Understanding and Using Feedback," for more advice about the type of feedback to leave in different situations.

The Absolute Minimum

Here are the key points to remember from this chapter:

■ When an auction is over, eBay notifies both you and the seller via email.

■ If you're paying by credit card, you can initiate payment directly from the end-of-auction email.

■ After you receive the merchandise, let the seller know that you're satisfied (or not) and leave feedback on the eBay site.

IN THIS CHAPTER

- Protecting Yourself Before You Buy
- Protecting Yourself After the Auction
- Reporting Inappropriate Behavior
- Tips for Protecting Yourself on eBay

7

DEALING WITH FRAUDULENT SELLERS

When you're bidding for and buying items on eBay, you're pretty much in "buyer beware" territory. You agree to buy an item, almost sight unseen, from someone whom you know practically nothing about. You send that person a check and hope and pray that you get something shipped back in return—and that the thing that's shipped is the thing you thought you were buying, in good condition. If you don't like what you got—or if you received nothing at all—the seller has your money. And what recourse do you have?

Remember, when you buy something through an eBay auction, when it comes down to making the financial transaction, you're dealing with an individual—*not* eBay. And as you'll soon learn, every person you deal with behaves differently and expects different behavior of you. In the course of your eBay dealings, it's not unlikely that you might run into a shady seller who never sends you the item you purchased—or tries to pass off a lower-quality item for what was described in the item listing. What can you do to protect yourself against other users who aren't as honest as you are?

Fortunately, you can do several things to protect yourself on eBay—and, in general, shopping at eBay is no more dangerous than shopping at a local garage sale. This chapter details some of the standard guidelines and procedures you can follow to ensure that your eBay buying and selling experience is not only successful, but profitable and enjoyable as well.

note

To learn more about feedback and the Member Profile page, see Chapter 27, "Understanding and Using Feedback."

Protecting Yourself Before You Buy

The first line of defense against frauds and cheats is to intelligently choose the people you deal with. On eBay, the best way to do this is via the Feedback system.

You should always check a seller's Feedback rating before you bid. If it's overwhelmingly positive, you can feel safer than if the seller has a lot of negative feedback. For even better protection, click the seller's name in the item listing to view his Member Profile, where you can read individual feedback comments. Be smart and avoid those sellers who have a history of delivering less than what was promised.

You can also use the Member Profile page to view the user's ID history (shifty users sometimes change IDs frequently) and other items for sale. You can even email the seller to ask for more information; just click the Contact Member button. If the seller won't work with you—or if the information doesn't check out—then don't deal with him!

" **Mike Sez** "

eBay regards its Feedback system as the best protection against fraudulent transactions. I certainly recommend that, whether a transaction went swell or went south, you leave feedback about your partner in every transaction. I know that I check the feedback rating of every seller I choose to deal with; it really is a good way to judge the quality of the other party in your eBay transactions.

Protecting Yourself After the Auction

What do you do if you follow all this advice and still end up receiving unacceptable merchandise—or no merchandise at all?

First, know that eBay doesn't accept any responsibility for any transactions conducted on its site. It's not the buyer or the seller, only a relatively disinterested third party.

However, that doesn't mean you shouldn't contact eBay if you're the recipient of a sour deal—you should, and eBay encourages you to do so. At the very least, eBay will start tracking the seller's other activities and perhaps kick the seller off the site if a pattern of fraudulent activity can be shown. Best case scenario, eBay will actually refund some of the money you've lost.

tip

In addition, you should leave formal negative feedback about any bad sellers you encounter; it's your duty to warn other buyers before they get suckered, too.

Getting Help from eBay

eBay offers a Purchase Protection Program that protects you up to $200 (with a $25 deductible) for any auction transaction gone bad. This Purchase Protection Program is the final step in a long process with an equally long name—the Item Not Received or Significantly Not as Described Process. (Whew!)

note

Learn more about The Process at pages.ebay.com/help/tp/inr-snad-process.html.

Understanding the Process

The Item Not Received or Significantly Not Described Process (let's just call it The Process) outlines specific steps you need to follow if you don't receive an item you've purchased, or if the item isn't what you thought you were buying. You can initiate The Process between ten and sixty days after the end of an auction, and it goes like this:

1. **Contact the seller.** If, after a reasonable waiting period, you haven't received an item (or think the seller pulled a "bait and switch" on you), try to work it out with the seller first. Email the seller directly (and politely) and see how he responds.

2. **Open a dispute**. If the seller doesn't respond to your satisfaction, you can open an Item Not Received or Significantly Described dispute. You can do this by going to eBay's Security & Resolution Center (pages.ebay.com/securitycenter/), checking the Item Not Received option, and then clicking the Report

Problem button. When the next page appears, as shown in Figure 7.1, enter the item number and click Continue. Follow the onscreen instructions from there. Note that the dispute has to be opened within 10 to 60 days after the end of the auction.

FIGURE 7.1

Opening a dispute for an item not received.

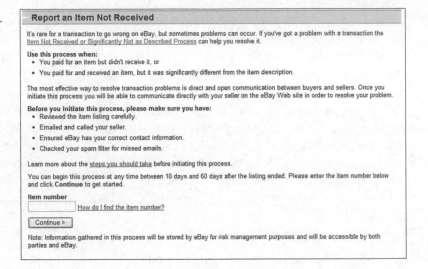

Report an Item Not Received

It's rare for a transaction to go wrong on eBay, but sometimes problems can occur. If you've got a problem with a transaction the Item Not Received or Significantly Not as Described Process can help you resolve it.

Use this process when:
• You paid for an item but didn't receive it, or
• You paid for and received an item, but it was significantly different from the item description.

The most effective way to resolve transaction problems is direct and open communication between buyers and sellers. Once you initiate this process you will be able to communicate directly with your seller on the eBay Web site in order to resolve your problem.

Before you initiate this process, please make sure you have:
• Reviewed the item listing carefully.
• Emailed and called your seller.
• Ensured eBay has your correct contact information.
• Checked your spam filter for missed emails.

Learn more about the steps you should take before initiating this process.

You can begin this process at any time between 10 days and 60 days after the listing ended. Please enter the item number below and click **Continue** to get started.

Item number

[   ] How do I find the item number?

[Continue >]

Note: Information gathered in this process will be stored by eBay for risk management purposes and will be accessible by both parties and eBay.

3. **eBay contacts the seller**. eBay will now send an automated email to the seller, encouraging him to contact you and work out the problem. More often than not, this prompting will cause the seller to resolve the issue.

4. **The seller responds**. The seller should then respond to eBay's email, either by noting how the issue was resolved, or by requesting further communication.

5. **You communicate with the seller.** If the seller hasn't already shipped the item, eBay now encourages the two of you to talk some more. (Via eBay's online posting system, of course.) This is yet another opportunity to work out the problem.

6a. **Close the dispute**. If the issue is resolved to your satisfaction, you should now close the dispute. Or...

6b. **File a claim**. If 30 days have passed since the end of the auction and you haven't been able to work out your dispute, you're now eligible to file a claim under eBay's Purchase Protection Program, which we'll discuss next.

caution

Be reasonable before you file a dispute. For example, if you paid by personal check, the buyer will hold the check for up to two weeks before he ships the item—so you can't expect to receive the item in 10 days. Also factor in weekends and holidays before you determine that you're not going to receive an item.

Understanding eBay's Purchase Protection Program

eBay's Standard Purchase Protection Program is available to all buyers with non-negative feedback. Here are some of the details you need to know:

- You're insured (for up to $200) on items with a final value over $25. If the item is priced under $25, you're on your own.

- There's a $25 deductible on each claim. If you submit a claim for a $35 item, you'll get $10 back ($35 minus the $25 deductible). If you submit a claim for $200, you'll get $175 back.

- You'll be reimbursed only for the final bid price, not for any other fees—such as shipping, handling, or escrow fees.

- To qualify, both your feedback rating and the seller's feedback rating have to be zero or above.

- All items that meet eBay's user agreement are covered; items that violate the user agreement aren't covered.

- You can get reimbursed if you send money to a seller and you don't receive the item. You can also get reimbursed if you receive the item, but it's significantly different than described in the auction listing. However, you won't be reimbursed if something happens to the item in transit; if the shipping company loses or damages the item, that's the company's problem to fix.

- You have to wait until 30 days after the auction to begin the complaint process—and have to file within 60 days of the auction end.

- If you paid by credit card, you can only file a Buyer Protection claim if the credit card company has denied your request for a refund—which means that you contact your credit card company first, and eBay second.

- You can file a maximum of three claims in a six-month period.

Filing a Claim

How do you get your money back if you've been burned? Here are the basic steps to take:

1. Go through the Item Not Received or Significantly Not Described Process, as previously described.

2. Somewhere between 30 and 60 days after the end of the auction, close your dispute and select "I feel I have no other option but to escalate this to a claim."

3. If your transaction is eligible for coverage, you'll be presented with a link to the Standard Purchase Protection claim form; click this link. (You can also access this form by clicking the Disputes Console link on your My eBay page.)

4. Fill out the Standard Purchase Protection Claim form, and then click the Submit button to file your claim.

5. Within 14 days of submitting your claim, an eBay claims administrator will contact you via email. If you're asked to provide proof of payment, you'll need to send eBay a copy of a receipt, money order, personal, check, and so on. If you paid by credit card, eBay will require proof of denial of reimbursement through your credit card company. You can mail or fax this information to eBay.

6. If you're filing a claim for an item "significantly not as described," the eBay claims administrator may ask you to provide a letter of authenticity or appraisal from an independent authenticator.

7. Sometime in the next 45 days you will be contacted by the eBay claims administrator. If your claim is approved, you'll be sent a check for the disputed amount (less the $25 deductible).

I hope you'll never have to use eBay's Purchase Protection Program. But if you are the unfortunate recipient of an unscrupulous seller, it's good to know that eBay is looking out for you.

Resolving Conflicts

Sometimes a problem auction doesn't have a clear-cut good guy and bad guy. If you ever find yourself in an extreme finger-pointing situation, it might be time to engage in online dispute resolution.

To negotiate these sticky types of disputes, eBay offers mediation services through SquareTrade (www.squaretrade.com). This site settles disputes through a possible two-part process. You start out with what SquareTrade calls Online Dispute Resolution; this free service uses an automated negotiation tool to try to get you and the seller to neutral ground. Communication is via email; the process helps to cool down both parties and let you work out a solution between the two of you.

If the two of you can't work it out in this manner, you have the option of engaging a SquareTrade mediator to examine the case and come to an impartial decision. This will cost you $20, and both parties agree to abide with the results. If the SquareTrade mediator says you're owed a refund, the seller has to pay you. If the representative says there's no basis for your claim, you have to stop complaining. (At least to the other person.)

Beyond eBay

Beyond eBay, you can contact other agencies if you've been disadvantaged in a deal. For example, if mail fraud is involved (which it is if any part of the transaction—either payment or shipping—was handled through the mail), you can file a complaint with your local U.S. Post Office or state attorney general's office. If you've had a large amount of money ripped off or if your credit card number was stolen, you should also contact your local police department.

You can also register a complaint with the National Fraud Information Center (www.fraud.org), which is a project of the National Consumers League. This site will transmit the information you provide to the appropriate law enforcement agencies.

Finally, you can file a complaint about any fraudulent auction transaction with the Federal Trade Commission (FTC). Although the FTC doesn't resolve individual consumer problems, it can and will act if it sees a pattern of possible law violations. You can contact the FTC online (www.ftc.gov/ftc/consumer.htm) or via phone (877-FTC-HELP).

Reporting Inappropriate Behavior

There is a long list of activities that buyers and sellers can engage in that eBay expressly prohibits. Most of these offenses—detailed in the list that follows—involve blatantly manipulating auction results, whether by the seller or by an overly interested bidder. If eBay catches a user doing any of these, that user will be either temporarily suspended (kind of a first warning) or permanently banned from the service.

Of course, you have to be caught before you can be punished. The main way eBay finds out about these activities is from other users—the real victims of these offensive behaviors.

If you suspect any of these bidding offenses in any specific auction (even if you yourself are not participating in the auction), you should notify eBay at pages.ebay.com/help/tp/programs-investigations.html. Be sure to include all relevant information and copies of all email correspondence with the suspected offender.

What activities are we talking about? Here's a short list:

■ **Shill bidding**, which involves bidding on your own item in a deliberate attempt to artificially drive up its price. A shill bid can involve the use of secondary eBay registrations, user aliases, family members, friends, or associates to pump up the price; other bidders then have to top a higher price to stay in the game.

■ **Bid shielding**, which is the practice of using shill bidding (but not a shill associated with the seller) to artificially increase the price of an item temporarily, in an attempt to protect the low bid level of a third bidder. Essentially, the artificially high bid scares off other bidders, and then the shill retracts the superhigh bid at the last moment, leaving the bidding wide open for the initial, lower bidder.

■ **Bid siphoning**, which happens when a third party (unrelated to the seller or bidder) emails bidders in a currently open auction, offering a similar or identical item at a price below the current bid level. This siphons off potential sales away from the registered seller and makes an end-run around eBay's fee system.

- **Bid discovery**, which happens when the bidder places a very high bid on the item (well over the current high bidder's assumed maximum bid level) and then retracts the bid. This returns the high bid to the former high bidder, but at that bidder's maximum bid level—which wasn't previously public.

- **Unwanted bidding**, which happens when a buyer is warned away from an auction (because of poor feedback, past experience, or other reasons) yet persists on placing a bid. If the seller reports you to eBay for this offense, you can be indefinitely suspended from the service.

- **Repeatedly backing out of transactions.** Backing out of one or two transactions won't win you any friends, it also won't get you kicked off eBay. However, if you back out of a lot of transactions—as either a buyer or a seller—eBay will toss you off. It's chronic incomplete transactions that eBay notices.

- **Auction interference**, which happens when a bidder sends threatening emails to other bidders to warn them away from a seller or an item. You're not allowed to interfere with in-process auctions—and you're *definitely* not allowed to threaten other users! eBay will bump you if they find out.

- **Transaction interception**, which is out-and-out fraud. You represent yourself as another eBay seller, intercepting the ended auctions of that seller (generally with forged email messages) and convincing buyers to send you payment for the items. Getting caught at this one will cause you more trouble than just a simple eBay expulsion.

- **Spamming**, which occurs when you send bulk email (spam) to masses of other users. If eBay finds out, it'll kick you off, simple as that.

Tips for Protecting Yourself on eBay

When all is said and done, eBay is a fairly safe environment to conduct person-to-person transactions. The vast majority of eBay users are honest individuals, and you'll no doubt enjoy hundreds of good transactions before you hit your first bad one.

That said, here are some tips on how to better protect yourself when you're dealing on eBay:

- Remember that you're dealing with human beings. Be nice, be polite, and, above all, *communicate!* Send emails confirming receipt of payment or shipment of merchandise. Say "please" and "thank you." And don't send short, snippy emails in the heat of the moment. Be tolerant and friendly, and you'll be a better eBay citizen.

- Realize that, in most cases, you're dealing with individuals, not businesses. Keep that in mind if things don't go quite as smoothly as they would if you ordered from Amazon.com or L.L.Bean. Most folks don't have automated shipping systems installed in their living rooms!

■ Know that experienced eBay users take the feedback system very seriously—if not obsessively. Positive feedback is expected for every successful transaction, and negative feedback should be used in only the most dire of circumstances. When in doubt, just don't leave any feedback at all.

■ If you have questions about an item for sale, or about any part of the transaction, ask! Email the seller if you're not sure about payment or shipping terms. Good communication eliminates surprises and misinterpretations; don't assume anything.

■ When the item you purchased arrives, inspect it thoroughly and confirm that it's as described. If you feel you were misled, contact the seller immediately, explain the situation, and see what you can work out. (You'd be surprised how many sellers will go out of their way to make their customers happy.)

■ If the merchandise doesn't arrive in a timely fashion, contact the seller immediately. If the item appears to be lost in transit, track down the letter/package via the shipping service. If the item never arrives, it's the seller's responsibility to file an insurance claim with the carrier (if the item was insured), and you should receive a refund from the seller.

THE ABSOLUTE MINIMUM

Here are the key points to remember from this chapter:

■ Buying an item on eBay is generally about as safe as buying something from a local garage sale—with the caveat of "buyer beware."

■ That said, most eBay buyers and sellers are honest and trustworthy.

■ To protect you against those who aren't, eBay offers its Standard Purchase Protection Program, which includes $200 worth of insurance per transaction for aggrieved buyers.

■ You're better protected if you pay by credit card or use an escrow service.

■ If you do get ripped off, contact the auction site, your local authorities, and the FTC.

■ You should always leave feedback about the people you deal with—whether positive or negative.

8

OTHER WAYS TO BUY ON EBAY

eBay was born as an online auction site, and is still known for its auction-format listings. But there's more to eBay than auctions; you can also buy merchandise on eBay without all that bidding and waiting.

If you want your merchandise *now*, you need to check out eBay's various fixed-priced item listings. Whether it's an auction with a Buy It Now option or an item for sale (not auction) in an eBay Store, there's a lot of merchandise available, no bidding required!

Get It Quick with Buy It Now

Tired of waiting around for the end of an auction—only to find out you didn't have the winning bid? Well, there's a way to actually *buy* some items you see for auction—without going through the bidding process. All you have to do is look for those auctions that have a Buy It Now (BIN) option.

Buy It Now is an option that some (but not all) sellers add to their auctions. With Buy It Now, the item is sold (and the auction ended) if the very first bidder places a bid for a specified price. (For this reason, some refer to Buy It Now auctions as "fixed-price" auctions—even though they're slightly different from eBay's *real* fixed-priced listings.)

Buying an item with Buy It Now is really simple. If you see an item identified with a Buy It Now price (as shown in Figure 8.1), just enter a bid at that price. You'll immediately be notified that you've won the auction, and the auction will be officially closed.

note

eBay also offers true fixed-price listings—that is, item listings with no bidding allowed. These work pretty much like Buy It Now auctions, except that your only option is to buy at the stated price; you can't place a lower bid.

FIGURE 8.1

A Buy It Now auction.

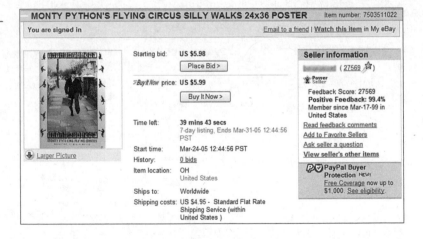

Of course, you don't have to bid at the Buy It Now price. You can bid at a lower price and hope that you win the auction, which then proceeds normally. (The Buy It Now option disappears when the first bid is made—or, in a reserve price auction, when the reserve price is met.) But if you want the item *now*—and you're willing to pay the asking price—you can use the Buy It Now option to make an immediate purchase.

Shopping at eBay Stores

There's something else you might find as you're browsing for items on eBay—fixed-price items. These items are different from Buy It Now items in that they're not up for auction at all; they're only available for sale outright.

Most fixed-price items are available from eBay sellers who run *eBay Stores*. An eBay Store is an online storefront where eBay merchants can sell their goods without putting them up for auction.

You can browse through thousands of different eBay merchants at the eBay Stores page (www.stores.ebay.com), shown in Figure 8.2. eBay Stores merchants are organized by the same categories as the eBay auction site—Antiques, Art, Books, and so on. You can also search for a specific store or a store selling a certain type of item, or view an alphabetical list of all stores.

"Mike Sez"

You should use Buy It Now only if you really, really, really want the item; if you think the Buy It Now price is reasonable; if you fear that the final price will be higher than the Buy It Now price; or if you don't want to wait for the auction to run its course to complete your purchase.

tip

You can also access eBay Stores from the regular eBay site. Just click the eBay Stores link in the Specialty Sites box on eBay's main page.

Browsing and Buying from an eBay Store

As you can see in Figure 8.3, the typical eBay Store offers fixed-price merchandise that isn't available for auction on eBay, as well as any auction items the merchant currently has listed. When you access a particular eBay Store, you have access to this entire collection of merchandise; if you tried searching on eBay proper, you wouldn't find the non-auction items the retailer might have for sale.

Buying an item from an eBay Store is a little like buying from any other online merchant, and a little like winning an item in an eBay auction. On the one hand, you're buying from an actual merchant at a fixed price, and you can always pay by credit card (typically via PayPal). On the other hand, you have all the niceties you have on eBay, including the ability to check the merchant's feedback rating.

FIGURE 8.2
The home page
for eBay Stores.

FIGURE 8.3
Shopping for
fixed-price items
at an eBay Store.

After you locate an item you want, you're taken to the "virtual storefront" of the
eBay Store that is selling the item. When you're in a specific store, you can purchase the item you were looking at or shop for additional items. Your checkout is
handled from within the store.

Searching eBay Stores

Here's the thing about eBay Stores; the merchandise they offer doesn't show up in standard eBay searches. This is too bad, since you can sometimes find items for sale in eBay Stores that you can't find in eBay's normal auctions. If you want to search for items available at eBay Stores, you have to perform a special search.

Follow these steps:

1. Click the Advanced Search link at the top of the eBay home page.

2. When the Find Items page appears, click the Items in Stores link in the left-hand column.

3. When the Search: Items in Stores page appears, enter one or more keywords in the Enter Keyword or Item Number box.

4. Define other search parameters, as necessary.

5. Click the Search button to start the search. eBay displays your results on a separate Items Matching page.

tip

You can also search eBay Stores from the eBay Stores page; use the Search for Items in Stores section at the top of the page.

Just Like Amazon: Half.com

eBay Stores isn't the only place you can find fixed-price merchandise on the eBay site. eBay also runs a site called Half.com, which offers new and used merchandise for sale from a variety of merchants.

As you can see in Figure 8.4, the Half.com home page (half.ebay.com) looks a little like Amazon.com. That's by design; Half.com was originally conceived as an Amazon competitor. Today, Half.com offers merchandise from both large and small retailers, and from individuals, too. The site specializes in books, CDs, DVDs, video games, computers and software, and other consumer electronics items.

When you search for a specific item on the Half.com, the site returns a list of all the sellers who have that item for sale, like the one in Figure 8.5. The list is sorted into new and used items, with the used items further sorted by condition—like new, very good, good, acceptable, and so on. This is a great way to compare prices between sellers; click the More Info link next to a specific seller link to learn more, or click the Buy button to make your purchase.

When you make a purchase at Half.com, you're buying directly from the individual seller, just as you do in an eBay auction. The big difference, of course, is that it's not an auction; you're buying an item (new or used) at a fixed price. The other difference is that you don't pay the seller separately; all your Half.com purchases end up in the same shopping cart, just like at Amazon.com. As you can see in Figure 8.6, you check out once for all your purchases, and make just one payment (to Half.com). Half.com then pays the individual sellers, who ship you your merchandise separately. It's fairly painless.

FIGURE 8.4

eBay's Half.com site.

FIGURE 8.5

Searching for items for sale on Half.com.

FIGURE 8.6

Items from multiple sellers end up in the same Half.com shopping cart.

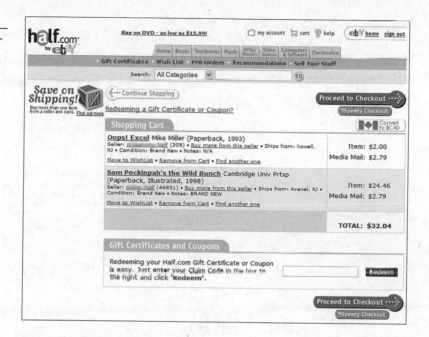

Express Shopping for Books, CDs, DVDs, and Video Games

If you're in the mood for a specific book, CD, DVD, videotape, or video game, you can use eBay's new Express Zone feature to search for exactly what you want. The Express Zone (pages.ebay.com/express/), shown in Figure 8.7, lets you search by ISBN, UPC, title, author, or artist. All you have to do is enter the exact information into the Express Product Search box, select the type of product you're looking for, and click the Search button. eBay now displays a list of items that match your query. Select the one you want, and eBay lists all the current auctions for that item. It's a quick and easy way to find exactly what you want.

FIGURE 8.7

Shop the Express Zone for books, CDs, DVDs, and video games.

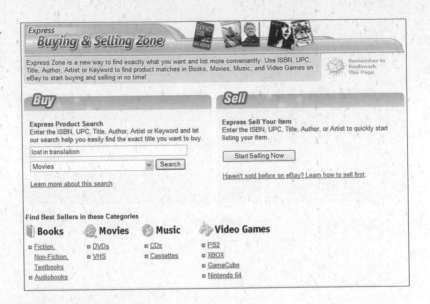

Want It Now? Then Ask for It!

If you can't find exactly what you want on the eBay site, all hope is not lost. eBay offers a new feature called Want It Now, which lets you post the online equivalent of an "item wanted" ad; sellers who have what you want can then contact you to make a deal.

To get to the Want It Now page (shown in Figure 8.8), click the Want It Now link in the Specialty Sites section of the eBay home page or go directly to pages.ebay.com/wantitnow/. Click the Post to Want It Now button, and eBay displays the Post to Want It Now page, shown in Figure 8.9. Enter a description of what you're looking for, click the Post to Want It Now button, and your request now appears in eBay's Want It Now database. Your request stays live for 60 days, or until you find something to buy.

Sellers can either browse or search the Want It Now listings from the main Want It Now page. If they have an item that fits your request, they click the Respond button in the listing. This automatically sends you an email with a link to the seller's item listing, like the one in Figure 8.10. Click the View This Item button to view the item listing; you can then decide to bid on or buy the item—or not. It's a great way to locate otherwise hard-to-find items.

FIGURE 8.8

eBay's Want It Now page.

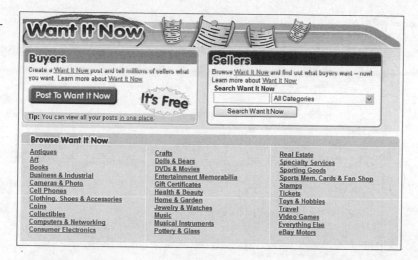

FIGURE 8.9

Creating a Want It Now request.

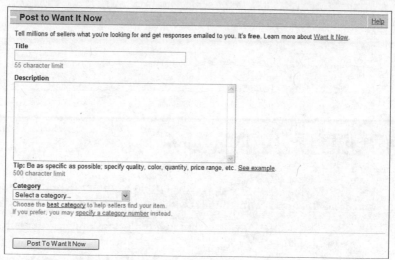

FIGURE 8.10

Somebody has
something you
might want
to buy!

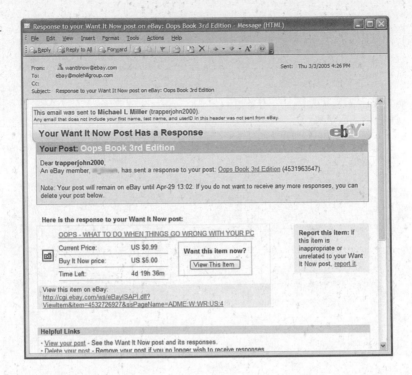

THE ABSOLUTE MINIMUM

Here are the key points to remember from this chapter:

- Many sellers offer a Buy It Now option in their auctions; this lets you purchase the item immediately, without waiting for the auction to end.

- eBay Stores offer fixed-price merchandise not otherwise available via eBay auctions.

- eBay's Half.com also offers fixed-priced merchandise for sale from both individuals and merchants—all from one common shopping cart and checkout.

- To shop for a specific book, CD, DVD, or video game, use eBay's Express Zone.

- If you can't find what you're looking for, use eBay's Want It Now feature to post a request for a particular item.

9

SECRETS OF SUCCESSFUL BIDDERS

You want to be a player. You want to bid with the best of them. When you bid, you want to win. When you win, you don't want to overpay.

This is the chapter you've been waiting for. Discover the secrets and strategies that will help you be a successful eBay bidder!

The Guaranteed Way to Win an Auction—Be Sneaky and Snipe

If you have any experience with eBay auctions, you've seen the following phenomenon. On day one of the auction, there are a few initial bids. On day two, the number of new bids trails off. On days three through six, few if any bids are placed. Then, on the seventh and last day of the auction, all hell breaks loose—with the heaviest bidding taking place in the auction's final minutes.

What's happening here? It's simple: Interested bidders are employing a technique called *sniping*, and saving their best bids for last.

Sniping is a technique used to win auctions by not bidding at all over the course of the auction, but then swooping in at the very last minute with an insurmountable bid. The thinking behind this strategy is simple. By not disclosing your interest, you don't contribute to bidding up the price during the course of the auction. By bidding at the last minute, you don't leave enough time for other bidders to respond to your bid. The successful sniper makes one bid only—and makes it count.

Sniping happens on eBay because the end time of each auction is rigidly enforced. If you know that an auction ends at 12:01:30, you can time your snipe to hit at 12:01:29, leaving no time for any other bidders to trump your bid. Some other auction sites, such as Yahoo! Auctions, have flexible end times; if there is bidding within the last five minutes of an auction, the auction is automatically extended by another five minutes, giving extra time for other bidders to respond to a snipe.

Sniping: Pros and Cons

eBay management doesn't have an official position on sniping, although it has the company's tacit approval. Many experienced eBay users not only participate in sniping, but also regard it as a kind of game. (Sellers like sniping, of course, as long as it helps to drive up the prices of their items.) It's the community of less-experienced users—or those used to more traditional auctions—that is less likely to embrace sniping as a practice.

Most bidders who despise sniping say that it takes all the fun out of the auction process. Experienced snipers say that sniping itself is fun, that it can be kind of a game to see just how late you can bid and still make it count before the auction closes.

Whether you like it or not, sniping works. After all, if you place a high enough bid at the last second, there's no time for anyone to respond with a higher bid. The last high bidder always wins, and a sniper stands a very good chance of being the last high bidder.

Can a sniper lose an auction? Yes, under these scenarios:

■ First, there might be another sniper in the queue who places a higher snipe than your maximum bid. A last-second bid of $35 will beat out a last-second bid of $30 any day.

■ Second, your snipe might be too early, allowing time for the previous high bidder to receive an outbid notice and respond with a higher bid.

■ Third, your snipe might not be high enough to beat out an existing high bid. (That's why I told you earlier to always bid the maximum amount you want to pay—it can ward off some cheap snipers.) If the current bid is $25 but the high bid (not known to you) is $35, you'd be beat if you "only" bid $30.

If you've ever been outbid on an item at the very last moment, you know that sniping can win auctions. Even if you hate sniping, the only way to beat a sniper is to snipe yourself.

Successful Sniping, Step-by-Step

Successful sniping requires large amounts of patience and split-second timing—but will reward you with a higher number of winning bids. Just follow these steps:

1. Identify the item you want to buy—and then *don't bid!* Resist the temptation to place a bid when you first notice an item. Make a note of the auction (and its closing time), or even put the item on your watch list; but don't let anyone else know your intentions.

2. Five minutes before the close of the auction, make sure you're logged on to the Internet, and access the auction in question.

3. Open a second browser window to the auction in question.

4. Display the Windows clock on your desktop, and configure it to display both minutes and seconds. (Or just grab a watch with a second hand or a stopwatch.)

5. In your first browser window, enter your maximum bid and click the Submit button to display the confirmation screen. *Don't confirm the bid yet!* Wait for the confirmation screen.

6. In your second browser window, click the Refresh or Reload button to update the official auction time. Keep doing this until the time remaining until close is 60 seconds.

> **"Mike Sez"**
>
> It's a good idea to synch your Windows clock with eBay's official time. To view the current eBay time, go to cgi3.ebay.com/aw-cgi/ eBayISAPI.dll?TimeShow.

7. Now, using either the Windows clock or your watch or stopwatch, count down 50 seconds, until there are only 10 seconds left

in the auction. (You might want to confirm the synchronization midway through your countdown by refreshing your second browser window again.)

8. When exactly 10 seconds are left in the auction, click the Confirm Bid button in your first browser window to send your bid.

9. Wait 10 seconds, and then click the Refresh or Reload button in your second browser window. The auction should now be closed, and (if your sniping was successful) you should be listed as the winning bidder.

Why bid 10 seconds before close? It takes about this long to transmit the bid from your computer to the online auction site and for the bid to be registered. If you bid any earlier than this, you leave time for the auction to send an outbid notice to the previous high bidder—and you don't want that person to know that until it's too late to do anything about it.

Using Software to Snipe

If you can't personally be present to snipe at the end of an auction, check out an automated sniping program or Web-based sniping service. These programs and services let you enter the item number of the auction and your maximum bid beforehand, and then go online at precisely the right time to place a last-minute snipe—even if you're not at home or you're otherwise occupied.

The best of these auto-snipe tools are listed in Table 9.1.

note

For more details on these and other third-party auction programs and services, see Chapter 28, "Using Auction Software and Services."

TABLE 9.1 Automated Sniping Programs and Web Sites

Tool	Type	Pricing	Website
Auction Sentry	Software	$14.95 ($24.95 for Deluxe edition)	www.auction-sentry.com
AuctionSniper	Web service	1% of final price ($0.25 min/ $5.00 max)	www.auctionsniper.com
AuctionStealer	Web service	$11.99/month	www.auctionstealer.com
BidNapper	Web service	$9.95/month	www.bidnapper.com
BidRobot	Web service	$19.95/6 months	www.bidrobot.com
BidSlammer	Web service	$0.10/losing bid or 1% of final price ($0.25 min/$5.00 max)	www.bidslammer.com
Cricket Power Sniper	Software	$19.99	www.cricketsniper.com

TABLE 9.1   (continued)

Tool	Type	Pricing	Website
eSnipe	Web service	1% of final price ($0.25 min/ $10.00 max)	www.esnipe.com
HammerSnipe	Web service	Free	www.hammertap.com/ HammerSnipe.html
Merlin Auction Magic	Software	$12.95	www.merlinsoftware.com
Vrane	Web service	Free	www.vrane.com

Forty Sure-Fire Tips for Placing a Winning Bid—And Getting the Most for Your Money

Whether you snipe or not, you can do many other things to increase your chances of winning an auction without overpaying for the item in question. Here are my top tips that can help anyone be a more successful eBay bidder.

> **tip**
>
> Want even more advice? Then check out my companion book, *Tricks of the eBay Masters* (Que, 2004). It's filled with 600 tricks and tips that any eBay buyer can use!

Tip #1: Bid in the Off Season

You already know that the final minute of the auction is the best time to place your bid. But are there specific times of the year that offer better bargains for bidders?

The answer, of course, is yes. Although there is some category-specific seasonality, the best overall time of the year to pick up eBay bargains is during the summer months. Summer is the slowest period on eBay, which means fewer people bidding—and lower prices for you.

Tip #2: Look for Off-Peak Auctions

Believe it or not, some auctions are set to end in the wee hours of the morning—when there aren't a lot of bidders awake to make last-minute snipes. Look for auctions ending between midnight and 5:00 a.m. Pacific time if you want some competition-free sniping.

Tip #3: Do Your Research

Don't bid blind; make sure you know the true value of an item before you offer a bid. Look around at auctions of similar items; what prices are they going for? And don't neglect researching outside of eBay; sometimes, you can find what you're looking for at a discount store or in a catalog or at another online site—where you'll probably get a real warranty and a better return policy. Shop around, and don't assume that the price you see at an auction is always the best deal available.

Be informed, and you won't bid too high—or too low.

Tip #4: Don't Bid on the First Item You See

Probably several other items on the same auction site are similar to the first item you saw. Look at the entire list of items before you choose which one to bid on. Seldom is the first item you see the one you really want or the best deal.

Tip #5: Know When to Say No

Be disciplined. Set a maximum price you're willing to pay for an item, and *don't exceed it!* It's okay to lose an auction.

Don't automatically rebid just because you've been outbid. It's too easy to get caught up in the excitement of a fast-paced auction. Learn how to keep your cool; know when to say no.

Tip #6: Don't Let the Proxy Bid Things Up

If two or more people are bidding on the same item, eBay's proxy bidding software can automatically (and quickly) rocket up the price until the bidder with the lower maximum bid maxes out. It's kind of an automated bidding frenzy conducted by two mindless robots.

Some bidders refuse to participate in proxy bidding. If the price is to increase, they want to do it manually. If you want to hold total control over the entire bidding process, how do you defeat the automatic bidding software? Simple: Make sure that your maximum bid is the same price as the next incremental bid and no higher. It might take a bit more work—and it's not the way I like to do things, personally—but it does put you in total control of the bidding process.

Tip #7: There Are Other Fish in the Sea

In 99.9% of eBay's auctions, that "one of a kind" item really isn't one of a kind. In fact, some sellers (especially merchant sellers) will have multiple quantities of an item, which they release to auction in dribs and drabs over time. In addition, some collectibles are bought and sold and bought and sold by multiple buyers and sellers over time, continually changing hands via new auctions. If you don't get this particular item, there's a good chance you'll get to bid on something similar soon.

Tip #8: If It Sounds Too Good to Be True, It Probably Is

A rare copy of *Action Comics* #1 for only $25? A brand-new laptop computer for only $100? There has to be a catch. That *Action Comics* is probably a facsimile reprint, and the brand-new laptop PC is actually a remanufactured unit missing some key parts. Be suspicious of improbable or impossible deals; always ask questions that confirm or reject your suspicions.

Tip #9: Ask Questions

If you're unclear about any aspect of an item you're interested in, ask the seller questions via email. In addition to answering your specific questions, some sellers have additional information or pictures they can send you one-on-one. There's no excuse for ignorance; if you're not sure, ask!

Tip #10: Check the Feedback

Check out the seller's feedback rating. Make sure that the seller of the item you want has a good feedback rating—and avoid any sellers who don't. You should also click the seller's numerical feedback rating to display actual comments from other users who have dealt with this user before. The best way to avoid bad sellers is to find out that they're bad sellers beforehand.

Tip #11: Check the Seller's Past Auctions

While you're checking up on the seller, use eBay's search function to display all the seller's completed auctions. See whether the seller has sold multiples of this particular item in the past. There's no need to get into a bidding war if the same item will come up for auction again next week.

Tip #12: Check the Seller's Other Current Auctions

You'd be surprised how many times a seller has more than one item you're interested in. Click the View Seller's Other Auctions link to see everything else the seller has for auction—and bid accordingly!

Tip #13: Search; Don't Browse

If you know what you're looking for, don't go through the time-consuming hassle of clicking and loading and clicking and loading to access a particular item category. Using an auction's search function will find what you want a lot quicker.

Tip #14: Search Smart

Searching for an item on eBay is easy; finding what you really want is hard. You're more likely to find what you're looking for if you can use the auction site's advanced search capabilities to fine-tune your query. Some specific search tips can help you perform more effective—and efficient—searches:

- **Narrow your search.** Some of the more popular categories on eBay will list thousands of items. If you do a search on nba, for example, you'll be overwhelmed by the results; narrow your search within these large categories (to nba jerseys or nba tickets) to better describe the specific item you're looking for.

- **Make your queries precise—but not too precise.** When you're deciding which keywords to use, pick words that are precise, but not overly restrictive. If you must use a very general word, modify it with a more specific word—or you're apt to generate a huge number of results that have little relevance to the specific information you're searching for. As an example, model is a pretty general keyword; Star Wars Death Star model is a much more precise query. On the other hand, if you search for an old Star Wars Death Star model partially assembled without instructions not painted, you probably won't return any matching results. If you get few if any results, take some of the parameters out of your query to broaden your search.

- **Use wildcards.** If you're not sure of spelling, use a wildcard to replace the letters in question. Also, wildcards help you find variations on a keyword. For example, if you want Superman, Supergirl, and Superdog, enter super* to find all "super" words.

- **Vary your vocabulary—and your spelling.** Don't assume that everyone spells a given word the same way—or knows how to spell it properly. Also, don't forget about synonyms. What you call pink, someone else might call mauve. What's big to you might be large to someone else. Think of all the ways the item you're looking for can be described, and include as many of the words as possible in your query.

- **Fine-tune your results.** Did eBay's search engine return an overwhelming number of matching items? If so, you need to fine-tune your search to be more specific. Look at the results generated from your initial search. Think about the good matches and the bad matches and why they ended up in the results list. Then, enter a new query that uses additional or different keywords and modifiers. Your goal is to make the next list of results a higher quality than the last.

- **Different day, different results.** Remember that new items are constantly added to any given auction site, and closed auctions are constantly removed from the listings. If you didn't find anything that matched your query today, try again tomorrow; you'll probably find a different list of items for sale. (Another good reason to save your favorite searches and use eBay's email notification service.)

Tip #15: Search for Misspellings

Here's a good way to take advantage of other users' mistakes. Some eBay sellers aren't great spellers—or are just prone to typing errors. This means you'll find some items listed for auction under misspelled titles. It's not hard to find the occasional Dell per-sonal *commuter*, Apple *ipud*, or jewel *neklace*.

The problem for these sellers—and the opportunity for you—is that when you're searching for an item (correctly), listings with misspellings won't appear in the search results. If potential bidders can't find the listings, they can't bid on them, either—leaving these misspelled listings with few if any bidders. If you can locate these mis-spelled listings, you can often snap up a real deal without competition from other bidders.

The key, of course, is figuring out how an item might be misspelled. Let's say you're looking for a bargain on a toaster. Instead of searching for toaster, you might search for toster, toastter, toastor, and toester. Give it a try—you'll be surprised what you find!

Tip #16: Search for Last-Minute Bargains

When you search the eBay listings, be sure to display the results with auctions ending today listed first. Scan the list for soon-to-end items with no bids or few bids, and pick off some bargains that have slipped others' attention.

Tip #17: Don't Show Your Hand

Part and parcel of the sniping strategy: Don't place an early bid on an item. That just signals your interest and attracts other bidders—which results in a higher price.

Tip #18: Watch, Don't Bid

Expanding on the previous tip, use eBay's Watch This Item feature to watch auctions in process without first placing a bid. (Just click the Watch This Item link on the item listing page, and then watch the items on your My eBay page.)

Tip #19: Use the eBay Toolbar

eBay offers a neat little add-on for your Web browser that makes it easy to track auc-tions you've bid on, or that are on your watch list. When you install the eBay Toolbar, it appears as part of your Web browser, under all your normal toolbars. (Figure 9.1 shows the eBay Toolbar as it appears in Internet Explorer.)

FIGURE 9.1

Track your auc-
tions in your
Web browser
with the eBay
Toolbar.

The eBay Toolbar also includes some other useful features, including the capability to search auction listings from the toolbar, go directly to your My eBay page, and view the top picks in selected categories. The eBay Toolbar is free, and available for downloading at pages.ebay.com/ebay_toolbar/.

Tip #20: Watch the Finish

Don't forget the downside to sniping—that you can be sniped, too. Don't get outbid at the last minute. Because most auction activity occurs at the very end of the auction, track the last hour of your most important auctions, and be prepared to react quickly to last-second snipers.

Tip #21: Get in Sync

Make sure that you're in sync with eBay's official clock (cgi3.ebay.com/aw-cgi/eBayISAPI.dll?TimeShow). If you're a few seconds slow, you could lose a sniping contest!

Tip #22: Put Your Best Foot Forward

When you do bid, don't weasel around. Make your bid the maximum amount the item is worth to you, and be done with it.

Tip #23: Bid in Odd Numbers

When you bid, don't bid an even amount. Instead, bid a few pennies more than an even buck; for example, if you want to bid $10, bid $10.03 instead. That way, your bid will beat any bids at the same approximate amount—$10.03 beats $10 any day—without your having to place a new bid at the next whole bid increment.

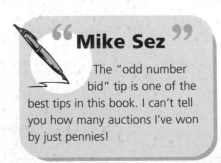

Mike Sez

The "odd number bid" tip is one of the best tips in this book. I can't tell you how many auctions I've won by just pennies!

Tip #24: Don't Be a Deadbeat

Don't bid unless you really intend to buy. Nobody likes a deadbeat—and if you do it often enough, you'll get kicked off the auction site, permanently.

Tip #25: Use My eBay to Track Your Auctions

Don't let your auction activity get away from you. If you're a regular eBay user, the best way to track all your auction activity on a single page is by using My eBay. My eBay can also track your favorite auction categories, as well as your account status—and let you access the pages you use most often, without having to click through useless parts of the site. Personalize My eBay the way you like and then bookmark it; it's a great home page for the heavy auction trader.

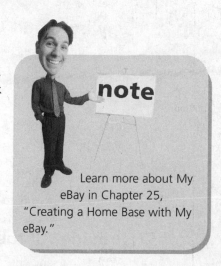

note

Learn more about My eBay in Chapter 25, "Creating a Home Base with My eBay."

Tip #26: Read the Fine Print

What methods of payment can you use? What about shipping? Any other details that might impact your decision to bid? Read the entire item listing before you place your bid—so you aren't surprised by the fine print in any auction.

Tip #27: Don't Forget Shipping Costs...

When you're placing your bid, remember that you'll actually have to pay more than you bid; you have to pay shipping and handling to put the item in your hands. If s&h costs aren't detailed in the item listing, figure them out yourself, or email the seller to get a reasonable estimate. That ultra-cheap $2 item looks pretty expensive if you have to add $5 shipping and handling to the base price.

Tip #28: ...But Don't Overpay for Shipping

Not only should you not get taken by surprise by shipping costs, but you also shouldn't be taken advantage of by unrealistic shipping and handling charges. Get a ballpark feel for shipping on a specific item from the seller's location to where you live. Expect a little overage on the seller's part (she has to buy packing materials, labels, and such), but not too much. If you know that shipping should be in the $2 range, accept a $3 charge—but question a $5 charge.

Tip #29: Pay Quickly

Don't delay—*pay!* Look, the seller needs the money, and the sooner you pay, the sooner you'll get what you paid for.

Tip #30: Pay by Credit Card

Now that most auctions are credit card enabled (via PayPal), use that option. Paying via credit card is relatively safe and leaves a good paper trail—and ensures that your item will be shipped quickly.

Tip #31: Money Orders Cost Money

The seller says that money orders or cashier's checks speed shipment. Depending on your bank, it might cost a few dollars to cut a money order or cashier's check. Be sure to factor these costs into your total expenditure—and question whether you really want to pay to cut a money order for a $5 item.

Tip #32: Provide All the Information Necessary

When you send your payment, be sure to include your name, shipping address, email address, and item name and description. Even better, enclose a copy of the item's Checkout or listing page, with additional information written on it. (I can't tell you how many envelopes I've opened with only a check or money order inside; you gotta tell 'em who the payment is from and what it's for!)

Tip #33: Use a Middleman for Expensive Items

If you buy a high-priced item through a person-to-person auction, consider using an escrow service. Although you'll pay for the service (in the neighborhood of 5%, typically paid by you, the buyer), it's a good safety net in case the seller doesn't ship or the item isn't what was described. In addition, you can use escrow services to accept credit card payments when the seller doesn't or can't accept credit cards directly.

Tip #34: Insure It

If you bought a rare or high-priced item, ask the seller to insure the item for shipping. Pay the extra cost; it's worth it in peace of mind alone.

Tip #35: Document Everything

In case something goes south, it helps to have good records of all aspects of your transaction. Print copies of the confirmation email, plus all email between you and the seller. Be sure to write down the seller's user ID, email address, and physical address. If the transaction is ever disputed, you'll have all the backup you need to plead your case.

Tip #36: Keep a Log

Not only should you document all the correspondence for an individual auction, but you also should keep a log of all the auctions you've won. If you do a lot of bidding, it's all too easy to lose track of which items you've paid for and which you've received. You don't want to let weeks (or months!) go by before you notice that you haven't received an item you paid for!

Tip #37: If You Win It, Inspect It

When you receive the item you paid for, open it up and inspect it—*immediately!* Don't wait a month before you look at it and then expect the seller to rectify a situation that was long considered closed. Okay the item, and then send the seller an email saying you got it and it's okay. If you sit on it too long, it's yours—no matter what.

Tip #38: If You Get Ripped Off, Tell eBay About It

If you have a problem with a seller, first try working it out between the two of you. If things don't get resolved, contact eBay with your grievance; you can use eBay's Purchase Protection Program to register your complaint and (hopefully) get reimbursed for your loss. (And don't forget to leave negative feedback on the snake who did you wrong!)

Tip #39: Communicate!

Don't assume anything; communicate what you think you know. If you have questions during an auction, ask them. When the auction is over, email the seller. When the seller emails you, email him or her back to confirm. Email the seller when you send payment and again to confirm receipt of the item. The more everyone knows, the fewer surprises there are.

Also, remember that not everyone reads his email daily, so don't expect immediate response. Still, if you don't receive a response, send another email. If you're at all concerned at any point, get the seller's phone number or physical address from the auction site and call or write her. A good phone conversation can clear up a wealth of misunderstandings.

Tip #40: Be Nice

You're dealing with another human being, someone who has feelings that can be hurt. A little bit of common courtesy goes a long way. Say please and thank you, be understanding and tolerant, and treat your trading partner in the same way you'd like to be treated. Follow the golden rule; do unto other auction traders as you would have them do unto you.

The Absolute Minimum

Here are the key points to remember from this chapter:

- Sniping—a literal last-second bid—is the most successful tool for winning eBay auctions.

- Keep track of items you haven't yet bid for by using the Watch This Item and My eBay features.

- When you place your bid, make it the highest amount you're willing to pay—and then walk away if the bidding goes higher.

- The best time of year to pick up good deals is during the summer.

- You can sometimes win an auction by bidding in an odd amount—$20.03 instead of $20.00, for example.

- The faster you pay, the faster you'll receive the item you won!

PART III

eBay for Sellers

SELLING 101: A TUTORIAL FOR BEGINNING SELLERS

You've poked around eBay some. Maybe you've bid on an item or two; maybe you've even been fortunate to be the high bidder in an auction for something you really wanted. Now you're looking at your collection of...well, whatever it is you collect, and you're thinking that maybe you ought to be getting some of that online auction action.

In other words, you're ready to put your first item up for bid on eBay.

Getting Ready to List

Before you list your first item, you need to get all your ducks in a row. That means determining what you're going to sell and for how much, as well as how you're going to describe and promote the item. If you try to list an item "cold," you'll find yourself stopping and starting as you move through the listing process; you'll be constantly running around trying to gather more information or make important listing decisions on-the-fly. Better to prepare for these decisions up front, as described in the following checklist.

Checklist: Before You List an Item for Auction

☐ Make sure that the item exists and is at hand, and has been cleaned up and spruced up as much as possible. (This includes putting the item in the original box, if you have it.)

☐ Determine what you think the final selling price will be, and then choose an appropriate minimum bid price.

☐ Take a picture or a scan of the item and prepare a JPG-format file for uploading.

☐ If you're selling a commonly sold item, such as a book, CD, or DVD, write down the item's UPC number or ISBN number—this is the product code typically found on the back or bottom of the packaging.

☐ Determine what listing options you might want to purchase—such as bold-facing the title or placing the item in the Gallery.

☐ Think up a catchy yet descriptive headline for the item.

☐ Write out a detailed description of the item.

☐ Determine what payment options you'll accept. (If you haven't yet signed up with PayPal, now is the time.)

☐ Determine how you want to ship the item.

☐ Weigh the item, and then try to determine the actual shipping costs. Use that information to set an up-front shipping and handling charge, if you want.

☐ If you haven't yet registered as an eBay user and entered your credit card information, do that now.

☐ Determine what day of the week—and what time of the day—you want your auction to end.

When all this is done, *then* you can create your listing!

Getting Started: Creating an Item Listing

Remember that before you can list an item for sale, you have to be a registered eBay user. It also helps to have your credit card on file so that you can pay the fees you will soon incur. (If you need to do either of these things, turn immediately to Chapter 2, "Joining Up and Getting Started.")

Assuming you're registered and filed, now what do you do? Well, listing an item for sale on eBay is pretty simple; all you have to do is work through the following series of steps.

Step 1: Get Ready to Sell

This is the easiest thing you'll do in the whole process. All you have to do is click the Sell link in the eBay Navigation Toolbar.

The very first time you try to sell an item, this process is subtly different. First, if you haven't already created a Seller account, you'll be asked to do so. Second, the Sell hub might only show a Sell Your Item button; clicking this button will take you to a separate Choose Selling Format page.

Step 2: Choose the Type of Auction

eBay now displays the Sell hub, shown in Figure 10.1. You can choose from several types of selling formats (although if you're a new user, not all options may be displayed):

- **Online Auction.** This is eBay's traditional auction format; you'll probably choose this option.

- **Fixed Price**. Choose this option only if you want to sell your item at a fixed price. (Items listed in eBay's Fixed Price Format appear in all item listings and searches, but users can't bid on them; they can only use the Buy It Now option.)

- **Store Inventory**. This option is available if you already have an eBay Store, and wish to add an item to its inventory.

- **Real Estate**. Choose this option if you want to create a real estate listing, instead of a typical auction. (Learn more about real estate auctions in Chapter 23, "Other Ways to Sell on eBay.")

Items listed in the Fixed Price Format are charged the same insertion and final value fees as regular auction items.

Most users will choose the Online Auction option. Click the Start a New Listing button to proceed.

FIGURE 10.1
Decide whether
you want a regu-
lar auction or a
fixed-price sale.

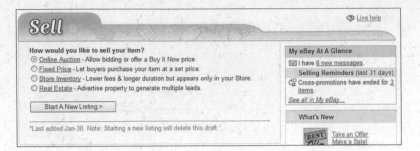

Step 3: Choose Your Category

The Select Category page, shown in Figure 10.2, appears next; you use this page to choose the selling category and subcategory for your item.

FIGURE 10.2
Select the cate-
gory and subcat-
egory for your
item.

There are two ways to select a category. You can browse through all of eBay's available categories until you find the one you want, or you can let eBay suggest a category for you. We'll examine the first method first.

Browse Categories

To browse through all available categories, start by selecting a major category from the first category list, then select a subcategory from the next list, then a further subcategory from the next list, and so on. Continue selecting subcategories until there aren't any more subcategories to select.

tip

If you've previously listed a similar item, you can save a little time by skipping the choosing process. Just pull down the Select a Previously Used Category list and make a selection. Or if you already know the category number (each category has one), enter that number into the Category # box, below and to the right of the Previously Used Category list.

Search for Suggested Categories

If you're not sure which category you should list in, use eBay's Category Search feature. All you have to do is enter a few descriptive keywords into the Enter Item Keywords to Find a Category box, and then click the Find button. eBay now displays the Find a Main Category page (in a separate window), as shown in Figure 10.3; select the best category from this list and click the Sell in This Category button to continue.

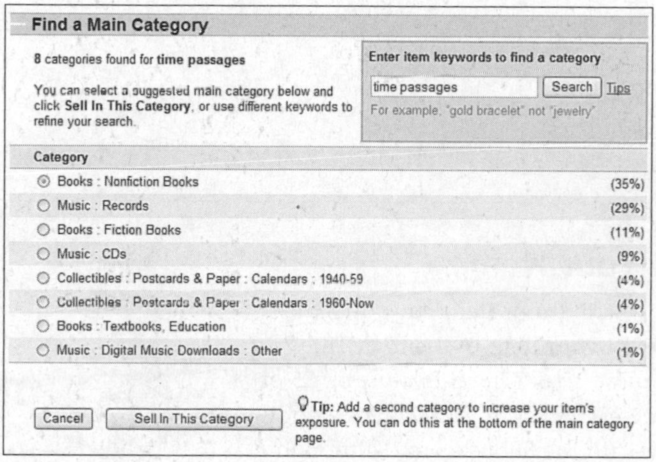

FIGURE 10.3

Let eBay search for the best category for your item.

Find a Main Category

8 categories found for **time passages**

You can select a suggested main category below and click **Sell In This Category**, or use different keywords to refine your search.

Enter item keywords to find a category

time passages   [Search] Tips

For example, "gold bracelet" not "jewelry"

Category	
◉ Books : Nonfiction Books	(35%)
○ Music : Records	(29%)
○ Books : Fiction Books	(11%)
○ Music : CDs	(9%)
○ Collectibles : Postcards & Paper : Calendars : 1940-59	(4%)
○ Collectibles : Postcards & Paper : Calendars : 1960-Now	(4%)
○ Books : Textbooks, Education	(1%)
○ Music : Digital Music Downloads : Other	(1%)

[Cancel] [Sell In This Category] ♀Tip: Add a second category to increase your item's exposure. You can do this at the bottom of the main category page.

List in More Than One Category

If you want to list your item in more than one category, scroll down to the Second Category section and click the List Your Item in a Second Category link. From there you see a new Select Category page; follow the same procedures to either browse or search for a category and subcategory. Know, however, that listing in two categories will cost you double your normal listing fee.

Step 4: Choose a Listing Option

Depending on the type of item you're selling, you may now see the Choose a Listing Option page shown in Figure 10.4. This page is shown when you're selling certain types of commonly sold products, such as books, CDs, DVDs, video games, digital cameras, and the like.

This page provides two options: creating your listing the standard way, or creating your listing with pre-filled item information. We'll discuss the pre-filled option in the "Selling Commonly Sold Items with Pre-Filled Item Information" section, later in this chapter. For now, let's assume you're listing the standard way—so click the Continue button in the List the Standard Way section.

FIGURE 10.4

Choose how you want to enter your item listing.

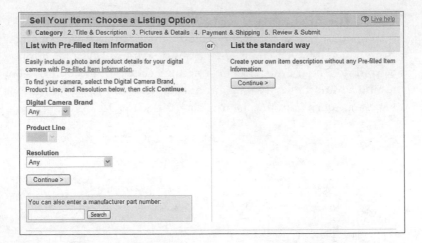

Step 5: Describe Your Item

When the Describe Your Item page appears, enter a title for your item in the Item Title box shown in Figure 10.5. (The title must be 55 or fewer characters.) You can also enter a subtitle for your item (in the Subtitle box), although it will cost you an extra $0.50.

Some categories prompt you to enter specific information in addition to your general description, via an Item Specifics section like the one shown in Figure 10.6. For example, if you're selling a DVD, you can enter the item's region code, genre, subgenre, condition, and display format (full screen or widescreen). If you're selling a digital camera, you're asked for the camera's type, brand, resolution, condition, and other features. Entering these details is optional, but it provides useful information for potential buyers.

note

The Item Title field must contain standard numbers and text, and cannot contain any HTML code. The Item Description field, on the other hand, can contain HTML code (if you click the Enter Your Own HTML Code tab); see Chapter 16, "Creating a Great-Looking Listing," for more information.

FIGURE 10.5

Provide a title and optional subtitle for your item.

FIGURE 10.6

Enter item
specifics.

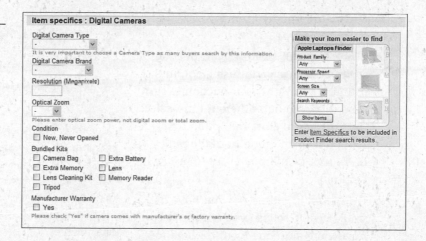

Below this section is the Item Description box, shown in Figure 10.7. This is where you
enter a description—of any length—of the item you're selling. Provide as much information as you feel appropriate, format the text as you like, and then click Continue to
proceed.

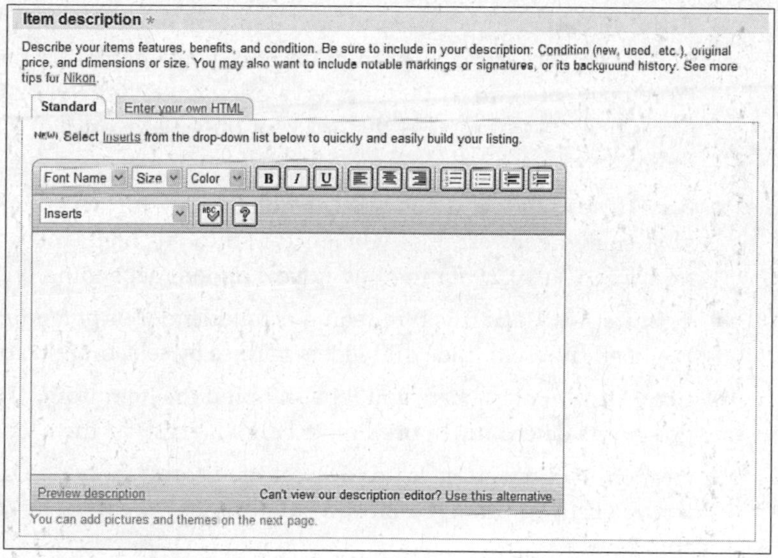

FIGURE 10.7

Enter a detailed
description of
your item.

Step 6: Fill in the Details

When the Provide Pictures & Item Details page appears (as shown in Figures 10.8,
10.9, 10.10, and 10.11), you have a lot of entering to do. You'll need to provide the following details:

- **Duration**. Choose from 1, 3, 5, 7, or (for $0.40 extra) 10 days.

- **Start Time.** By default, your auction starts as soon as you finish creating the listing. If you want your auction to start (and thus end) at a different time, select the Schedule to Start On option and select a date and time from the pull-down lists. (You'll pay $0.10 to use this feature.)

- **Quantity.** In most cases you have a single item to sell, so you enter 1. If you have more than one identical item to sell, enter the number you have—which means you'll be holding a Dutch auction, as described later in this chapter.

- **Starting Price.** Enter the price you want bidding to start at.

> **" Mike Sez "**
>
> The most common duration for an eBay auction is 7 days. Unless you're in a rush for cash (or are up against some other deadline), there is no reason to go for any auction lasting less than a week. On the other hand, 10 days is probably overkill, given that so much bidding takes place in the auction's final minutes. The best option is the 7-day auction, which exposes your item to a week's worth of bidders.

- **Reserve Price.** If you want to hold a reserve price auction (discussed later in this chapter), enter the minimum price you'll accept for the item here. (You'll pay an extra $1.00 for reserve prices up to $49.99, $2.00 for reserve prices from $50.00 to $199.99, or 1% of the reserve price of $200.00 or more.)

- **Buy It Now Price.** If you want to add the Buy It Now option to your auction, enter the lowest price you'll accept into this box. (You pay anywhere from $0.05 to $0.25 for the Buy It Now option, depending on the BIN price.)

- **Private Auction.** If you're selling a confidential or potentially embarrassing item, choose to hide all bidders' names by selecting this option.

- **City, State.** Enter where you'll be shipping the item from. (This helps potential buyers determine approximate shipping costs to their location.)

- **Region.** Pull down the list and select the nearest metropolitan area. (This lets you list your item in eBay's local auctions—great for large and hard-to-ship items.)

- **Country.** This is the United States by default; if you live elsewhere, click the Edit link to make changes.

- **Add Pictures.** If you have a picture of your item and want eBay to host the picture for you, select the eBay Picture Services tab, click the Add Pictures button in the 1 (Free) box, and, when prompted, locate the picture on your hard drive. If you have additional pictures, click the Add Picture buttons next to the picture 2 box, picture 3 box, and so forth. (You'll pay an extra

$0.15 for each picture past the first one.) Next, select a layout for your pictures: Standard (one picture, no charge), Picture Show (multiple picture slideshow, $0.25), Supersize Pictures (one or more bigger pictures, $0.75), or Picture Pack (up to six pictures, Gallery, and Supersize Pictures, for $1.00).

If you want to host your pictures on another web server (instead of via eBay Picture Services), select the Your Own Web Hosting tab and enter the file's web address in the Picture URL box. Or, if you've added pictures via HTML code in your item description, select the option The Description Already Contains a Picture URL for My Item.

Listings with pictures are more successful than those without; turn to Chapter 15, "Using Pictures in Your Listings," to learn more about creating and inserting pictures for your item listings.

- **Listing Designer.** eBay lets you create fancy listings without the need for additional listing creation software—for a paltry $0.10 per listing. It's a two-part process; you start by selecting a theme, and then choose what kind of layout you want. The themes are pretty simple, with different borders and colors. The layouts affect the placement of your pictures—on the left, right, top, or bottom. When you select a layout, it's previewed in a thumbnail to the right of the Theme list. You can also preview your full-size listing, complete with theme, by clicking the Preview Your Listing link.

- **Gallery Picture.** If you want to include a picture of your item in the Gallery (for $0.35 extra), select the Gallery option; if you want your item listed in the Featured section of the Gallery (for a whopping $19.95 extra), select the Gallery Featured option. If you don't want to use the Gallery, make sure that the No Gallery Picture option is selected.

- **Listing upgrades.** Select or deselect any of the following for-a-charge listing upgrades: Bold ($1.00), Border ($3.00), Highlight ($5.00), Featured Plus! ($19.95), or Home Page Featured ($39.95).

- **Gift Services.** If you think your item would make a nice gift, select the Show as a Gift option. For an extra $0.25, you can then select any of the following gift-related services that you offer: Gift Wrap/Gift Card, Express Shipping, or Ship to Gift Recipient.

- **Free Page Counter.** To display a hit counter (free, from ándale) at the bottom of your listing, scroll down to the Free Page Counter selection and select either ándale Style, Green LED, or Hidden. (Hidden counters can be seen only by you—not other users.) If you don't want to display a counter, select Do Not Add a Counter.

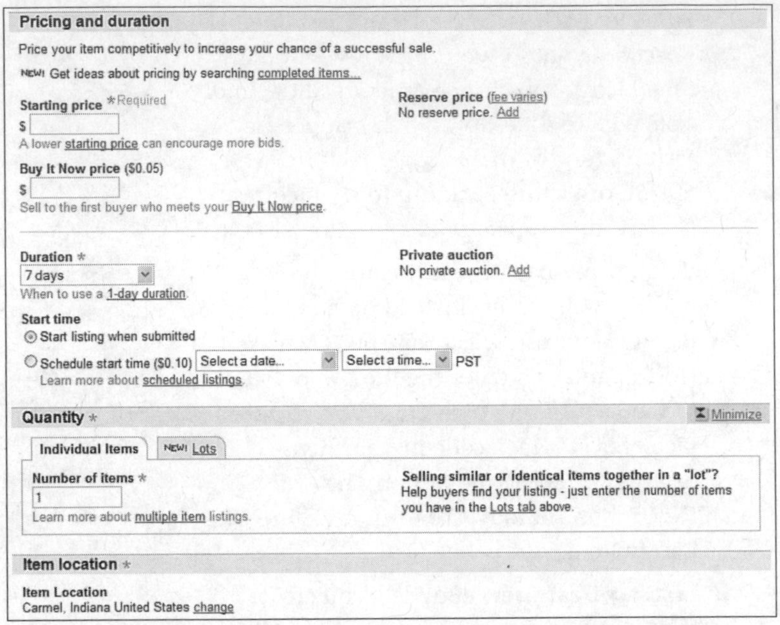

FIGURE 10.8

Enter the starting price, duration, and quantity available.

FIGURE 10.9

Add pictures to your listing.

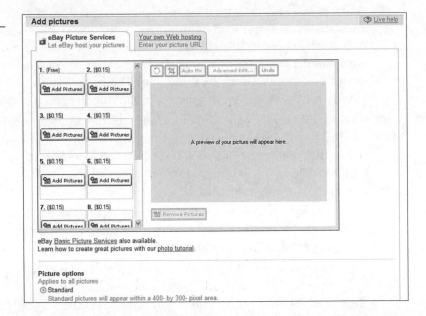

These options are all discussed in more detail in Chapter 13, "Choosing the Right Listing Options." Click Continue when you're ready to proceed.

FIGURE 10.10

Create a fancier listing with Listing Designer templates.

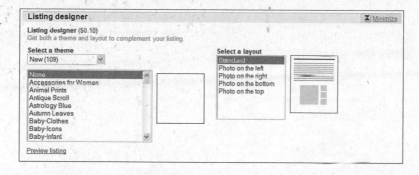

FIGURE 10.11

Select various extra-charge listing enhancements.

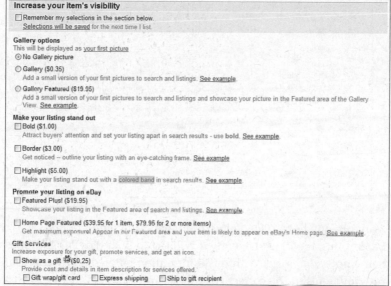

Step 7: Enter Payment and Shipping Info

When the Enter Payment & Shipping Page appears, as shown in Figure 10.12, select which payment methods you'll accept. You can opt for payment by PayPal, Money Order or Cashier's Check, Personal Check, C.O.D., or Other Online Payment Services. You can also leave all the other options unchecked and select See Item Description instead; if you choose this option, be sure to describe your payment options in the Description section of your item listing.

You can opt to accept payment via PayPal even if you don't currently have a PayPal account. Just enter your email address in the PayPal–Payment

note

If you accept credit cards directly (not through PayPal), check the Visa/MasterCard, Discover, or American Express options in the Merchant Credit Cards section.

Will Go To box, and PayPal will contact you if the buyer chooses to pay via PayPal. At that point PayPal will walk you through creating a PayPal Premier account so that you can receive your funds.

FIGURE 10.12

Choose your payment options.

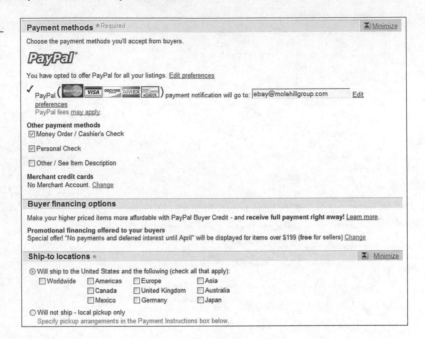

If you already have a PayPal account, enter the email address you use for that account into the PayPal–Payment Will Go To box. (PayPal identifies members by their email addresses.) With this information entered, eBay can route any credit card payments to the correct PayPal account—*yours.*

Next up on the page is the Shipping Costs section, shown in Figure 10.13. Start by selecting who will pay shipping costs (the Buyer, in most cases), and then choose whether to include shipping rates in your listing. If you choose to list shipping rates, you can then choose to charge a flat rate or have eBay automatically calculate the rate based on the buyer's location.

To charge a flat rate, select the Flat Shipping Rates tab and enter the amount you want to charge into the Shipping & Handling box. You can also specify the shipping insurance for the item, and the sales tax (if you charge it; most nonprofessional sellers don't) .

If you don't know the exact shipping charge for your item, have eBay insert a Shipping Calculator into your listing. Select the Calculated Shipping Rates tab, and then enter the package weight and size, which shipping service you'll be using, and your ZIP Code. You can also enter a Packaging & Handling Fee over and above the actual shipping costs, which will be automatically added to the total. Finish this up by entering shipping insurance and sales tax information.

Next you should enter any specific payment instructions into the Payment Instructions & Returns Policy box. You should then select whether you'll ship to the U.S. only, worldwide, or to the U.S. and specific countries. Finally, select whether you'll accept escrow payments for this item, and then click Continue.

note

Learn more about using eBay's Shipping Calculator—and determining shipping costs—in Chapter 21, "Shipping It Out—Cheaply and Safely."

FIGURE 10.13

Enter your shipping and handling charges.

> **Shipping costs** *
>
> ☒ Minimize   💬 Live help
>
> Specify a flat cost for each shipping service you offer, or have costs calculated automatically based on your package and the buyer's address. Learn more about specifying shipping costs.
>
> | **Flat:** same cost to all buyers | **Calculated:** based on buyer's address |
>
> **Domestic Shipping** (offer up to 3 services)
> US Postal Service Priority Mail ▾ $ [   ]   📄 Research rates and services
>
> Add service Remove service and have buyers contact me later
>
> **International Shipping** (offer up to 3 services)
>
> Add service
>
> **Shipping Insurance**   **Sales Tax**
> Not offered. Change   I don't charge tax. Change

Step 8: Review and Submit Your Listing

The next page, shown in Figure 10.14, provides a preview of your listing page and the options you've selected. If you see something that needs to be changed, click the Edit link next to that item. (For example, to edit the item description, you'd click the Edit Title & Description link.) If everything looks right, click the Submit Listing button.

You're Done!

When you're all done, eBay displays the Congratulations page. This page confirms your listing and presents you with important details about your auction—including your item listing's URL, in case you want to publicize your auction elsewhere on the Internet.

After you see the Congratulations screen, your completed listing should appear immediately on the eBay website—although it might take a few hours to be listed in the appropriate category listings.

FIGURE 10.14

Confirm your listing before you submit it.

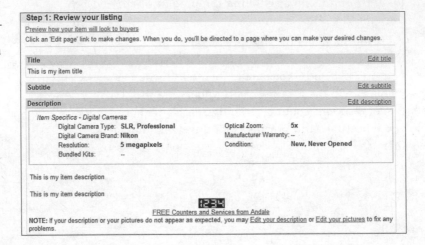

Selling Commonly Sold Items with Pre-Filled Item Information

Back in step 4 we discussed the Choose a Listing Option page. If you recall, you had two options to choose from: listing the standard way or listing with pre-filled item information. Let's discuss that pre-filled option now.

eBay has created a huge database of commonly sold products—books, audio books, audiocassettes, CDs, DVDs, and the like. If you're selling one of these items, you can have eBay create your item description for you, using the information stored in its database—and add a stock photo of the item, as well. All you have to do is tell eBay what you're selling, and eBay will do the hard work for you. (Figure 10.15 shows an item listing with eBay's pre-filled information and product photo.)

Start on the Choose a Listing Option page (shown back in Figure 10.4). Depending on the type of item you're selling, you can choose to search for that item by title, artist, director, author, UPC, or ISBN code. Make a selection from the Search By list, enter the appropriate information into the box, and then click the Continue button.

tip

The most accurate way to search is via the UPC code, which is typically located on the back of the DVD box or CD case—or, if you're selling a book, via the ISBN, which is typically found on the back or inside cover.

FIGURE 10.15

Let eBay provide the item information for you.

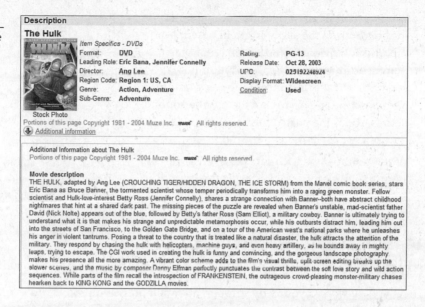

You now see a Select Your Item page, like the one in Figure 10.16. All items matching your search are displayed here; find the item you're selling, and then click the Sell One Like This button.

FIGURE 10.16

Select the exact item you want to sell.

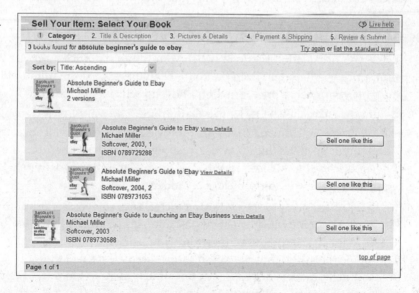

eBay now moves to the standard Describe Your Item page, but with the item title entered for you. Above the Item Description box is a stock photo of the item (if available), and two options that you probably want to check—Include Stock Photo and Include Additional Information. If you're not sure what information is included, click the Additional Information link to view the details that eBay provides.

You'll note that eBay adds its database information outside the standard item description area, which means you can still enter your item description into the Description box, if you want. In this instance, I typically use the item description box to provide any personal details about the particular item I'm selling—if it's used, worn, damaged, or so on.

When you're done with this page, click the Continue button to proceed with the normal listing creation process.

"Mike Sez"

I like using eBay's pre-filled item information, especially when I'm selling books, CDs, and DVDs. eBay's database includes a lot more information than I'm willing to type by hand—and it saves me from capturing and uploading a product photo. It's a real time-saver!

Dealing with Different Types of Auctions

As you've worked your way through eBay's item listing process, you've discovered that there are four variations on the main auction theme—and that's not counting those high-priced real estate auctions! The four variations, which you first learned about in Chapter 3, "Bidding 101: A Tutorial for Beginning Bidders," are Reserve Price, Dutch, Private, and Buy It Now auctions. We'll look at each of these in turn.

Set a Higher Minimum with a Reserve Price Auction

A reserve price auction is one in which your initial bid price really isn't the minimum price you'll accept. Even though bids might exceed the initial bid price, if they don't hit your reserve price, you don't have to sell.

Many buyers—especially those just getting started—don't like reserve price auctions, and shy away from them. That's probably because they appear more complicated than regular auctions (and they are, just a little), and also because the reserve price is never disclosed to bidders. In this case, lack of familiarity definitely breeds contempt, at least from a certain class of bidders.

But there's something to the confusion factor. Let's say you set a minimum price of $5 for an item (really low, to get a buzz going and attract some early bidders) but a reserve price of $50 (because that's what you believe the item is really worth). If the high bidder bids $25, that bid doesn't win—because it's less than the $50 reserve. Unfortunately, bidders have no idea how much more to bid to hit the undisclosed reserve price. Messy and confusing, eh?

Why, then, would you opt for a reserve price auction? There are two possible scenarios:

- When you're unsure of the real value of an item—and don't want to appear to be asking too much for an item—you can reserve the right to refuse to sell the item if the market value is below a certain price.

- When you want to use a low initial bid price to get the bidding going more quickly than if the true desired minimum price (now the reserve price) was listed; the reserve price still guarantees that you won't have to sell below a minimum acceptable price.

If you insist on running a reserve price auction, it's easy enough to do. On the Provide Pictures & Item Details page, enter a price (higher than your Starting Price) in the Reserve Price box. That's all you have to do; after that, the auction runs as normal—or as normal as a reserve price auction gets.

Remember, if no one bids the reserve price or higher, no one wins.

Sell Larger Quantities with a Dutch Auction

When should you place a Dutch auction? Simple: when you have more than one copy of an item to sell.

Dutch auctions are those in which you have more than one quantity of an identical item to sell. It's great if you have a dozen Scooby Doo PEZ dispensers, 10 copies of *Lord of the Rings* on DVD, or a hundred units of bright orange extra-large boxer shorts to sell.

To set up a Dutch auction, all you have to do is enter a quantity greater than 1 in the Quantity

tip

If your auction ends and the high bid is below your reserve price, you don't have to do anything—you are not obligated to sell the item. However, you may want to use the Second Chance link on the item listing page to contact the high bidder and see whether he or she is willing to pay the reserve price for the item, or perhaps you can negotiate a fair price in between the high bid and your reserve. If you don't want to do this, you can always *relist* the item in a new auction, in the hope that a new round of bidders will push the price up to what you expect to receive. If you do relist, however, you might want to edit the item's description to make it more appealing, or even rethink your reserve price to make the item more affordable.

" Mike Sez "

I personally don't like reserve price auctions, and I run them only on the rarest of occasions. My experience is that you turn a lot of potential bidders off by using a reserve price; it's better to create a regular auction with a higher minimum bid price, and be up-front about everything.

box on the Provide Pictures & Item Details page. When you do this, eBay automatically registers your auction as a Dutch auction.

The way Dutch auctions work is a little complicated, so I'll refer you to the explanation in Chapter 3. Suffice to say that the highest bidder always wins something—but doesn't always have to pay the highest price. To be precise, all bidders pay the lowest winning price, even if they bid higher. (I told you it was complicated!)

In any case, eBay handles all the details automatically as long as you specify multiple quantities.

Keep It Anonymous with a Private Auction

The next oddball auction type is relatively simple, compared to the others. If you're auctioning off something that is relatively high priced, or perhaps a little delicate, sensitive, or downright embarrassing, choose a Private auction and none of the bidders' names will ever be revealed publicly. It's great for items in the Adult category, although some bidders on ultra-high-priced items might also want to remain anonymous.

caution

You can't make a Dutch auction private.

To activate a Private auction, all you have to do is check the box next to the Private Auction option on the Provide Pictures & Item Details form.

End It Quick with Buy It Now

eBay's Buy It Now (BIN) option lets you add a fixed-price option to your auction listings. The way BIN works is that you name a fixed price for your item; if a user bids that price, the auction is automatically closed and that user is named the high bidder. Note, however, that the BIN price is active only until the first bid is placed. If the first bidder places a bid lower than the BIN price, the BIN price is removed and the auction proceeds normally.

Why would you add the BIN feature to your auction? I find that most sellers who use BIN just happen to be retailers with a lot of similar inventory. That is, they're likely to place the same item up for auction week after week; in this scenario, the BIN price becomes the de facto retail price of the item.

You might also want to consider BIN around the Christmas holiday, when buyers don't always want to wait around seven days to see whether they've won an item; desperate Christmas shoppers will sometimes pay a premium to get something *now*, which is where BIN comes in.

You activate BIN on the Provide Pictures & Item Details page. Just enter your BIN price into the Buy It Now Price box. And remember: Your BIN price should be higher than your Starting Price.

Managing Your Item Listing

When your listing is complete, the auction itself begins. But what if, for whatever reason, you need to make a change to your listing—or cancel the auction altogether?

Editing Your Listing

One thing I heartily recommend doing is to look over your ad carefully after you've posted it. Maybe you like it—great. Maybe you don't—not so great. Fortunately, if you don't like your listing, eBay lets you revise it.

If you haven't received any bids yet (and there's more than 12 hours left before the end of your auction), you can edit anything you want about your listing—the title, description, pictures, starting price, you name it. If the item *has* received a bid, you can only add information to your description—you can't change the existing description or other information. (And if there's less than 12 hours left, you're stuck—you can't change anything.)

To edit your listing, go to your item listing page and click the Revise Your Item link (located at the top of your listing, just below the item title). This leads you to an editing screen where you can change whatever information you want.

Canceling an Auction

What if your auction starts and you decide you really don't want to sell that item? You need a good excuse, but you *can* cancel eBay auctions.

Canceling an auction is a two-step process:

1. **Cancel any existing bids on your item.** Go to the Bid Cancellation page (cgi.ebay.com/aw-cgi/eBayISAPI.dll?CancelBidShow—or go to the Site Map page and click Cancel Bids on My Item) and cancel the first bid on your item. Then return to this page as many times as necessary to cancel all the outstanding bids.

2. **Officially end your auction.** (You can't end an auction that has open bids, which is the reason you had to cancel all the bids first.) Go to the End My Listing page (cgi3.ebay.com/aw-cgi/eBayISAPI.dll?EndingMyAuction—or go to

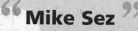

Mike Sez

There's no sense using Buy It Now if you're not going to make any more money from it than you would a normal auction. If you want to use Buy It Now, set a BIN price 20% or so *above* your most wildly optimistic selling price. (So if you think your item might possibly, if all the stars align properly, sell for $10, set a BIN price of $12.) That way if an enthusiastic buyer does end your auction prematurely, you'll be well compensated for it.

the Site Map page and click End My Auction Early) and enter the auction item number. Click the Continue button to proceed, and then click the End Auction button to officially cancel your auction.

Blocking Buyers

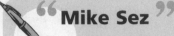

" Mike Sez "

You can also use the bid canceling feature to delete bids from undesirable bidders. Let's say you stipulated in your item listing that your auction is for U.S. bidders only, and you discover that someone from Japan has placed a bid. Just cancel the bid. (And maybe email the bidder and tell him why.) Or maybe you stated that you only wanted bidders with positive feedback, and a no-feedback newbie (or below-zero slime) places a bid anyway. Just cancel the bid. (And no emails are necessary!)

Here's something else you'll eventually run into. Not every member of eBay is worth dealing with. When you run into a deadbeat bidder or otherwise slimy customer in one of your auctions, you don't want to have to deal with that person *again*. The best way to remove this person from your life is to block that bidder from all your future auctions.

To block a bidder, you have to add that user to your Blocked Bidder/Buyer List. Follow these steps:

1. From the Site Map page, click the Blocked Bidder/Buyer List link (or go directly to pages.ebay.com/services/buyandsell/biddermanagement.html).

2. When the Bidder/Buyer Management page appears, scroll to the Blocked Bidder/Buyer List section and click Continue.

3. When the Blocked Bidder/Buyer List page appears, add the buyer's user name to the list; separate multiple names with commas.

4. Click the Submit button when you are done.

You can remove blocked buyers from your list at any time. Just return to the Blocked Bidder/Buyer List page and delete the user name you want to unblock, and then click Submit.

Relisting an Item

This is maybe getting a little ahead of things, but it's a good place to talk about the subject. What happens if your auction ends and you don't have any bidders?

The answer is simple: If at first you don't succeed, try, try again!

When you relist an unsold item, eBay lets you request a refund for the second insertion fee, assuming the following conditions are met:

- You didn't receive any bids on a regular (no-reserve) auction or, in a reserve price auction, you didn't receive any bids that met or exceeded your reserve price.

  or

- The original buyer backed out of the deal, resulting in your filing an Unpaid Item alert.

- You are relisting an item within 90 days of the closing date of the first auction.

- If you're relisting a reserve price auction, the new reserve price is the same as or lower than the original reserve price.

One last thing. If your item *doesn't* sell the second time, eBay won't waive the insertion fee. In other words, if you have a real loser item, eBay won't give you a free ride!

To relist an item, follow these steps:

1. Go to the item listing page for your completed auction, and click the Relist Your Item link.

2. Proceed through the normal listing creation procedure. Your information from the previous listing will already be entered, although you can make any changes you want for this new listing.

caution

You can't take advantage of the relisting offer if you tried to sell a fixed-price item at your eBay Store.

eBay will refund your listing fee for this second listing time, although you'll still be charged a final value fee if it sells. (That's only fair.) If your item *doesn't* sell the second time around, there's no third chance.

Five Common Selling Mistakes

You'll learn some tips for being a better seller in Chapter 24, "Secrets of Successful Sellers." But let's take a moment and examine some of the things you can do *wrong*—actions that can keep you either from selling your item or from getting the highest possible final price.

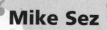

" Mike Sez "

If your item didn't sell the first time around, there was probably a good reason for it—maybe the starting price was too high, or the description stank, or you didn't include a picture. When you relist an item, take the opportunity to spruce up the listing, revisit the pricing, and so on, to try to make the item more attractive to potential bidders.

Mistake #1: List in the Wrong Category

You have to put your item where people will expect to see it. The problem is that eBay has all those categories—almost too many of them, especially if you're not sure just what it is you're selling.

If you list your item in the wrong category, many people looking for that type of item simply won't see it. Take the time to search for similar items currently on auction, and see what category they're listed in. Go where the others go—and, if you're still not sure, use the second category option to list in *two* different categories!

Mistake #2: Set Too High a Starting Price

I know that you want to get as high a price as possible for the item you're selling. But if you try to start the bidding at too high a level, you'll scare off potential bidders—especially if your idea of a fair price is higher than the going market price. It's better to start with a lower starting price and let the bidding take the price to its natural level. Or, if you honest-to-goodness don't want to sell at too low a price, use the reserve price option to protect yourself if the bidding doesn't go high enough.

Mistake #3: Don't Adequately Describe the Item

Let's face it. People shopping on eBay are bidding on items more or less sight unseen—so you have to help them feel comfortable about what they're bidding on. That means describing the item in words, to the best of your abilities. The better you describe the item, the more comfortable potential bidders will feel about it—and the more likely you'll be to sell the thing.

And describing the item also means describing its faults. If you're selling a used or distressed item, you better let potential bidders know about all the dings and dents. You most certainly don't want to misrepresent what you're selling—so be up-front about every little thing.

Mistake #4: Don't Include a Picture

It's a fact. Auction listings with pictures are more likely to sell than those without. Don't include a picture, and you start the auction with two strikes against you. Don't make this all-too-common mistake; get out your digital camera and start snapping—before you create your item listing!

Mistake #5: Don't Charge Enough Shipping and Handling

Oh, how many times I've been burned by not charging enough shipping and handling! This is probably *the* most common seller mistake. You want to include a flat shipping and handling charge in your item listing, so you do a little homework, weigh the item, look up the shipping rate on the postal service site, and enter a number. But when you take the item to the post office, you find your guestimate to be off by a buck or two, and you end up eating that additional shipping cost. The difference might even be big enough that you end up losing money on the transaction.

How do you avoid this problem? First, be sure to weigh the item ahead of time—don't just guess at the weight. And don't stop at weighing just the item; you also have to weight the box you'll ship it in, and all the packing materials. (And that includes those Styrofoam peanuts or shredded newspapers you pack inside the box.) Then be sure to pick the appropriate shipping method (don't change your mind after you've placed the listing!) and the correct distance.

Ah, the correct distance—now there's a problem! You know your ZIP Code, but you don't know the buyer's ZIP Code—because you don't know who the buyer will be. This is one very good reason to use eBay's Shipping Calculator. As you'll learn in Chapter 21, the Shipping Calculator does the distance calculation for you, so you don't have to guess at a flat shipping and handling charge.

The lesson here? When it comes to shipping and handling charges, *don't guess!* Or if you absolutely, positively have to guess, guess high. The best answer, though, is to fig-ure out the weight ahead of time, and then use the eBay Shipping Calculator.

The Auction's Over! Now What?

The days go by, and finally your auction is over. If you're fortunate, you've received a high bid that far exceeds your opening bid or reserve price—which means that you have a buyer.

The question is, now what do you do?

You've sat around watching the bidding for seven days or so, but now it's time to go to work. You need to contact the high bidder, figure out the final selling price (including shipping and handling), deal with the payment process, pack the darned thing up and ship it out, sit around for another couple of days hoping it gets to where it's going in one piece, and then leave feedback for the buyer. Whew! That sounds like a lot of hard work—and it is.

To learn about the post-auction process in more detail, turn to Chapter 19, "After the Auction: Concluding Your Business." And to learn more about how to ship items to buyers, turn to Chapter 21, "Shipping It Out—Cheaply and Safely."

THE ABSOLUTE MINIMUM

Here are the key points to remember from this chapter:

- Before you sell an item, you have to be a registered eBay user and have a credit card on file.

- To start an auction for an item, click the Sell link on the Navigation Bar, and work your way through the Sell Your Item pages.

- You can choose from 1-, 3-, 5-, 7-, or 10-day auctions—although the default 7-day auction is the most popular.

- You can opt for four major auction variations—reserve price, Dutch, private, or Buy It Now.

- If you're selling a commonly sold item, you can have eBay fill in the product details for you—all you have to do is enter the item's UPC/ISBN number or name.

- When the auction is over, you'll be notified by eBay; you then should contact the buyer and communicate payment and shipping terms and information.

11

DETERMINING WHAT TO SELL—AND FOR HOW MUCH

Selling your first item on eBay can be a real rush—and a genuinely stressful experience. What's the right price to set? What category should it go into? What do I do if it doesn't sell—or if it does? As you gain more experience selling, you still run into a lot of these same issues. Pricing is always a guessing game, as is category placement. But as you sell more and more items on eBay, you run into a new issue: Where do you get more stuff to sell?

Now, to anyone with a garage full of junk, that might not seem like a real issue. You want more stuff to sell? Just go out to the garage and grab something! For those of you who want to make some big bucks, however, you need to find a constant flow of merchandise to put up for auction. The more you have to sell, the more money you can make.

Finding Items to Sell

Most eBay users get started by selling items they find in their attics, garages, and basements. (Makes you think of eBay as a giant garage sale, doesn't it?) But what do you do when you've completely cleaned out the attic?

There are many places to find quantities of items to sell on eBay. We'll discuss a few of the more popular ones here—although it's likely you have a few ideas of your own. Just remember that you need to buy low and sell high—so be on the lookout for places where you can buy stuff *cheap*.

You should also be on the lookout for *trends*. Just because something's hot today doesn't mean it's going to be hot tomorrow. You wouldn't have wanted to be the proud owner of a garage-full of Pokemon cards just as the Poke-bubble burst, would you? So when you're hunting for merchandise you can auction on eBay, try to stay on top of the coming trends—and don't buy in at the tail end of an old trend.

Of course, it's difficult to stay on top of the trends in thousands of different categories. For that reason, many eBay power sellers specialize in a half-dozen or fewer types of merchandise. You can track the trends in a handful of categories (by watching the current auctions—and the current selling prices); you can't be as aware of the trends in a larger number of categories.

So specialize, stay on top of trends, and keep your eyes open!

Garage Sales and Yard Sales

If eBay is like a giant garage sale, you might as well start with the bona fide original source. Many eBay sellers scrounge around their local garage and yard sales, looking for any merchandise that they can sell for more money on eBay. It isn't difficult; you can pick up a lot of stuff for a quarter or a dollar, and sell it for 5 or 10 times that amount online. Just be sure to get to the sale early, or all the good bargains will be picked over already!

Flea Markets

Flea markets offer merchandise similar to what you find in garage sales. The bargains might be a little less easy to come by, however, but if you keep a sharp eye you can find some items particularly suited for eBay auction.

Estate Sales

Not to be insensitive, but dead people provide some of the best deals you can find. It's the equivalent of raiding somebody else's garage or attic for old stuff to sell. Check out the weekly estate sales and auctions in your area, be prepared to buy in quantity, and see what turns up.

Live Auctions

Any live auction in your area is worth checking out, at least once. Just don't let yourself get caught up in the bidding process—you want to be able to make a profit when you resell the merchandise on eBay!

Vintage and Used Retailers

Head down to the funky side of town and take a gander at what the various "vintage" and used-merchandise retailers have to offer. These are particularly good sources of collectibles, although you might have to haggle a little to get down to a decent price.

Thrift Stores

Think Goodwill and similar stores here. You can typically find some decent merchandise at low cost—and help out a nonprofit organization, to boot.

Discount and Dollar Stores

These "big lot" retailers are surprisingly good sources of eBay-ready merchandise. Most of these retailers carry overruns and closeouts at attractive prices. You can pick up merchandise here cheap, and then make it sound very attractive in your eBay listing. ("Brand new," "last year's model," "sealed in box," and so on.)

Closeout Sales

You don't have to shop at a cheap retailer to find a good deal. Many mainline merchants offer terrific deals at the end of a season or when it's time to get in next year's merchandise. If you can get enough good stuff at a closeout price, you have a good starting inventory for your eBay sales.

Going Out of Business Sales

Even better, look for a merchant flying the white flag of surrender. When a retailer is going out of business and says "everything must go," that means that bargains are yours to be had—and don't be afraid to try to make a lower-priced deal.

Classified Ads

This isn't as good a source as some of the others, but if you watch the classifieds on a regular basis, you might stumble over some collectibles being sold for less than the going price online. Just buy a daily newspaper and keep your eyes peeled.

Friends and Family

You can sell stuff you find in your garage—what about your neighbor's garage? Think about cutting a deal as a "middleman" to sell your friends' and family's stuff on eBay, especially if they're ignorant of the process themselves. (And remember to keep a fair share of the profits for yourself; you're doing all the work, right?)

Liquidators and Wholesalers

There are several websites that specialize in selling liquidated merchandise, typically in bulk lots. These items might be closeouts, factory seconds, customers returns, or overstocked items—products the manufacturer made too many of and wants to get rid of. If you're interested in investing in some liquidated merchandise to sell, a good site to check out is Liquidation.com (www.liquidation.com), which offers various goods from many manufacturers.

In addition, many wholesalers operate over the Web, providing you the opportunity to buy large lots of new merchandise. The best way to search for a distributor is to use the directory provided by Wholesale411 (www.wholesale411.com).

tip

If you're looking for particular types of items to sell, check out Ándale Suppliers (www.ándale.com). This is a free service that tries to match merchandise suppliers with potential buyers—like you!

If you're interested in buying large quantities for resale, check out eBay's Wholesale Lots listings (pages.ebay.com/catindex/catwholesale.html).

eBay!

This leads us to the final place to look for items to sell on eBay: eBay itself! Yes, it's possible to make money buying something on eBay and then turning around and selling it to someone else on eBay later. The key is timing. Remember, you have to buy low and sell high, which means getting in at the start of a trend. It's possible—although it takes a lot of hard work, and not a little skill.

Picking the Right Category

This one sounds simple. You have an item, you find the category that best describes the item, and you're done with it. To be fair, sometimes it is that simple. If you have *Singin' in the Rain* on DVD, you put it in the "DVDs & Movies: DVD" category, no questions asked.

What if you have a model of an American Airlines jet? Does it go in the "Collectibles: Transportation: Aviation: Airlines: American" category, or the "Toys & Hobbies: Models: Air" category?

Where you put your item should be dictated by where the highest number of potential bidders will look for it. Search the completed auction listings to get an idea of which items are in what categories, and for those categories that have a higher success rate. In the American jet model example, if there are more bidders traipsing through the Collectibles category, put it there; if there are more potential buyers who think of this as a model toy thing, put it in that category. (In reality, you'll probably find listings for this sort of item in both categories.) Think like your potential buyers, and put it where you would look for it if you were them.

If you really can't decide—if your item really does belong in more than one category—eBay lets you list your item in two categories. It costs twice the regular listing fee, but it potentially doubles your exposure. Just scroll down to the Second Category section on the Category page, and enter a second category. Your item listing will show up in both categories, just like that.

tip

If you're not sure how to research eBay auctions, take a look at the research tools offered by Ándale (www.andale.com). Ándale's various research reports analyze all of eBay's closed auctions to help you determine eBay's hottest categories, the best categories to list in, how to price your items, and so on. Prices vary by report, but start at $3.95 per month.

Setting the Right Price

How should you price your item? If you set your minimum price too high, you might scare off potential buyers. If you set your minimum price too low, you'll probably get more interested bidders, but you might end up selling your item for less than you want or than what it's worth.

So what's the right starting price?

Set It Low Enough to Be Attractive...

I like setting a price that's low enough to get some interested initial bidding going, but not so low that it won't get up to the price I think the item can really sell for. So how do you know what the final selling price will be? You don't. But you can get a good idea by searching eBay for completed auctions of similar items. eBay keeps most auctions on file for 30 days, so if anything similar has sold in that period of time, you can find it from eBay's advanced search page.

At the least, you want to be sure you're not setting the starting bid higher than the similar items' final selling price. If you do a search for completed auctions and find that *Star Wars* DVDs have been selling between $4 and $6, don't put a $10 starting price on the *Star Wars* DVD you want to sell. Ignore precedence and you won't get any bids. Instead, gauge the previous final selling prices and place your starting price at about a quarter of that level. (That would be a buck or so for our *Star Wars* example.)

Of course, you can always go the reserve price auction route—in which you get to set a low initial price and a high selling floor. In our *Star Wars* example, that might mean starting bidding at a penny (very attractive to potential bidders), but setting a reserve price of $4 or so. But when you run a reserve price auction, you run a very real risk of scaring away a lot of viable bidders. If you want to run that risk, fine; reserve auctions do let you get bidding started at a very attractive level, while protecting you if bids don't rise to the price you're looking for.

...But Don't Set It So Low That It's Not Believable

In some instances you need to worry about setting the starting price too *low*. If you set too low a minimum bid for your item, some potential bidders might think that something is wrong. (It's the old "if it's too good to be true, it probably is.") Although you might assume that bidding will take the price up into reasonable levels, too low a starting price can make your item look too cheap or otherwise flawed. If you start getting a lot of emails asking why you've set the price so low, you should have set a higher price.

Make Sure You Recover Your Costs...

Another factor in setting the starting price is what the item actually cost you. Now, if you're just selling some junk you found in the attic, this isn't a big concern. But if you're selling a large volume of items for profit, you don't want to sell too many items below what you paid for them. Many sellers like to set their starting price at their item cost—so if the item cost you $5, you set the minimum bid (or reserve price) at $5, and see what happens from there.

...But Not So High That You Pay Too High a Listing Fee

Of course (and there's always another "of course"), if you set a higher starting price, you'll pay a higher insertion fee. Here's where it helps to know the breaks—in eBay's fee schedule, that is. Table 12.1 shows the fee breaks as of March 2005.

TABLE 12.1   eBay's Insertion Fee Breaks

Price Point	Fee
$0–$0.99	$0.25
$1.00–$9.99	$0.35
$10.00–$24.99	$0.60
$25.00–$49.99	$1.20
$50.00–$199.99	$2.40
$200.00–$499.99	$3.60
$500.00 and up	$4.80

Let's think about what this means. At the very least, you want to come in just below the fee break. Which means that you want to list at $9.99 (which incurs a $0.35 fee) and not at $10.00 (which incurs a $0.60 fee). That extra penny could cost you $0.25!

It's in your best interest to minimize any and all fees you have to pay. If you're almost positive (based on completed auction activity) that your item will sell in the $20 range no matter what you price it at, price it as low as is reasonable.

Make Sure You Can Live with a Single Bid

What happens if you set the starting price at $5 and you get only one bid—at $5? Even if you thought the item was worth twice that, you can't back out now; you have to honor all bids in your auction, even if there's only one of them. You can't email the bidder and say, sorry, I really can't afford to sell it for this price. If you listed it, you agreed to sell it for any price at or above your minimum. It's a binding contract. So if the bidding is low, you'd better get comfortable with it—it's too late to change your mind now!

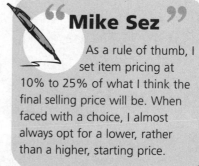

"Mike Sez"

As a rule of thumb, I set item pricing at 10% to 25% of what I think the final selling price will be. When faced with a choice, I almost always opt for a lower, rather than a higher, starting price.

THE ABSOLUTE MINIMUM

Here are the key points to remember from this chapter:

- You can find items to sell on eBay just about anywhere, from garage sales to estate auctions to dollar stores. Just remember to buy low and sell high!

- When it comes time to pick the item category, think about where the most potential buyers would think to look for that item. If you can't decide between two categories, list the item in two categories—if you can absorb the double listing fees.

- Setting the starting price for an auction is more of an art than a science. In general, lower prices are best—if you can live with an item actually selling for the minimum price.

12

Deciding On Your Payment Methods—And Using PayPal

When you're listing an item for auction on eBay, you can choose which types of payment you'll accept from the winning bidder. This may seem like an easy decision, but each type of payment needs to be handled differently on your end.

This chapter talks about the types of payment you can choose to use. As any experienced eBay seller will tell you, not all dollars are worth the same; a dollar paid by one method might actually be worth less (or be more risky) than a dollar by another method. And you *do* want the biggest dollar, don't you?

Fortunately, you're not forced to use any one payment method. For example, you can limit your payments to credit cards only; there's no law that says you have to accept cash or checks. So read on to learn which types of payment provide the biggest return for your efforts!

Accepting Cash

As a seller, there's nothing better than opening up an envelope and finding a few crisp new bills inside. Unfortunately, sending cash through the mail is not one of the smartest things a buyer can do; cash is too easily ripped off, and virtually untraceable. You can ask for cash payment (not that you should, of course), but unless the selling price is extremely low (under $5), don't expect buyers to comply.

Accepting C.O.D. Payments

Cash on delivery (C.O.D.) might sound good on paper. You ship the item, with the stipulation that the delivery man (or woman) collect payment when the item is delivered.

There are problems with this method, however. What happens if the buyer isn't home when the delivery is made? What if the buyer is at home, but doesn't have the cash? What if the buyer refuses to pay—and rejects the shipment? I've heard stories of up to 25% of all C.O.D. orders being refused, for one reason or another. And if the item is refused, you (the seller) have to pay postage in both directions.

Even worse, C.O.D. service often comes with a high fee from the carrier—and it's a fee that you, the seller, have to pay. The additional fee alone rules out C.O.D. for many sellers.

All things considered, it's easy to see why few eBay sellers offer C.O.D. payment. The problems with this payment method tend to outweigh the benefits, and I can't recommend it.

Accepting Personal Checks

Many people still prefer to pay for their purchases via personal check. Buyers like paying by check because it's convenient, and because checks can be tracked (or even canceled) if problems arise with the seller.

Sellers like personal checks a little less, because they're not instant money. When you deposit a check in your bank, you're not depositing cash. That $100 check doesn't turn into $100 cash until it tracks back through the financial system, from your bank back to the buyer's bank, and the funds are both verified and transferred. That can take some time, typically 10 business days or so.

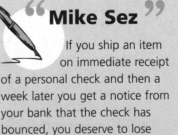

" Mike Sez "

If you ship an item on immediate receipt of a personal check and then a week later you get a notice from your bank that the check has bounced, you deserve to lose every single penny of that transaction. Eager shippers and personal checks just don't mix—and you *will* learn from your mistake.

Because some buyers still prefer paying by check, you should prob-ably be prepared to handle this payment method. When you receive a check, deposit it as soon as possible—but do *not* ship the item. Wait until the check clears the bank (two weeks if you want to be safe—longer for checks on non-U.S. banks) before you ship the item. If, after that period, the check hasn't bounced, it's okay to proceed with shipment.

If you are on the bad end of a bounced check, all hope is not lost. The first thing to do is get in touch with your bank and ask them to resubmit the check in question. Maybe the buyer was just temporarily out of funds. Maybe the bank made a mistake. Whatever. In at least half the cases, bounced checks "unbounce" when they're resub-mitted.

> **caution**
>
> If a check bounces, the depositor (you) will likely be assessed a fee from your bank. (The writer of the bad check will also have a fee to pay.) If the buyer who wrote the check offers to make good on the payment, make sure that they reimburse you for your bad check fee, over and above the final auction price.

Whether you resubmit the check or not, you should definitely email the buyer and let him know what happened. At the very least, you'll want the buyer to reimburse you for any bad check fees your bank charged you. The buyer might also be able to pro-vide another form of payment to get things moving again. (Credit cards are nice—as are money orders.)

Accepting Money Orders and Cashier's Checks

Money orders and cashier's checks are, to the seller, almost as good as cash. You can cash a money order imme-diately, without waiting for funds to clear, and have cash in your hand. When you receive a money order or cashier's check, deposit it and then ship the auction item. There's no need to hold the item.

The only bad thing about money orders and cashier's checks is that you have to wait for them to arrive. Even if the buyer puts payment in the mail the very next day, you'll still wait anywhere from three to five days after the auction to receive payment. Still, there's a lot to like about this method of payment—it's hard to get burned with either a money order or a cashier's check.

> **caution**
>
> Beware of scammers who send you a money order or cashier's check in excess of the amount due, and then ask you to send them the difference. That's a sure sign that the payment is fraud-ulent—and you make it worse by sending the scammer some or your money in return!

Accepting Credit Cards—Via PayPal

There was a time that if you wanted to accept credit card payment for your auction items, you had to be a real retailer, complete with merchant account and bank-supplied charge card terminal. This limited the number of sellers who could accept credit card payment, which probably cut down on potential bidders, because many buyers like the convenience and relative safety of paying by credit card.

Today, however, just about any seller can accept credit card payments, by signing up to use an online payment service, such as PayPal. When a buyer uses his or her credit card to pay via PayPal, PayPal charges the credit card and then notifies you (via email) that you've been paid. Upon this notification, you ship the item and then access your account on the PayPal site and instruct PayPal to either cut you a check or transfer the funds into your bank account.

note

PayPal accepts payments by American Express, Discover, MasterCard, and Visa. Although it's primarily a U.S.-based service, it also accepts payments to or from 45 other countries.

Signing Up for PayPal

Before you can use PayPal as a seller, you must sign up for PayPal membership. You do this by going to the PayPal website (www.paypal.com), shown in Figure 12.1, and clicking the Sign Up Now button or Sign Up link.

FIGURE 12.1
The PayPal home page.

You can choose from three types of PayPal accounts:

- A **Personal** account is great for eBay buyers, but not quite enough for sellers. You can send money free, but can receive only non–credit card payments. (For no charge, though.)

- A **Premier** account is the best way to go for most eBay sellers. You can still send money free, and you can now accept both credit card and non–credit card payments (for a fee).

- A **Business** account is necessary if you're receiving a high volume of payments. With this type of account, you can do business under a corporate or group name, and use multiple logins.

> **"Mike Sez"**
>
> I recommend you sign up initially for a Premier account. If your sales volume gets high enough, PayPal will automatically switch you to a Business membership.

There is no charge for becoming a PayPal member—although there are fees for actually using the service. (The exception is the Personal account, which charges no fees for anything—but doesn't let you accept credit card payments.)

Paying for PayPal

The fee you pay to PayPal is separate from any other fees you pay to eBay. The way PayPal works is that the buyer doesn't pay any fees; it's the seller who is assessed a fee based on the *amount of money transferred.*

This last point is important. PayPal charges fees based on the total amount of money paid, *not* on the selling price of the item. That means that if a $10 item has a $5 shipping and handling cost, the buyer pays PayPal a total of $15—and PayPal bases its fee on that $15 payment.

PayPal's fees range from 1.9% to 2.9%, depending on your monthly sales volume. Table 12.1 presents PayPal's fee schedule as of March 2005:

TABLE 12.2 PayPal Transaction Fees (U.S.)

Monthly Sales	Transaction Fee
$0–$3,000.00	2.9%
$3,000.01–$10,000.00	2.5%
$10,000.01–$100,000.00	2.2%
>$100,000.00	1.9%

The lower fees apply only to those members with a qualified Business account. You're also charged a flat $0.30 per transaction, regardless of your sales volume. All fees are deducted from your account with every transaction.

Choosing PayPal in Your New Auction Listing

The easiest way to accept PayPal payments in your eBay auctions is to choose the PayPal option when you're creating an item listing. This is as simple as checking the PayPal box and entering your PayPal ID on the Enter Payment & Shipping page.

When you choose this option, a PayPal payments section is added to your item listing. PayPal will also appear as a payment option on your post-auction item listing page and in eBay's end-of-auction email to the winning bidder.

Collecting PayPal Payments

When a buyer makes a PayPal payment, those funds are immediately transferred to the seller's PayPal account, and an email notification of the payment is sent to the seller. In most cases, this email will include all the information the seller needs to link it to a specific auction and ship the item to the seller.

When you sign into the PayPal site, you're taken to the My Account tab, and the Overview tab within that. As you can see in Figure 12.2, this displays an overview of your recent PayPal activity, including payments made by buyers into your account. Click any item to view more detail about the activity.

FIGURE 12.2
An overview of your PayPal activity.

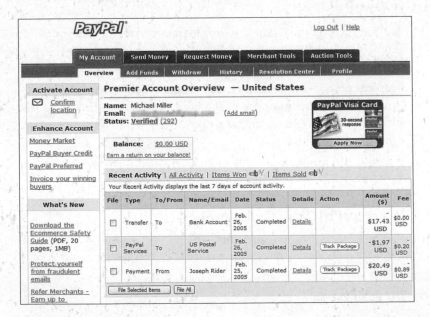

In most cases, the buyers' payments come into your account free and clear, ready to be withdrawn from your checking account. The exception to this is an eCheck payment, in which a buyer pays PayPal from his or her personal checking account. Because PayPal has to wait until the "electronic check" clears to receive its funds, you can't be paid until then, either. PayPal will send you an email when an electronic payment clears.

Withdrawing PayPal Funds

You can let your funds build up in your PayPal account, or you can choose (at any time) to withdraw all or part of your funds. You have the option of okaying an electronic withdrawal directly to your checking account (no charge; takes three to four business days) or requesting a check for the requested amount ($1.50 charge; takes one to two weeks). Just click the Withdraw tab (from the Overview tab) and click the appropriate text link.

Which Way Is Best?

The more payment options you offer, the more potential bidders you'll attract. Still, some methods are better than others for different types of sellers; use Table 12.2 to determine which methods work best for you.

"Mike Sez"

I prefer to empty my PayPal account at the end of each day, via an electronic transfer to my checking account. I find this the fastest, no-hassle way to receive PayPal funds due.

In all my auctions, I accept personal checks, money orders, cashier's checks, and credit cards (via PayPal). Most buyers these days end up using PayPal, so I make sure to factor those charges into my cost of doing business.

TABLE 12.2   Payment Methods Rated

Payment Method	Pros	Cons
Cash	Relatively fast payment, no hassles	Unattractive to buyers
C.O.D.	Cash payment	High noncompletion rate; lots of paperwork
Personal check	Convenient for buyers	Slow, have to wait to clear
Money order/cashier's check	Like cash	Hassle for buyers
Credit cards (via PayPal)	Fast payment, buyers like online payment services	Fees involved

THE ABSOLUTE MINIMUM

Here are the key points to remember from this chapter:

■ The fastest way to get your money is via credit card (using PayPal). You'll pay for the privilege, however—2.9% of the total selling price, plus $0.30 per transaction.

■ The slowest way to get your money is via personal check.

■ If you do accept payment by personal check, remember to wait at least 10 business days for the check to clear before you ship the merchandise.

■ The best compromise between speed and hassle is payment via cashier's check or money order. (And there are no fees involved.)

13

CHOOSING THE RIGHT LISTING OPTIONS

Back in Chapter 10, "Selling 101: A Tutorial for Beginning Sellers," you learned how to use the various forms on the eBay site to create an auction item listing. At the time, I told you about the various listing options available on the Provide Pictures & Item Details page, but I didn't go into a lot of detail.

Well, now it's time to fuss over all those particulars.

All the options I talk about in this chapter are found on the Provide Pictures & Item Details page, in eBay's Sell Your Item section. To be specific, this is the third page you encounter after you click the Sell link on eBay's home page.

Choosing the Right Length

The first listing option you encounter is one of Duration. eBay lets you choose from five lengths for your auctions: 1, 3, 5, 7, or 10 days. The first four options come at the standard listing price; 10-day auctions cost you an additional $0.40, which reduces their attractiveness.

When eBay first started out, it offered only a single auction length: 7 days. This is still the default length, and the length chosen by most sellers. What's nice about a 7-day auction is that it guarantees that your item is listed over a weekend; a 1-, 3-, or 5-day auction won't necessarily hit the busy weekend days, depending on the day you start the auction.

tip

More bidders log on to eBay on Saturday and Sunday than on any other days of the week—probably because more users are home from school and work.

Thinking about heavy weekend traffic, some users prefer a 10-day auction, starting on a Friday or Saturday, to get *two* weekends into the bidding schedule. However, a longer auction like this also means that you have to wait longer before you collect your money, so that needs to be figured in, as well—along with the $0.40 additional cost.

If you really need your money quickly, go with a 3- or 5-day auction, but try to time the listing so that you get in a bidding weekend. Also know that some buyers expect and plan on 7-day auctions, so you might not get as much last-minute sniping if you opt for the shorter length.

And if you're in a *real* hurry for your money—or if you list the same items over and over—then the 1-day auction might be worth considering. I don't see the sense in it personally—but eBay obviously had some call for it, so there it is.

❝ Mike Sez ❞

I opt for the 7-day auction for all my items. It's what users expect, and it allows for bidding on each day of the week—without taking *too* long to get the process over with.

Choosing a Different Start Time

eBay also lets you choose a specific start time for your auction—which, of course, also becomes your auction's end time. By default, an eBay auction starts as soon as the item listing is placed, so if you place your listing at 10:00 a.m., that's when the auction starts and ends. However, you can pay an extra $0.10 and schedule your auction to start (and stop) at a specified time different from when you created the item listing.

This is a good option if you have to create your auction listings at what would otherwise be a bad time to end an auction—in the morning or early afternoon, for example. It's better to end an auction during the evening, when more users are at home. So if you can't launch your auctions in the evening, spend the extra $0.10 so that eBay can automatically schedule the start of your auction for you.

To Reserve, Or Not to Reserve

After you decide on the duration of your auction, how many units you're selling, and your starting price, you run into the Reserve Price option. As you learned in Chapter 10, a reserve price auction is one in which you set a low starting price to get the bidding started, but keep a higher, hidden reserve price that serves as the lowest price you'll sell the item for. For example, you might start the bidding at $10 but have a reserve price of $50. You don't actually sell the item until you get a bid at $50 or above; a high bid of $49.99 wouldn't be a winning bid.

On the upside, reserve price auctions let you set however low a starting price you want—and low starting prices get a lot of buyer attention, and get the bids flowing. You're not obligated to sell at that low price, of course; that's why you have the reserve, as protection in case the bids don't go high enough.

On the downside, reserve auctions confuse a lot of potential bidders—newer users, in particular. They also foster a bit of suspicion from bidders, because you're not telling them the whole truth. (The reserve price is always hidden.) So you're apt to have fewer bidders on a reserve price auction, in spite of the lower starting price.

In addition, it costs money to use the reserve price option. You'll pay an extra $1.00 if your reserve price is between $0.01 and $49.99, $2.00 if your reserve price is between $50.00 and $199.99, or 1% of the reserve price for items priced $200.00 and over. That's a significant additional cost.

My advice is, in most cases, not to use the reserve price option. If there's an absolutely positively minimum price you have to get out of a

" Mike Sez "

Using eBay to schedule a start time for your auctions may be a necessary evil if you're not at home, at your computer, at the time of day you want your auctions to end. It may be better, however, to use an auction management program or service that includes this type of listing scheduling at a lower (or zero) additional cost.

" Mike Sez "

I hardly ever use the reserve price option; my auction-of-choice is the standard, nonreserve model. The only exception is when I have an item that should have a relatively high basement price (above $100), even though similar auctions are starting at much lower prices. For example, I might list an item that will probably sell in the $200 range with a $20 starting price. It's this kind of differential that makes you think about setting a reserve price.

particular item, set that price as your starting bid price. There's no need—and little to be gained—by setting a hidden reserve.

Sell It Now?

The next option on the Provide Pictures & Item Details page is the Buy It Now (BIN) price. Buy It Now is the option that lets you sell your item to the first bidder who offers a specific fixed price. If the first bidder bids lower than the Buy It Now price, the Buy It Now option disappears and the auction continues as normal. To add the BIN option to an auction, you'll pay anywhere from a nickel to a quarter extra, depending on the amount of the BIN price.

Should you use Buy It Now? The downside is that BIN adds to an auction's confusion factor, possibly scaring away some users. (The presence of a high BIN—relative to the starting price, in any case—is apt to tell some buyers that you're asking more for your item than it's worth, or that similar items are selling for.) The upside is that if you set a high enough BIN price and some chump ponies up, you get your money sooner than if you'd allowed the auction to continue to its natural conclusion.

If you're going to use Buy It Now, make sure that it's worth your while. You definitely *don't* want to set a BIN price lower than what you think your item will eventually sell for. For example, if you know that similar items have been selling for $20 on eBay, the absolute lowest you want to set your BIN price is $20. If you set the BIN price at $15, for example, some sharp buyer is going to swoop in and pay you $15 for an item that probably would have sold for $20.

In fact, if you use the BIN option, you probably want to set the BIN price at some point *higher* than the expected high bid price. Taking our $20 example, you might set the BIN at $25. If somebody wants to buy it now, they'll pay you a $5 premium for the privilege. If not, bidding will proceed as normal until a (presumably lower) high bid is realized.

> **❝ Mike Sez ❞**
>
> I seldom use Buy It Now in my auctions. That's because I typically sell unique items; if I were selling more-common items, I'd probably use the BIN option more often.

Public or Private?

Just below the Buy It Now option is the Private Auction option. When you choose this option, the bidders' names don't show up on the item listing page; bidders' identifications remain private.

The worth of a private auction comes when you have something controversial to sell—something that others might be embarrassed to be found bidding on.

Although most private auctions are for adult-only items, it's easy to imagine an auction for an exclusive high-priced item for which bidders don't want (or need) the publicity. So if you're selling either dirty pictures or items that Donald Trump might be interested in, going private is worth consideration.

A Pretty Picture

I devote an entire chapter of this book (Chapter 15, "Using Pictures with Your Listings") to including pictures with your eBay listings, so I won't go into a lot of detail here. Suffice to say that listings with pictures are more successful than listings without pictures. Whether you use eBay's picture hosting services or your own Web hosting, you'll increase your sell rate *and* your average final price when you add a picture to your text.

Grab Attention with Listing Upgrades

Next we come to that list of nickel and dime (and higher!) marketing devices that eBay calls "listing upgrades." These options are designed to make your listing stand out from the hundreds or thousands of similar listings in any particular category.

Subtitle

eBay recently added an option to insert a subtitle in your item listing, just below the main title. The charge is $0.50 for this option, and it's probably not worth it. After all, you can put all the details you want into the item description—what do you need the subtitle for? It's possible that an item with a subtitle may stand out on a search results page, but that's about it. Probably not a good use of your money.

> ## "Mike Sez"
>
> I don't think I've ever listed a private auction. Of course, the stuff I sell isn't that exclusive—or arousing.
>
> Unless there's a good reason *not* to include a picture (such as you don't have a camera), I always recommend including at least one picture with your item listings. You should know, however, that using eBay's picture hosting service can get expensive; eBay charges for every picture of yours (past the first one) that it hosts on its servers.
>
> In general, I find that spending money on most of these listing options isn't much different from just throwing your money away. Whether you're spending a buck or a hundred, these options just don't increase traffic that much—so I try to avoid them. (The exception is the Listing Designer templates, which I find are worth the extra dime to add some visual interest to my listings.)

FIGURE 13.1

A listing with a subtitle.

| | | IBM THINKPAD PENTIUM LAPTOP NOTEBOOK COMPUTER WOW!!! 100% Guaranteed, Internet Ready, Complete!! | 🖂 | $208.50 | 21 | 22m |

That said, in some categories a majority of sellers have adopted the use of subtitles, so if you don't choose this option, your listing will look naked and somehow inferior. Other categories have less frequent use of subtitles, which might make a subtitled listing stand out in the search results. Or not.

Gallery

Selecting the Gallery option does two things. First, it displays a thumbnail picture next to your item in all browsing category pages, as shown in Figure 13.2. Second, it enables your item to be displayed in eBay's Gallery section (pages.ebay.com/buy/gallery.html), as shown in Figure 13.3.

The latter option doesn't account for much, as few users browse the Gallery. The former option, though, is very important; users are more likely to click through to your listing if there's a picture displayed. For that reason, many sellers find the $0.35 Gallery fee to be money well spent.

> **" Mike Sez "**
>
> In general, I'm not a big fan of the subtitle option. My advice is to use it if you have to (in those categories where all the other listings employ it), but otherwise not.
>
> The Gallery option is one listing enhancement that I frequently use. It's a defensive measure; if you don't have picture next to your listing, many users simply won't click through. You have to show a picture to play the game, which makes the $0.35 fee necessary in most cases.

FIGURE 13.2

Two listings, one with a Gallery picture, one without.

FIGURE 13.3

Less useful— items displayed in eBay's Gallery.

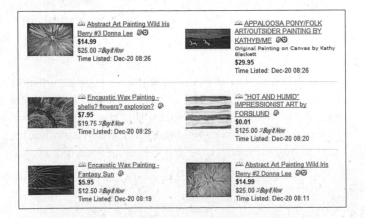

Gallery Featured

eBay also offers a second Gallery option, called Gallery Featured. When you pay for this option, your item will periodically show up in the special Featured section above the general Gallery. Pricing for the Gallery Featured option is $19.95.

> **" Mike Sez "**
>
> Gallery Featured is a fairly expensive enhancement, and I'm not sure it gets you much; most buyers look beyond the first listings on a page. Given the price, I can't recommend this option.

FIGURE 13.4

The Featured section at the top of a listings page.

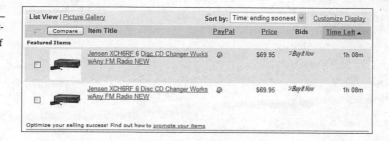

Bold

How do you make your item stand out on a page full of listings? By displaying the listing title in boldface. This option, which costs $1.00, displays your item title in bold in any category or search results listings. You can see how the Bold option looks in Figure 13.5.

> **" Mike Sez "**
>
> Because of the high price and minimal visual impact of the Bold enhancement, I can't recommend you use it.

FIGURE 13.5

Two item listings—the second one in bold.

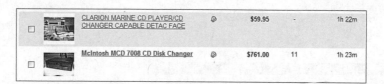

Border

Want something a little more attention-getting than a bold title? The Border option puts a dark frame or border around your listing on every search results page, as shown in Figure 13.6. This option is more expensive than the bold option, costing you $3.00.

> **" Mike Sez "**
>
> At three bucks extra, I don't think the Border option is worth the money.

FIGURE 13.6
An item listing
with the Border
option.

Highlight

If a border doesn't attract enough attention,
how about a *shaded* item listing? When you
select the Highlight option, your listing (on
any category or search results page) is displayed with a colored shade, as shown in
Figure 13.7. This little bit of color will cost
you $5.00.

Mike Sez

There's no way the
five-dollar Highlight
option is worth the price. I don't
recommend it.

FIGURE 13.7
Two item list-
ings—the second
one enhanced
with the
Highlight option.

Featured Plus!

The Featured Plus! option displays your item in
the Featured Items section on the appropriate
major category page, as well as in the Featured
Items section at the top of any search results
page. This option will set you back a whopping
$19.95.

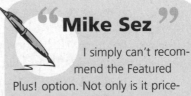

Mike Sez

I simply can't recom-
mend the Featured
Plus! option. Not only is it price-
prohibitive, it also puts your "featured" listing at the bottom of
the page—which is hardly a
prominent position!

FIGURE 13.8
The Featured
Plus! section at
the bottom of
the Antiques cat-
egory page.

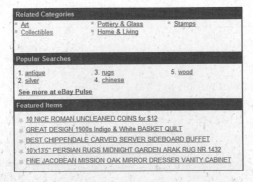

Home Page Featured

Ever wonder how much it costs to have your item featured on the eBay home page? Here's the answer: $39.95. (And it doesn't even guarantee how often your item will pop up. What a deal— *not*.) All you have to do is select the Home Page Featured option, and your item will *periodically* be displayed on the home page. (And for the same low price, your item also gets displayed in the Featured Items section of normal category and search results pages.)

"Mike Sez"

The Home Page Featured option is another one that I can't recommend, unless you're selling something really special.

FIGURE 13.9

The Featured Items section in the middle of eBay's home page.

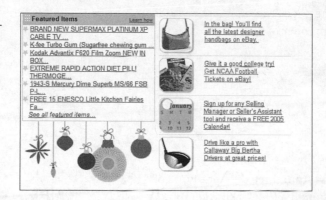

Gift Icon

Think your item would make a great gift for a specific occasion? Then pony up $0.25 to add a gift icon to your listing, like the one shown in Figure 13.10. When you pay for the Gift option, you can also choose to promote any extra gift-related services you might offer—in particular, Gift Wrap/Gift Card, Express Shipping, or Ship to Gift Recipient (instead of the buyer).

"Mike Sez"

The Gift icon is an okay option for some sellers during the Christmas season, but otherwise fairly ineffective.

FIGURE 13.10

An item enhanced with the Gift icon.

Listing Designer

This is a great feature that lets you spice up your listing with fancy-looking templates. The cost is just $0.10, and the results are much more attractive than the typical plain-text listing. (Learn more about the Listing Designer templates in Chapter 16, "Creating a Great-Looking Listing.")

Count 'em Up

The final option you can select on the Provide Pictures & Item Details page is the free page counter, supplied (free of charge) by ándale, a third-party service firm. When you opt to put a counter at the bottom of your listing page (like the one in Figure 13.11), you and (in most cases) potential bidders can see how many other users have visited the page. The more page visitors, the more likely it is that you'll receive a substantial number of bids.

> **Mike Sez**
>
> Listing Designer is one listing enhancement I like. It's worth the dime to give your listing some pizzazz!

FIGURE 13.11
An Ándale counter at the bottom of an eBay listing page.

You can choose from three different types of counters, all supplied (free of charge) by ándale. The Andale Style counter is a black-and-white "odometer"-type counter; the Green LED Counter is a little more colorful, displaying bright green "digital" numbers against a black background; and the Hidden counter is hidden to bidders but visible to you, the seller. Choose one of these three, or the Do Not Add a Counter option—no payment necessary!

> **Mike Sez**
>
> If you think you're going to get a lot of traffic to your item listing page, by all means display a counter. A high number on a counter will make bidders think they have to bid *now* to get in on the action. If, on the other hand, you don't want to tip your hand as to how many potential bidders you might have, go with the hidden counter. After all, it doesn't matter whether you have 2 or 200 visitors, as long as you have one really good bid!

THE ABSOLUTE MINIMUM

Here are the key points to remember from this chapter:

- eBay offers various listing enhancements on the Provide Pictures & Item Details page.

- Most of these listing enhancements cost money.

- Few of these listing enhancements are worth the money—although the Gallery and Listing Designer options are probably worth the money.

- Having an item that a lot of buyers want will produce many more bidders than you'll get by using expensive listing options.

14

WRITING A LISTING THAT SELLS

Did you know that only about half the items listed on eBay at any given time actually sell during the current auction? That's right; in about half the current auctions, no one meets the minimum bid.

How do you increase the odds of *your* item selling? It's all about creating a powerful, effective item listing—in both the title and the item description.

Write a Title That SELLS!

Let's start right at the top, with the title of your item listing. You can use up to 55 letters, numbers, characters, and spaces, and you need to accomplish two things:

- Include the appropriate information so that anyone searching for a similar item will find your item in his search results.
- Make your title stand out from all the other titles on those long listing pages.

Do those two things, and you significantly increase your chances of getting your item noticed and sold.

Include Key Information

Let's tackle the first point first. You have to think like the people who will be looking for your item. Most users will be using eBay's search feature to look for specific items, so you want to put the right keywords into your item title, to make your item pop up on as many search results pages as possible.

As an example, let's say you have an original 1964 Superman model kit, manufactured by Aurora, still in its shrink-wrapped box. How do you list this item?

You have to make sure you get all the right keywords in your title. For this example, it's obvious that Superman should be a keyword, as should Aurora and maybe 1964. Then, it gets iffy-er. Should you call it a model kit or a plastic model kit or a plastic model? Should you call it unassembled or still in box or original condition?

When dealing with collectibles, you often can use accepted abbreviations and acronyms. (I'll list some of these acronyms later in this chapter.) In this case, you could use the abbreviation MISB, which stands for *mint in sealed box*. True collectors will know what this means, and it saves precious "real estate" in your title. (By the way, if this model wasn't in the box but was instead already assembled, you could use the abbreviation BU, for *built-up*.) Continuing this example, a title that included all the keywords users might search on would be 1964 Superman Aurora Plastic Model Kit MISB. (And this comes in at well under 55 characters!)

> **tip**
>
> If you're unsure how best to word the title for your item listing, check out auctions for similar items and "borrow" their wording.

Note the inclusion of the year in the title. That's a good thing, because it helps to narrow down or better identify the item. Someone looking for a 1964 Superman model is not going to be interested in the 1978 or 2001 reissues, so including the date helps to narrow down your prospective customers.

If your item has a model number or series name, that's definitely something to include. As an example, you might be selling a `14" Pearl Export Select Snare Drum with Case`. In this case, Pearl is the manufacturer and Export Select is the series or line. Another example might be a listing for a `1956 Gibson ES-175 Red Jazz Guitar`. This title gets in the year (1956), the manufacturer (Gibson), the model number (ES-175), the color (Red), and a brief description of what it is (a jazz guitar)—which pretty much covers all the bases.

Make Your Title Stand Out

Beyond including as many relevant facts as possible in your title, how do you make your title stand out from all the other boring listings? Obviously, one technique is to employ the judicious use of CAPITAL LETTERS. The operative word here is *judicious*; titles with ALL capital letters step over the line into overkill.

Instead, I advise you to think like an advertising copywriter. What words almost always stop consumers in their tracks? Use attention-getting words such as FREE and NEW and BONUS and EXTRA and DELUXE and RARE—as long as these words truly describe the item you're selling and don't mislead the potential bidder. (And don't bump more important search words for these fluffier marketing terms—that won't help your item show up in bidder searches.)

Try this one on for size: Which would you rather bid on, a `1964 Superman Model Kit` or a `RARE 1964 Superman Model Kit`? I'm betting you go for the second one—and mentally prepare yourself to pay more for it, too!

In short, use your title to both inform and attract attention—and include as many potential search keywords as possible.

Write the Right Description

If the listing title is the headline of your ad, the listing description is your ad's body copy. Which means it's time to put on your copywriter's hat and get down to the nitty-gritty details.

Take All the Space You Need

What makes for good copy? First, you have all the space you need, so say as much as you need to say. Unlike with the title description, you don't have to scrimp on words or leave anything out. If you can describe your item adequately in a sentence, great; if it takes three paragraphs, that's okay too.

When you're writing the description for your ad, be sure to mention anything and everything that a potential bidder might need to know. Note any defects or imperfections of the item. Include your desired payment terms and your preferred shipping methods. If the object is graded or evaluated in any way, include that assessment in your description. In other words, include everything you can think of that will eliminate any surprises for the buyer.

First Things First

You should probably put the most important and motivating information in your initial paragraph because a lot of folks won't read any farther than that. Think of your first paragraph like a lead paragraph in a newspaper story: Grab 'em with something catchy, give them the gist of the story, and lead them into reading the next paragraph and the one after that.

The Bare Necessities

There are certain key data points that users expect to see in your item description. Here's the bare minimum you should include:

- Name (or title)
- Condition
- Age
- Original use (what you used it for)
- Value (if you know it)
- Important measurements, contents, colors, materials, and so on
- Any included accessories (including the original instruction manual, if you have it)
- Any known defects or damage

If you don't know any of this stuff, that's okay—as long as you admit it. If you're not that familiar with the type of merchandise you're selling, just say so. Better to plead ignorance up-front than to have a more savvy buyer cause problems for you after the sale.

Describe It—Accurately

Because other users will be bidding on your item sight unseen, you have to make the process as easy as possible for potential bidders. That means describing the item as accurately as possible, and in as much detail as possible. If the item has a scratch or blemish, note it. If the paint is peeling, note it. If it includes a few non-original parts, note it. Bidders don't have the item to hold in their hands and examine in person, so you have to be their eyes and ears.

That's right; you need to describe the item in painful detail, and be completely honest about what you're selling. If you're *not* honest in your description, it will come back to haunt you—in the form of an unhappy and complaining buyer.

Stress Benefits, Not Features

Although you need to be descriptive (and in some collectibles categories, you need to be *obsessively* so), it doesn't hurt to employ a little marketing savvy and salesmanship. Yes, you should talk about the features of your item, but it's even better if you can talk about your product's *benefits* to the potential buyer.

Let's say you're selling a used cordless phone, and the phone has a 50-number memory. Saying "50-number memory" is stating a feature; saying instead that the phone "lets you recall your 50 most-called phone numbers at the press of a button" is describing a benefit. Remember, a feature is something your item has; a benefit is something your item does for the user.

Break It Up

You should include as much descriptive copy as you need in your listing, but you should also make sure that every sentence sells your item.

And if your listing starts to get a little long, you should break it into more readable chunks. Use separate paragraphs to present different types of information, or just to break one long paragraph into several shorter, more readable ones. You can even use eBay's formatting options to use different type sizes and colors for different portions of your listing description.

caution

Don't forget to spell-check and proofread your listing. Bad grammar and misspellings can cause potential bidders to doubt your veracity and even to totally disregard your auction.

Don't Forget the Fine Print

Breaking up your description enables you to put a *lot* more info into your description. When it comes to informing potential buyers, it's impossible to be too complete. (And if you don't define a detail, the buyer will—in his or her mind.) Don't assume that buyers know *anything*; take the time to spell out all the details about payment and shipping and the like.

Here is some of the "fine print" you might want to include at the bottom of your item description:

- Bidding restrictions, such as "No bidders with negative feedback," "Bidders with positive feedback of at least 10 only," or "U.S. buyers only."

- Payment restrictions, such as "U.S. funds only," "No personal checks," or "Personal checks take two weeks to clear."

- Shipping/handling charges (if you know them) and restrictions, such as "Buyer pays shipping/handling" or "Shipping via USPS Priority Mail only."

- The grade of your item, if your item has been graded (discussed later in this chapter). Note that this information can also be included in the main body of the item description, as well as in the fine print section.

- Information about your other auctions.

Include Alternate Wording

The very last things you can put into your listing, at the bottom, are some extra words. Remember, not every person uses the same words to describe things. If you're selling a plastic model kit, for example, some users will search for model, others for kit, still others for statue or figure or styrene. Although you can't put all these variations into the item title, you *can* throw them in somewhere in the description—or, if all else fails, at the bottom of the item description. (Remember, they'll be picked up by eBay's search engine if they're *anywhere* in the description area.)

While you're at it, throw in any alternative spellings you can think of. For example, you might know that the correct spelling of Spider-Man includes the hyphen in the middle, but other users might search for the unhyphenated Spiderman. Whichever variation you use in your title, throw the other one in at the bottom of the description.

Making the Grade

When you're selling items on eBay, it helps to know what kind of shape your items are in. For many categories of merchandise, that means grading the item's condition—according to some very formal rules.

Grading is a way of noting the condition of an item, according to a predetermined standard. Collectors use these grading scales to help evaluate and price items within a category. If you know the grade of your item, you can include the grade in the item's title or description, and thus more accurately describe the item to potential bidders.

Making a Mint

Unfortunately, there is no such thing as a "universal" grading system for all items; different types of collectibles have their own unique grading systems. For example, trading cards are graded from A1 to F1; stamps are graded from Poor to Superb.

That said, many collectible categories use a variation of the Mint grading system, as shown in Table 14.1.

TABLE 14.1 Mint System Grading

Grade	Abbreviation	Description
Mint	MT, M, 10	An item in perfect condition, without any damage or imperfections.
Very Fine	VF	Similar to mint.
Near Mint	NM, 9	An item with a very minor, hardly noticeable flaw. Sometimes described as "like new."
Near Fine	NF	Similar to near mint.
Excellent	EX, 8	An item considered above average, but with pronounced signs of wear.
Fine	F	Similar to excellent.
Very Good	VG, 7	An item in average condition.
Good	GD, G, 6	An item that has clear indications of age, wear, and use.
Fair	F	An item that is heavily worn.
Poor	P, 5	An item that is damaged or somehow incomplete.

Degrees between grade levels are indicated with a + or –. (For example, an item between Fine and Very Fine would be designated as F+.) Naturally, the definition of a Mint or Fair item differs by item type.

Getting Graded

If you're not sure what grade an item is, you may want to utilize a professional grading and authentication service. These services will examine your item, authenticate it (confirm that it's the real deal), and give it a professional grade. Some services will even encase your item in a sealed plastic container or bag.

Where can you get your items graded? Table 14.2 lists some popular websites for grading and authenticating collectible items.

tip

eBay provides a page of links to "authorized" authentication services at pages.ebay.com/help/ community/auth-overview.html.

TABLE 14.2 Grading and Authentication Services

Collectible	Site	URL
Autographs	OnlineAuthentics.com	www.onlineauthentics.com
	PSA/DNA	www.psadna.com
Beanie Babies	Peggy Gallagher Enterprises, Inc.	www.beaniephenomenon.com
Books	PKBooks	www.pkbooks.com
Coins	American Numismatic Association Certification Service	www.anacs.com
	Numismatic Guaranty Corporation of America	www.ngccoin.com
	Professional Coin Grading Service	www.pcgs.com
Comic books	Comics Guaranty	www.cgccomics.com
Jewelry	International Gemological Institute	www.e-igi.com
Sports cards	Professional Sports Authenticator	www.psacard.com
	Sportscard Guaranty, LLC	www.sgccard.com
Stamps	American Philatelic Society	www.stamps.org
	Professional Stamps Experts	www.psestamp.com

The cost of these authentication services varies wildly, depending on what you're authenticating, the age or value of the item, and the extent of the service itself. For example, Professional Sports Authenticator rates range from $5 to $100 per sports card; Professional Stamps Experts rates range from $15 to $500 per stamp. Make sure that the item you're selling is worth it before you go to this expense—and that you can recoup this expense in your auction.

Other Ways to Describe Your Item

There are some other grading-related abbreviations you can use in your item listings. As you can see in Table 14.3, these abbreviations help you describe your item (especially in the title) without wasting a lot of valuable space.

TABLE 14.3 Grading-Related Terms

Abbreviation	Description	Meaning
ARC	Advanced readers copy	A pre-publication version of a book manuscript, typically released to reviewers and bookstores for publicity purposes
BU	Built up	For models and other to-be-assembled items; indicates that the item has already been assembled

TABLE 14.3 (continued)

Abbreviation	Description	Meaning
CC	Cut corner	Some closeout items are marked by a notch on the corner of the package
CO	Cut out	Closeout item
COA	Certificate of authenticity	Document that vouches for the authenticity of the item; often found with autographed or rare collectible items
COC	Cut out corner	Same as CC (cut corner)
COH	Cut out hole	Some closeout items are marked by a small hole punched somewhere on the package
FS	Factory sealed	Still in the original manufacturer's packaging
GP	Gold plate	Item is gold plated
HC	Hard cover	Used to indicate hardcover (as opposed to softcover, or paperback) books
HE	Heavy gold electroplated	Item has heavy gold plating
HTF	Hard to find	Item isn't in widespread circulation
LE	Limited edition	Item was produced in limited quantities
LSW	Label shows wear	Item's label shows normal usage for its age
MCU	Might clean up	Might show a higher grade if cleaned or otherwise restored
MIB	Mint in box	Item in perfect condition, still in the original box
MIMB	Mint in mint box	Item in perfect condition, still in the original box—which itself is in perfect condition
MIP	Mint in package	Item in perfect condition, still in the original package
MISB	Mint in sealed box	Item in perfect condition, still in the original box with the original seal
MNB	Mint, no box	Mint-condition item but without the original packaging
MOC	Mint on card	For action figures and similar items, an item in perfect condition still in its original carded package
MOMC	Mint on mint card	Item in perfect condition, still on its original carded package—which is also in mint condition
MONMC	Mint on near-mint card	Same as MOMC, but with the card in less-than-perfect condition
MWBMT	Mint with both mint tags	For stuffed animals that typically have both a hang tag and a tush (sewn-on) tag, indicates both tags are in perfect condition

TABLE 14.3 (continued)

Abbreviation	Description	Meaning
MWBT	Mint with both tags	Same as MWBMT, but with the tags in less-than-mint condition
MWMT	Mint with mint tag	Mint-condition item with its original tag, which is also in mint condition
NIB	New in box	Brand-new item, still in its original box
NOS	New old stock	Old, discontinued parts in original, unused condition
NR	No reserve	Indicates that you're selling an item with no reserve price
NRFB	Never removed from box	An item bought but never used or played with
NWOT	New without tags	Item, unused, but without its original tags
NWT	New with tags	Item, unused, that still has its original hanging tags
OOP	Out of print	Item is no longer being manufactured
P/O	Punched out	Same as CC (cut corner)
RR	Re-release	Not the original issue, but rather a reissue (typically done for the collector's market)
SC	Soft cover	A paperback (non–hard cover) book
SS	Still sealed	As it says, still in the original sealed package
SW	Slight wear	Only minor wear commensurate with age
VHTF	Very hard to find	Self-descriptive
WOC	Writing on cover	Item has markings on front surface

The big problem with any grading system is that grading is subjective. Although there may be guidelines for different grading levels, the line between very good and excellent is often a fine one. You should be very careful about assigning your own grading levels; even better, supplement the grade with a detailed description and photographs so that bidders can make up their own minds as to your item's true value.

THE ABSOLUTE MINIMUM

Here are the key points to remember from this chapter:

- Your item title must be no more than 55 characters long—and can include letters, numbers, characters, and spaces.

- Pack as much info into your title as possible, using common abbreviations and grading levels.

- The description of your item can be as long as you want—so take the space to include as much detailed information as is practical.

- Include an accurate description of the item's condition, including any flaws or damage.

- Include all necessary fine print for your transaction at the bottom of the item description.

- Use grading (Fair, Good, Mint, and so on) to describe the condition of your item.

15

USING PICTURES IN YOUR LISTINGS

A picture in your listing greatly increases the chances of actually selling your item—and also increases the average price you will receive.

Knowing that, you'd think more eBay ads would include pictures. The reason they don't is that adding a picture to an eBay listing requires more work than checking a check box. Basically, you have to go through four steps to insert a picture into your item listing:

1. Take a picture of your item.

2. Convert that picture to a digital graphics file.

3. Edit the image file (so that it looks pretty).

4. Upload your image file to a server somewhere on the Internet—or use eBay's Picture Services.

We'll look at each of these steps individually, but first, here's a checklist of what you need in order to take effective pictures for your eBay listings:

Checklist: eBay Pictures

☐ Digital camera

☐ Lighting (built-in flash can work)

☐ Tripod (optional)

☐ Clean space with plain black or white background

☐ Scanner (for flat items)

☐ Graphics editing software

☐ Web picture hosting service (optional)

" Mike Sez "

Is there any time when you *don't* want to include a picture of an item? If the item is nothing more than a black box—or a blank book cover—there's not a lot of point in showing it. However, don't think that if an item is damaged you shouldn't show it—just the opposite! You want bidders to know what they're getting into, regarding damage and flaws, and showing a picture is the best way to do this.

Take a Picture—Or Make a Scan

It all starts with a picture. But it had better be a darned good picture, or potential bidders won't find it much use.

Tips for Taking Great Product Photos

Although this really isn't the place for a basic photography lesson, I can give you a few tips on how to take the right kinds of pictures to use in your eBay listings.

■ **Use a digital camera.** Although you can take pictures with a normal film camera, develop the film, and have your film processor transfer your photos to graphics files on a photo CD, it's a lot easier if you start with digital at the source—especially if you plan on listing a lot of items on eBay. You can pick up a good low-end digital camera

caution

Whatever you do, resist the temptation to simply copy someone else's picture file to use in your listing. Not only is this unethical, but it misrepresents the exact item you're selling. You could also find yourself on the wrong side of a copyright lawsuit if the owner of the photo takes particular offense.

for $200 or less these days, and going direct from camera to computer (and then to eBay) is a lot easier than any other method.

■ **Shoot in strong light.** One of the worst photographic offenses is to shoot under standard indoor room light. Although you can touch up the photo somewhat afterward (see the "Edit the Image File" section, later in this chapter), you can't put in light that wasn't there to begin with. Open all the windows, turn on all the room lights, use a flash (but judiciously—you want to avoid glare on your item), or just take the item outdoors to shoot—do whatever it takes to create a well-lighted photograph. (Figure 15.1 and Figure 15.2 show the same item shot in low light and with stronger lighting; Figure 15.2 definitely works best.)

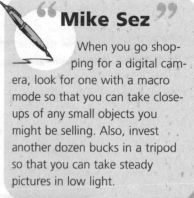

" Mike Sez "

When you go shopping for a digital camera, look for one with a macro mode so that you can take close-ups of any small objects you might be selling. Also, invest another dozen bucks in a tripod so that you can take steady pictures in low light.

FIGURE 15.1
An item shot in low lighting—bad.

FIGURE 15.2
An item shot in stronger lighting—good.

- **Avoid glare.** If you're shooting a glass or plastic item, or an item still in plastic wrap or packaging, or just an item that's naturally shiny, you have to work hard to avoid glare from whatever lighting source you're using—like that shown in Figure 15.3. This is one reason why I typically don't recommend using a single-point flash—without any fill lighting, it produces too much glare. You avoid glare by not using a flash, adding fill lighting (to the sides of the object), diffusing the lighting source (by bouncing the light off a reflector of some sort), or just turning the item until the glare goes away. A simpler solution is to shoot in an area with strong natural light—like outside on a nice day.

FIGURE 15.3

A shrink-wrapped item with glare from a flash—bad.

- **Shoot against a plain background.** If you shoot your object against a busy background, it detracts from the main point of the photograph, as you can see in Figure 15.4. Hang a white or black sheet (or T-shirt) behind the item; it will make the main object stand out a lot better.

- **Focus!** Okay, this one sounds obvious, but I see a lot of blurry pictures on eBay—like the one shown in Figure 15.5. Make sure you know how to focus your camera, or how to use the auto-focus function. Also—

tip

If you're shooting a small item, your camera may have difficulty focusing if you get too close. Use your camera's macro focus mode to enable sharp focus closer to the object.

and this is particularly important if you're shooting in low-light conditions—remember to hold the camera steady. A little bit of camera shake makes for a blurry photo. Either learn how to steady the camera or buy a cheap tripod to hold the camera for you.

FIGURE 15.4
An ugly back-ground detracts from the item you're shooting.

FIGURE 15.5
An out-of-focus photo—bad.

■ **Frame.** To take effective photographs, you have to learn proper composition. That means centering the item in the center of the photo, and getting close enough to the object so that it fills up the entire picture. Don't stand halfway across the room and shoot a very small object; get close up and make it *big!* (Figure 15.6 shows a poorly framed item—bad!)

FIGURE 15.6
Bad composition—the object's way too small!

■ **Take more than one.** Don't snap off a quick picture and assume you've done your job. Shoot your item from several different angles and distances—and remember to get a close-up of any important area of the item, such as a serial number or a damaged area. You may want to include multiple photos in your listing—or just have a good selection of photos to choose from for that one best picture.

Scan Instead of Shoot

Of course, if you're selling relatively flat items (books, comics, CDs, and so on), you might be better off with a scanner than a camera. (And remember that boxes have flat sides that can be scanned.) Just lay the object on a flatbed scanner and scan the item into a file on your computer. It's actually easier to scan something like a book or a DVD case than it is to take a good steady picture of it!

tip

When you're scanning compact discs, take the CD booklet out of the jewel case to scan.

Use eBay's Stock Photos

If you're selling a book, an audio book, an audio cassette, a CD, a DVD, a VHS tape, or a video game, you might not need any photos at all. That's because eBay automatically inserts a stock product photo when you use the pre-filled item description option to create your item listing. (You learned about this back in Chapter 10, "Selling 101: A Tutorial for Beginning Sellers.") If the item you're selling is listed in eBay's product database—and you like the photo they provide—save yourself the trouble and let eBay insert the picture for you.

Convert a Picture to a Digital Graphics File

If you took your pictures with a digital camera, all your pictures are in digital format, ready to transfer to your computer for editing. You can now skip to the next section.

If your pictures were shot on film, you have to get those film images into digital format. This is done by running your photograph through a scanner, which digitizes the image and stores it in a computer graphics file. You can buy your own flatbed scanner for $100 or so, you can ask a friend with a scanner to scan your photo for you, or you can pay around $10 to have FedEx Kinko's or some similar establishment do the job professionally.

note

There are several file formats you can use for your graphics files. The preferred format is the JPG format; most cameras and scanners will save files in this format.

When you have the scanned images on a disk or CD, you can then copy them to your computer, and get ready to edit them.

Edit the Image File

After your photograph has been converted to a JPG file (the graphics file type of choice on the Internet), you can do a little editing to "clean it up" for eBay use.

Things to Edit

What kinds of editing are we talking about? Here's a short list:

- Lighten up photos shot in low light.
- Correct the color and tint in poorly shot photos.
- Crop the picture to focus on only the subject at hand. (Figure 15.7 shows a picture being cropped in the Adobe Photoshop Elements program.)

■ Resize the image to fit better in your eBay listings. (Too big a picture won't fit within a normal web browser window.)

■ Decrease the resolution or color count to produce a smaller-sized file. (Files that are too big will take longer to load onto a bidder's PC—and may even be rejected by eBay.)

FIGURE 15.7

Cropping a photo in Adobe Photoshop Elements.

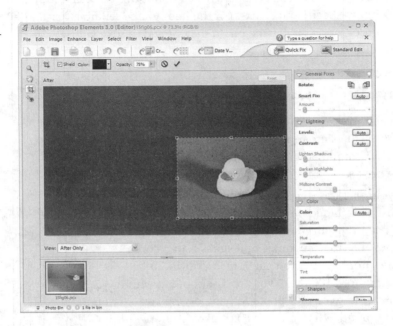

Graphics Editing Software

How do you do all this? You need an image-editing program. Although hard-core picture fanatics swear by the extremely full-featured (and very expensive) Adobe Photoshop CS, there are several lower-cost programs that perform just as well for the type of editing you'll be doing. These programs include the following:

■ Adobe Photoshop Elements (www.adobe.com)

■ CorelDRAW Essentials (www.corel.com)

■ IrfanView (www.irfanview.com)

■ Paint Shop Pro (www.corel.com)

■ Microsoft Picture It! (www.microsoft.com/products/imaging/)

■ Roxio PhotoSuite (www.roxio.com)

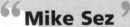
" Mike Sez "

My favorite of these programs is Adobe Photoshop Elements—not to be confused with the much more expensive (and harder to use) Adobe Photoshop CS. The Elements program is extremely easy to use, with one-button operation for most common photo editing tasks. To learn more, check out my companion book *Bad Pics Fixed Quick* (Que, 2004).

Most of these programs cost under $100 and have similar features. Or, if you'd rather not muck around with this sort of picture editing, you can always have somebody else do it for you; here again, FedEx Kinko's is a good place to start.

Resizing Your Photos

While you're editing, remember to resize your photo to best fit within your eBay listing. (Most pictures you take in a digital camera will come out too big to fit on a Web page without scrolling.) eBay recommends that you size your image to no more than 400 pixels wide by 400 pixels tall.

Resizing Your Files

You should also reduce the amount of detail in your picture to keep the file size small—no more than 50KB for each picture. This keeps the loading time for each photo down to a reasonable level.

> **" Mike Sez "**
>
> Personally, I find 400×400 pictures to be a tad on the small side for some items. I see no harm in going up to 500 or even 600 pixels wide, especially if viewing the detail of the object is important. Note, however, that if you use a larger size for a picture hosted with eBay Picture Services, it will automatically be resized down to 400 pixels (on the longest side), which sometimes results in distorted images. So if you're using eBay Picture Services, stick with their 400×400 guideline; if you're using a different picture host, then you can use a larger picture size.

There are three ways to reduce the size of an image file. You can reduce the dots per inch (dpi); you can resize the width and height; or you can reduce the number of colors used. Depending on your pictures, you may need to use some or all of these techniques to get the file down to a workable size. Most image editing software lets you perform all three of these operations.

Your photo editing software should include settings that let you reduce both the physical size and the file size for your photographs. And, of course, the two go hand in hand: Reduce the physical size, and you'll also reduce the file size.

Upload Your Image File to the Internet—Or Use eBay Picture Services

When you have your photos ready, you need to do one of two things: Upload the photos to your own personal website or picture hosting service, or get ready to add these photos to your new eBay item listing.

You see, when it comes to photos, eBay gives you a choice. They can host your photos for you, or you can have someone else host your photos. Which one is the right solution for you?

Using eBay Picture Services

When you have eBay host your photos, you have some choices to make. If you want to show only one picture, you're okay with eBay. If you want to show more than one photo, or if you want to show larger photos, you can still use eBay—you'll just have to pay for it.

Here's how eBay Picture Services' fee structure works:

- First photo: free.
- Each additional picture (up to six, total): $0.15 each.
- Picture show (multiple pictures in a slideshow format): $0.25.
- Supersize pictures (allow users to click a photo to display at a larger size): $0.75
- Picture pack (up to six pictures, supersized, with Gallery display): $1.00

If you like to get fancy with your pictures, those costs can add up pretty fast. Let's say you have two pictures of your item (front and back, perhaps) that you want to display in large format. You'll pay $0.90 for this privilege—the first picture is free, but you pay $0.15 for the second picture, plus $0.75 for supersizing.

If you frequently include multiple pictures in your auctions, it might be cheaper for you to find another site to host your pictures, which we'll talk about next. But if you typically include only a single photo, eBay Picture Services is both affordable (free!) and easy to use, especially for beginners. Here's how you do it:

1. Start the process to create a new item listing, and work your way to the Provide Pictures & Item Details page.

2. Scroll down to the Add Pictures section and select the eBay Picture Services tab, shown in Figure 15.8.

3. Click the Add Picture button in the first picture box. An Open dialog box now appears on your computer desktop; use this dialog box to locate and select the photo you want to use. Click the Open button when done; the photo you selected now appears on the Provide Pictures & Item Details page.

4. To insert an additional picture (for $0.15 extra), click the Add Picture button in the second box and repeat the instructions in step 3.

5. To insert even more pictures, click the Add Picture button(s) in the next box(es) and repeat the instructions in step 3.

6. In the Picture Layout section, select which options you want—Standard (single picture), Picture Show, Supersize Pictures, or Picture Pack.

7. If you choose to use eBay's Listing Designer, scroll to the Listing Designer section and select a position for your photo from the Select a Layout list.

FIGURE 15.8

Using eBay Picture Services to insert photos into your item listing.

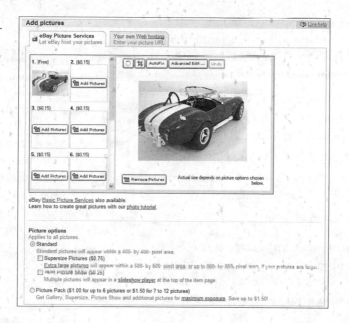

That's it. eBay will automatically upload the pictures from your hard disk to its picture hosting server, and automatically insert those pictures into your item listing.

Using Another Web Host

Many users are less than thrilled with eBay's picture hosting service. They find this service somewhat expensive (if you want to show a lot of pictures) and somewhat limited.

A better solution for some users is to use another Web hosting service to host their files. Here you have a lot of options.

tip

One plus to using eBay Picture Services is that you get a free picture of your item in the title bar of your item listing page—which you don't get if you host your pictures on another website.

First, if you have your own personal page on the Web, you can probably upload your pictures to that Web server. For example, if you have a personal page on Yahoo!, GeoCities, or Tripod, you should be able to upload your images to that site.

If you don't have a personal page but *could* have a personal page (via America Online or your Internet service provider), that's a potential place for you to upload picture files. If your company has a Web server, there's a chance it will let you use a little space there.

If you don't have any other options, you can go to a site that specializes in storing image files for eBay users. These sites include the following:

- Ándale Images (www.andale.com)
- Auction Pix Image Hosting (www.auctionpix.com)
- Photobucket (www.photobucket.com)
- PictureTrail (www.picturetrail.com)
- Vendio Image Hosting (www.vendio.com)

> **tip**
>
> eBay now offers its own advanced picture hosting service, dubbed eBay Picture Manager. Introductory pricing gives you 50MB of storage for $9.99 per month; more storage is available for additional fees. Learn more at pages.ebay.com/picture_manager/.

Most of these sites charge some sort of fee for hosting your pictures, either on a monthly basis for a certain amount of storage space or on a per-picture basis. Compare the fees at these sites with what you'll pay at eBay, and then make the smart choice.

After you have your pictures uploaded, you can add them to your new item listing. Just follow these steps:

1. Start the process to create a new item listing, and work your way to the Provide Pictures & Item Details page.

2. Scroll down to the Add Pictures section and select the Your Own Web Hosting tab, as shown in Figure 15.9.

3. Enter the full URL (including the http://) for the picture into the Picture URL box.

4. If you choose to use eBay's Listing Designer, scroll to the Listing Designer section and select a position for your photo from the Select a Layout list.

> **caution**
>
> The only problem with using a third-party Web hosting service in this manner is that eBay lets you insert only *one* picture into your listing. If you want to insert multiple photos, you either have to use eBay Picture Services, or insert your own picture links using HTML, as discussed in the following section.

FIGURE 15.9

Pointing to a picture file uploaded to another hosting service.

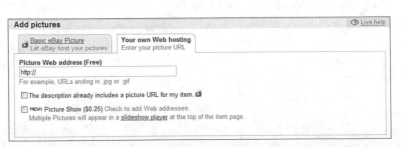

Adding a Picture Within Your Item Description

Another picture option is available for more advanced users—especially if you're comfortable adding a little HTML code to your item descriptions. This option lets you insert images directly within your item description. (And eBay won't charge you for it, either!)

As you'll learn in Chapter 16, "Creating a Great-Looking Listing," you can include HTML code in your item descriptions—and you can use this code to link to pictures you've already uploaded to a picture hosting service. This process isn't as hard as it sounds, assuming you've already found a hosting service, uploaded your picture file, and obtained the full URL for the uploaded picture. All you have to do is insert the following HTML code into your item description, where you want the picture to appear:

```
<img src="http://www.webserver.com/picture.jpg">
```

Just replace www.webserver.com/picture.jpg with the correct URL for your picture. Also, be sure to check the option The Description Already Contains a Picture URL for My Item. Your item will now display with the picture(s) you've selected—and you can expect the bids to start pouring in!

The Absolute Minimum

Here are the key points to remember from this chapter:

- Adding a picture to your item listing will increase the number of bids you receive—and the value of those bids.

- The easiest way to take pictures of the items you want to sell is with a digital camera—unless you have a small, flat item, in which case scanning is probably better.

- Take the best picture possible, and then edit the picture (in a graphics editing program) to make it look even better.

- Make sure that the picture will fit on your item listing page, and that the file size of the picture isn't too large.

- You can choose to let eBay host your pictures (with some potential cost), or you can find a third-party hosting service (that might also charge a fee).

- You add photos to your listings when you're creating the item listing, on the Provide Pictures & Item Details page.

16

CREATING A GREAT-LOOKING LISTING

Most of the item listings on eBay look the same: a paragraph or two of plain text, maybe a picture unceremoniously dropped in below the text. That's how a listing looks when you enter a normal, plain-text description for your item listing.

But then there are those ads that shout at you with colored text and different font faces and sizes and multiple columns and sizzling graphics and…well, you know the ones I'm talking about. How do you go about creating a dynamic listing like that?

Those colorful, eye-catching listings are created with Hypertext Markup Language (HTML). HTML is the engine behind every web page you've ever viewed, the coding language that lets you turn on and off all sorts of text and graphic effects.

Here's a secret known to successful sellers: eBay lets you use HTML in your item listings! All you have to do is know which HTML codes to enter in the Description box when you're creating your item listing—or you can use eBay's built-in HTML text editor and skip the coding altogether. Even easier, you can use eBay's Listing Designer or any number of third-party programs to create HTML-based listings without ever seeing the HTML code.

As you'll see, creating HTML-based listings isn't that difficult. And it's not just a tool for power sellers; it's a relatively common technique that *any* eBay seller can use to spruce up an eBay listing.

Apply Cool Templates with eBay's Listing Designer

The easiest way to create a listing that goes beyond plain text is with eBay's Listing Designer. This feature is available to all users, right from the Sell Your Item page—and it costs only $0.10 a listing.

As you can see in Figure 16.1, Listing Designer provides over a hundred predesigned templates, which eBay calls *themes*. You choose a theme from the Select a Theme list, and then choose a layout for your pictures from the Select a Layout list. This is without a doubt the easiest way to create HTML-based listings; eBay does all the work for you, and you never have to see the HTML code itself. (Figure 16.2 shows a listing enhanced with a Listing Designer theme.)

FIGURE 16.1
Use eBay's Listing Designer to choose a template for your item listing.

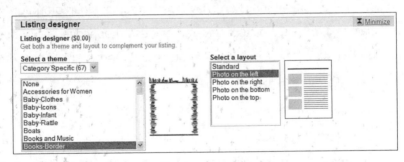

FIGURE 16.2
An eBay item listing enhanced with a Listing Designer template.

Create Fancy Listings with Listing-Creation Tools

Listing Designer isn't the only option you have for creating fancy eBay item listings. There are many software programs and web-based services that let you create great-looking listings without having to enter a line of HTML code. Most of these programs and services let you choose a design and fill in some blanks, and then they automatically write the HTML code necessary to create the listing. These programs and services are easy to use, even if they do come at a cost.

eBay Turbo Lister

Probably the most popular listing-creation program is eBay's Turbo Lister (pages.ebay.com/turbo_lister/). Turbo Lister uses the same templates found in eBay's Listing Designer, but it lets you create your listings in bulk, offline. We'll talk more about Turbo Lister in Chapter 17, "Automating Item Listing with eBay Turbo Lister," so turn there for more details.

Free Listing Templates

If you place a lot of listings, eBay's 10-cent Listing Designer fee can start to add up. Fortunately, there are lots of free auction templates you can use; it's always good when you can cut your auction costs.

Most of these free templates work by asking for specific input, and then let you choose from a number of colors and designs. This generates a batch of HTML code, which you copy from the template site into eBay's Sell Your Item form (using the Enter Your Own HTML tab). Other sites have predesigned template code you can download to your own computer. The results are similar.

Here are some of the most popular of these free auction template sites:

- Auction Riches Free Auction Ad Creator (www.auctionriches.com/freead/create.pl)
- AuctionSpice Templates (www.auctionspice.com)
- AuctionSupplies.com Free Auction Templates (auctionsupplies.com/templates/)
- K&D Web Page Design Custom Auction Creator (www.kdwebpagedesign.com/tutorials/tut_template.asp)
- ListTailor (www.listtailor.com/quickstart.html)
- Nucite Auction Templates (www.nucite.com/templates/)
- Wizard's Free Auction Template Creation Form (www.ambassadorboard.net/hosting/free-form.php)
- Xample.net Auction Templates (www.xample.net/templates.htm)

FIGURE 16.3

An eBay listing created with a Nucite auction template.

Third-Party Listing-Creation Tools

Of course, you're not limited to eBay's "official" listing creation tools. A plethora of listing creation programs and services are available, all of which provide various predesigned templates you can use for your item listings.

Most of these tools work in a similar fashion. You go to a particular web page or program screen, select a template from a list, choose available layout options, and then enter your normal listing title and description. The result varies from tool to tool, and depends on the choices you make; to give you an idea of what to expect, Figure 16.4 shows a listing created with Ándale Lister.

Here are some of the most popular of these third-party listing-creation tools:

- Ándale Lister (www.andale.com)
- Auction Hawk (www.auctionhawk.com)
- Auction Lizard (www.auction-lizard.com)
- AuctionWorks (www.auctionworks.com)
- Auctiva Poster (www.auctiva.com)
- EZAd (www.etusa.com)
- SpareDollar (www.sparedollar.com)
- Vendio (www.vendio.com)

Unlike the free auction template sites, you have to pay to use most of these third-party products and services. Make sure you can afford them before you sign up!

FIGURE 16.4

An eBay item listing created with Ándale Lister.

Insert Simple HTML Formatting with eBay's HTML Editor

Here's a secret known to successful sellers: eBay lets you use HTML to spruce up your item listings. While this isn't a task for the faint of heart, writing your own code lets you create highly individualized item listings—much fancier than you can do with a template-driven listing creator.

How HTML Works

HTML coding might sound difficult, but it's really pretty easy. HTML is really nothing more than a series of hidden codes that tell web browsers how to display different types of text and graphics. The codes are embedded in a document, so you can't see them; they're visible only to your web browser.

These codes are distinguished from normal text by the fact that they're enclosed within angle brackets. Each particular code turns on or off a particular attribute, such as boldface or italic text. Most codes are in sets of "on/off" pairs. You turn "on" the code before the text you want to affect and then turn "off" the code after the text.

note

I present only a handful of the huge number of HTML codes available to you. If you want to learn more about these and other HTML codes, I recommend that you check out the tutorials at the HTML Goodies (www.htmlgoodies.com). You can also pick up a copy of Todd Stauffer's *Absolute Beginner's Guide to Creating Web Pages, 2nd Edition* (Que, 2002), available wherever good books are sold.

For example, the code <h1> turns specified type into a level-one headline; the code </h1> turns off the headline type. The code <i> is used to italicize text; </i> turns off the italics. (As you can see, an "off" code is merely the "on" code with a slash before it.)

Entering HTML Codes

You enter HTML codes while you're creating your item listing. When you reach the Item Description section of the Sell Your Item: Title & Description page, click the Enter Your Own HTML tab (instead of the Standard tab). This displays eBay's HTML editor, shown in Figure 16.5. You can enter your raw HTML code into this form.

Codes to Format Your Text

We'll start off with some of the most common HTML codes—those used to format your text. Table 16.1 shows some of these text-formatting codes you can use in your item description.

note

If all you want to do is add some bold or color text to your listing, you don't have to learn HTML or use fancy listing-creation tools. eBay's standard text editor is available when you create your item listing with the Sell Your Item form. It lets you add HTML effects in a WYSIWYG environment, much the same way you add boldface and italics in your word processor. Just highlight the text you want to format and then click the appropriate formatting button. No manual coding necessary.

FIGURE 16.5

Enter your own HTML code on eBay's Sell Your Item page.

Item description ∗

Describe your items features, benefits, and condition. Be sure to include in your description: Condition (new, used, etc.), original price, and dimensions or size. You may also want to include notable markings or signatures, or its background history. See more tips for Fiction Books.

| Standard | **Enter your own HTML** |

New! Select Inserts from the drop-down list below to quickly and easily build your listing.

Inserts

This is a wonderful mystery book by the author of The Cuckoo. Only read once.

Preview description   Can't view our description editor? Use this alternative.

Enter <p> to start a new paragraph. Get more HTML tips. You can add pictures and themes on the next page.

Table 16.1—HTML Codes to Format Text

Effect	On Code	Off Code
Bold	`<b>`	`</b>`
Italic	`<i>`	`</i>`
Underline	`<u>`	`</u>`
Center	`<center>`	`</center>`
First-level headline	`<h1>`	`</h1>`
Second-level headline	`<h2>`	`</h2>`
Third-level headline	`<h3>`	`</h3>`

Just surround the text you want to format with the appropriate on and off codes, and you're ready to go. For example, to format a piece of text as bold, you'd write something that looks like this:

`<b>this text is bold</b>`

Codes for Font Type, Size, and Color

You can also use HTML to specify a particular font type or size, using the `<font>` code.

To specify a font type for selected text, use the `<font>` code with the `face` attribute, like this:

`<font face="xxxx">text</font>`

Replace the *xxxx* with the specific font, such as Arial or Times Roman—in quotation marks.

Another common use of the `<font>` code is to specify type size. You use the `size` attribute, and the code looks like this:

`<font size="xx">text</font>`

Replace the *xx* with the size you want, from –6 to +6, with –6 being the smallest, +6 being the biggest, and 0 (or no size specified) being "normal" size type.

You can also use the `<font>` code to designate a specific text color. In this instance, you use the `color` attribute, like this:

`<font color="#xxxxxx">text</font>`

Replace the *xxxxxx* with the code for a specific color. Table 16.2 lists some basic color codes.

caution

Just because you have a specific font installed on your computer doesn't necessarily mean that all the other web users who will be viewing your ad have the same font installed on their PCs. If you change fonts in your listing, change to a common font that is likely to be pre-installed on all Windows computers. Arial and Times Roman are always safe bets; choosing something more obscure could ensure an unpredictable display for your listing on many computers around the world.

TABLE 16.2 Common HTML Color Codes

Color	Code
White	FFFFFF
Red	FF0000
Lime Green	00FF00
Green	008000
Blue	0000FF
Fuchsia	FF00FF
Teal	00FFFF
Yellow	FFFF00
Black	000000
Silver	C0C0C0
Light gray	D3D3D3

note

For a complete list of the literally hundreds of different HTML color codes, check out the color charts at www.gotomy.com/color.html or www.annoyingwebsites.com/color_picker.htm.

Codes for Paragraphs, Line Breaks, and Rules

Some of the simplest HTML codes let you break your text into separate lines and paragraphs—and add horizontal rules between paragraphs. These codes are inserted into your text just once; there are no matching ending codes.

Table 16.3 lists these "on-only" codes.

TABLE 16.3 HTML Codes for Lines and Paragraphs

Action	Code
Line break	
New paragraph	<p>
Horizontal rule (line)	<hr>

Codes for Graphics

As you learned in Chapter 15, "Using Pictures in Your Listings," adding pictures and other graphics to your listings really brings some excitement to the normally plain-text world of eBay. You can add pictures the eBay way (described in Chapter 15), which puts all your pictures at the end of your text description—or you can put a picture *anywhere* in your text, using HTML.

Before you can insert a graphic into your listing, you need to know the address of that graphic (in the form of a web page URL). Then you use the following code:

```
<img src="URL">
```

No "off" code is required for inserted graphics. Note that the location is enclosed in quotation marks—and that you have to insert the `http://` part of the URL.

As an example, if your graphic is the file `graphic01.jpg` located at www.webserver.com/mydirectory/, you insert this code:

```
<img src="http://www.webserver.com/mydirectory/graphic01.jpg">
```

The nice thing about inserting graphics this way is that you can include more than just pictures—you can add logos, starbursts, you name it. (And you can put the graphics *anywhere* in your text description.) You use the same technique to link to any graphic image anywhere in your item listing.

Codes for Links

You can use HTML to add links to your own personal web pages (a great idea if you have additional images of this specific item) or to related sites. Many sellers also like to provide a direct email link in case potential bidders have questions they need answered.

To insert a link to another web page in your item listing, you use the following HTML code:

```
<a href="URL">this is the link</a>
```

The text between the on and off codes will appear onscreen as a typical underlined hyperlink; when users click that text, they'll be linked to the URL you specified in the code. Note that the URL is enclosed in quotation marks and that you have to include the `http://` part of the address.

You can also create a "mail-to" link in your listing; users will be able to send email to you by simply clicking the link. Here's the code for a mail-to link:

```
<a href="mailto:yourname@domain.com">click here to email me</a>
```

note

eBay allows links to pages that provide additional information about the item listed, additional photos of the item, and your other eBay auctions. eBay prohibits links to pages that attempt to sell merchandise outside eBay. Link at your own risk.

Codes for Lists

Finally, if you have a lot of features to list for your item, you might want to format them in a bulleted list. Using HTML codes, it's easy to create a neatly bulleted list for your ad.

First, you enclose your bulleted list with the `<ul>` and `</ul>` codes. Then, you enclose each bulleted item with the `<li>` and `</li>` codes.

The code for a typical bulleted list looks like this:

```
<ul>
    <li>item one</li>
    <li>item two</li>
    <li>item three</li>
</ul>
```

Bulleted lists are great ways to run through a list of attributes or specifications; it's a lot cleaner than just listing a bunch of stuff within a long text paragraph.

tip

When you're dealing with complex coding like this, it's easier to understand what's going on if you indent the different levels of code.

THE ABSOLUTE MINIMUM

Here are the key points to remember from this chapter:

- The easiest way to create a great-looking item listing is to apply a template via eBay's Listing Designer.

- You can also use listing-creation programs and services—such as eBay's Turbo Lister—to create template-based item listings.

- eBay lets you use HTML code to customize the appearance of your item's description (but not the item title!).

- For simple HTML coding, use eBay's built-in HTML Editor.

- For more complex formatting, you can apply HTML by hand—which means learning some basic HTML codes.

17

AUTOMATING ITEM LISTING WITH EBAY TURBO LISTER

As you learned in Chapter 10, "Selling 101: A Tutorial for Beginning Sellers," creating an item listing with eBay's standard Sell Your Item pages isn't that hard. However, if you have a lot of items to list, this page-by-page process can be time-consuming. Going through that cumbersome procedure for a dozen or more items isn't very appealing—trust me.

A better solution if you have a lot of items to list is to use a *bulk listing* program or service. These tools let you create a large number of item listings in advance, and even reuse saved listings—great if you run multiple auctions for similar items. You then schedule your auctions to launch at the time of your choosing, and you're done with it.

Several of these bulk listing tools are available, but the most popular one is available from eBay free of charge. This program is called Turbo Lister, and it also lets you create great-looking item listings through the use of predesigned templates.

Downloading and Configuring the Turbo Lister Software

Turbo Lister is a software program that you install on your own PC. When you run Turbo Lister, shown in Figure 17.1, you can create your eBay item listings offline, at your leisure. Then, when you're ready, it uploads all your listings at once, with the click of a button. Creating multiple auctions couldn't be easier.

> **" Mike Sez "**
>
> I'm a big fan of Turbo Lister. I use it to create *all* my item listings, even if I'm listing just a single item. It makes the listing creation process extremely fast and easy—and I can do it on my own time, offline!

FIGURE 17.1

Use Turbo Lister to create item listings in bulk.

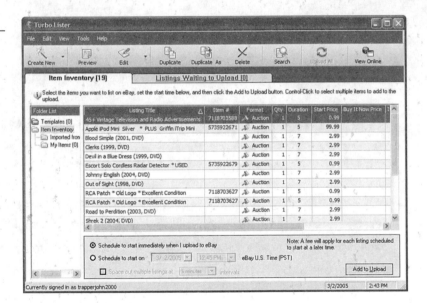

Downloading Turbo Lister

To download the Turbo Lister software, go to pages.ebay.com/turbo_lister/. The program is free and there are no monthly subscription fees—which makes it the program of choice for cost-conscious sellers.

Configuring Turbo Lister

Before you use Turbo Lister, you need to configure it for your specific auction listings. You do this from the Options & Preferences dialog box, which you open by pulling down the Tools menu and selecting Options.

As you can see in Figure 17.2, the Options & Preferences dialog box is divided into two parts. The left side contains a menu tree of options; the specifics for the selected option are displayed on the right.

FIGURE 17.2
Configuring
Turbo Lister via
the Options &
Preferences dia-
log box.

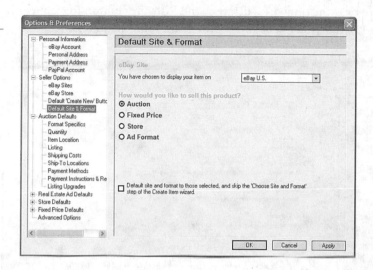

You'll want to go through each and every option to make sure that Turbo Lister is set up properly for your upcoming auctions. The options you set here determine the information used by default in your listings; you can always edit any piece of information when you create an individual auction.

Creating an Item Listing

The Turbo Lister software is quite easy to use. It uses a series of forms to request information about your listings. It also includes predesigned templates and a WYSIWYG editor that lets you create great looking listings.

You start out not by creating a listing, but rather by creating a new inventory item. After you've created the item, you then design a listing for that item. Here's how it works:

1. From the main Turbo Lister screen, click the Create New button.

2. When the Create a New Item screen appears, as shown in Figure 17.3, select the eBay Site (country) you're selling in and your preferred auction format—typically the Auction option. Click Next to proceed.

3. When the next screen appears, as shown in Figure 17.4, enter your item title and optional subtitle, and then select a category. Previously used categories are available from the pull-down list; if you don't

tip

If you're selling some common items (books, CDs, DVDs, video games, and the like), you have the option of using eBay's pre-filled information and stock photos. Read on to the "Creating Listings for Commonly Sold Items" section of this chapter to learn more.

know the category, click the Find Category button to display the Select a Category dialog box and browse through the full list.

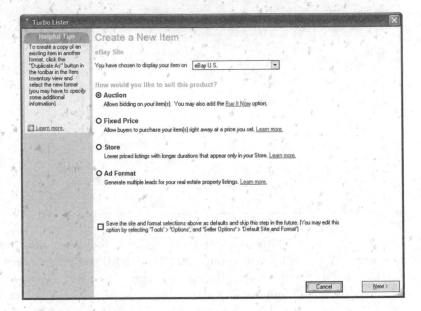

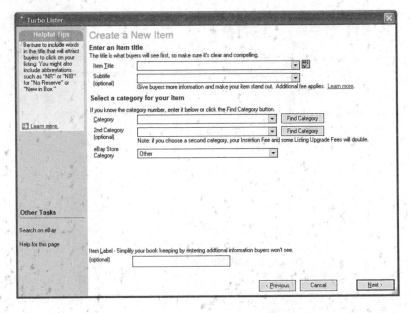

4. If the category for this item allows item specifics, you'll see an Enter Item Specifics screen, like the one in Figure 17.5. Enter the appropriate information, and then click Next.

FIGURE 17.5

Entering item specifics for your listing.

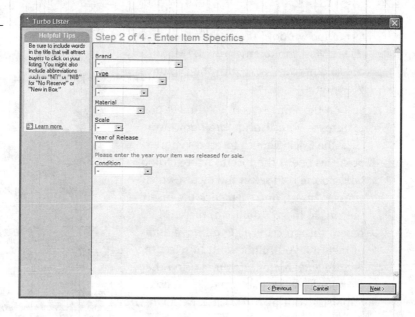

5. When the Enter Your Description screen appears, as shown in Figure 17.6, start by selecting an optional theme from the Theme list on the left, and then select a picture layout from the Layout list. (The Standard layout puts your pictures below your formatted description—but it also lets you use the Supersize option.)

FIGURE 17.6

Entering description, picture, and theme information.

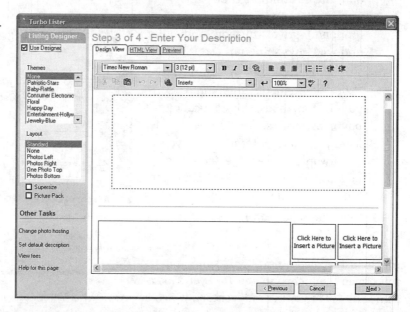

6. Still on the same screen, enter your item description into the Description box. (That's the one with the broken border.) Format the text by using the editing

controls (bold, italic, and so forth) at the top of the window. If you prefer, select the HTML View tab to enter raw HTML codes; otherwise, stay with the Design View tab.

7. Still on the same screen, it's time to add pictures to your listing. Scroll down and click the Click Here to Insert a Picture box; this opens the Insert Picture dialog box. Locate and select the picture you want to insert, and then click the Insert button. To insert additional pictures, repeat this procedure. If you have a lot of pictures, you might want to select the Picture Pack option; if you're using the Standard layout, you can also choose to Supersize your pictures. Click Next when you're ready to move on.

8. When the Format Specifics screen appears, as shown in Figure 17.7, enter the following information: duration, quantity, starting price, Buy It Now price (optional), reserve price (optional), private auction (optional), and who pays shipping costs.

9. Still on the same screen, examine the buyer requirements, shipping costs, payment methods, ship-to locations, payment address, item location, and listing upgrades information. If you don't want to accept the default values, click the appropriate Change button and enter new data.

10. Click the Save button to save this listing.

note

Step 7 assumes that you're using eBay's Picture Services. If your picture is hosted on another site, click the Change Photo Hosting link in the Other Tasks section; when the Photo Hosting dialog box appears, select the Your Own Web Hosting option. Now when you click the Click Here to Insert a Picture box, you'll be prompted for the URL of the picture you want to insert.

tip

To see how your listing will look on the Web, select the Preview tab.

To edit any listing you've created, select the Item Inventory tab and then double-click the item listing. This opens the Edit Item dialog box; make your changes and then click the Save button.

You've just created a new item listing—but you haven't launched the auction yet. This new item is added to your item inventory, which is what Turbo Lister calls your database of item listings. To turn this inventory item into a live auction, you have to upload it to eBay—which you'll learn how to do in the "Uploading Your Listings" section, later in this chapter.

FIGURE 17.7

Enter listing
details on the
Format Specifics
page.

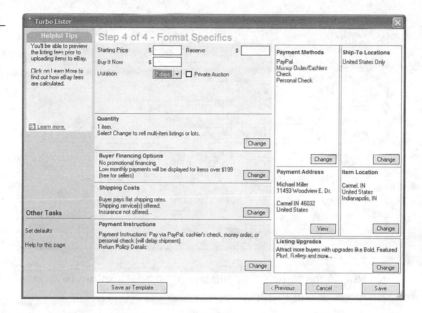

Creating Listings for Commonly Sold Items

As you learned back in Chapter 10, if you're selling commonly sold items—books, audio books, audio cassettes, CDs, DVDs, VHS tapes, or video games—you can use eBay's pre-filled item description feature to automatically create item descriptions, complete with stock product photos. Turbo Lister makes this feature even better by letting you create listings for multiple items at one time; all you have to do is enter the name or number of your items, and Turbo Lister will create multiple listings.

To create multiple listings of this type, follow these steps:

1. Click the down arrow next to the Create New button, and select Create Multiple Items with Pre-Filled Information.

2. When the opening screen appears, click Next.

3. When the Enter Multiple Items screen appears, as shown in Figure 17.8, pull down the Select Product Type list and select which type of items you're selling.

4. Still on the same page, pull down the Item 1 Search By list and select how you want to search for the item (UPC or ISBN is most accurate), and then enter the keywords or number into the adjoining box. Repeat this step to enter multiple items.

If you want to list more than 10 items, click the Add More Items button.

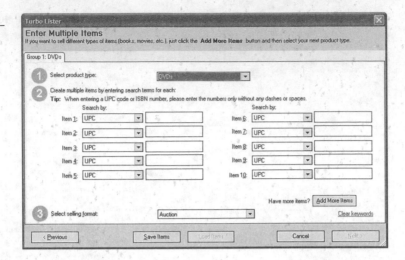

5. Still on the same page, pull down the Select Selling Format list and select Auction, and then click Next.

6. Turbo Lister now connects to the Internet and searches for the items you entered. Select the items that correctly match the items you're selling, and then click Next.

7. Turbo Lister downloads the appropriate information for each of these items, and then displays the You're Almost Done! screen. Click the Save button to proceed.

8. You're now taken to the Item Inventory tab in the main Turbo Lister window. Each of your newly created items is listed, along with a corresponding Edit button. You have to choose a listing category and enter auction details (such as starting price) for each item. Click the Edit button for each item to display the Edit Item screen, as shown in Figure 17.9; enter the required information and then click the Save button. Repeat this step for each item you've added.

When you've finished editing each of these new listings, they're ready to upload—which is what we'll do next.

FIGURE 17.9

Editing an inventory item before uploading.

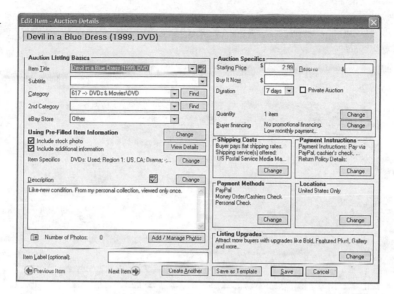

Uploading Your Listings

Turbo Lister keeps all your item listings—past and pending—in an inventory list. To view the items in your inventory, click the Item Inventory tab on the main Turbo Lister screen. This tab lists all the items you've created; from here you can edit, delete, or create duplicate items.

When you have an auction that you're ready to launch, follow these steps:

1. Select the Item Inventory tab.

2. Select the item(s) you want to launch.

3. Click the Add to Upload button; this copies the item(s) to your upload list. (The original items still appear in your inventory listing, so you can reuse them for additional auctions later.)

4. Turbo Lister displays the You're Almost Finished dialog box; click the Go Upload Listings button.

5. This action displays the Listings Waiting to Upload tab, shown in Figure 17.10. (You can also select this tab manually.) This tab shows all items waiting to be uploaded.

caution

Remember, just because an item appears in your inventory list doesn't mean that it has been launched as an eBay auction. You have to manually select which items you want to list, and then upload those items to eBay.

FIGURE 17.10

Items waiting to be uploaded to eBay.

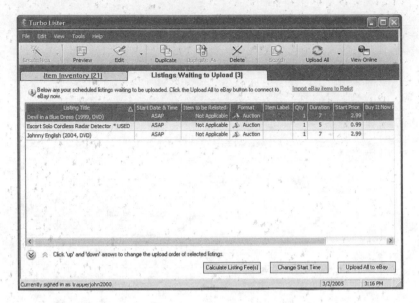

6. To calculate your listing fees for these items, click the Calculate Listing Fee(s) button.

7. To change the starting time for an item, select the item and then click the Change Start Time button. When the ReSchedule dialog box appears, make a new selection and then click OK. (Remember, you'll pay $0.10 per listing to schedule a later start time.)

8. When you're ready to upload these items, click the Upload All to eBay button.

Turbo Lister now connects to the eBay site and uploads the selected item listings. Those listings that are set to start immediately do so, and items with a future start time are sent to eBay's Pending Listings section. These auctions will go live at the time(s) you previously scheduled.

Pretty easy, huh? Just remember that you pay an extra $0.10 for every item you submit with Turbo Lister, due to the use of eBay's pay-per-use templates. (It's the same when you use these templates with the standard Listing Designer feature.)

THE ABSOLUTE MINIMUM

Here are the key points to remember from this chapter:

- Turbo Lister can create multiple listings—complete with fancy formatting and templates—offline, and then upload all these listings at one time.

- The Turbo Lister software is available for downloading from eBay—and it's free!

- Before you use Turbo Lister, you have to configure it to display various default information for your auction listings.

- The listings you create are added to Turbo Lister's inventory list; you then have to upload these listings to eBay in order to start the auctions.

- You can also use Turbo Lister to create multiple listings for commonly sold items, using eBay's pre-filled item description feature.

18

MANAGING THE AUCTION PROCESS

After you've placed your item listing and your auction is underway, you can just sit back and count the bids for the next seven (or so) days, right?

Wrong.

There's plenty for a motivated seller to do over the course of an eBay auction. Not only can you keep track of the current bids, but you also might have to answer questions from bidders, update your item listing, cancel bids from questionable bidders, and—on rare occasions—cancel the entire auction.

Auctioning an item on eBay is *work*!

Keeping Tabs on Your Current Auctions

When you're running only one or two auctions at a time, it's relatively easy to go directly to the item listing pages to check the status of those auctions. But what do you do if you're running a half-dozen, or a dozen, or several dozen auctions simultaneously?

If you're a busy seller, you need some way to consolidate all the information from all your auctions-in-process—the number of bidders, the high bids, and the time left until the auction ends. Fortunately, several tools are available to you for just this purpose.

Receiving Daily Updates from eBay

One of the most convenient ways to keep track of your in-process auctions is to let eBay do it for you. You can configure eBay to send you an email message every morning, containing key information about all your open auctions—as well as all the auctions in which you're currently bidding.

To automatically receive eBay's Daily Status report, follow these steps:

1. Click the My eBay link on the Navigation Bar, select the eBay Preferences link, and then click the View/Change link next to Notification Preferences (in the eBay Preferences section).

2. When the Change Your Notification Preferences page appears, as shown in Figure 18.1, check those emails you want to receive and uncheck those you don't. (In particular, check the two options in the Daily Status section.)

3. Go to the Transaction Emails delivery format section and select whether you want to receive these messages as simple text-only email or more appealing HTML email.

4. Click the Save My Changes button.

As you can see on the Change Your Notification Preferences page, eBay has lots of email messages that you can choose to receive. These messages include the following:

- Outbid notices (notification that you've just been outbid in a specific auction)

- End of item notices (notification for unsuccessful bidders that an auction has ended)

- Second-chance offer notices (offers from the seller on items you have bid on but not won)

- Bid notices (confirmation that you've completed a bid on an item)

- Bidding and selling daily status (daily update on all items you're selling or bidding on)

- Item watch reminder (daily notification of all items on your watch list that end within 36 hours)

- Listing confirmation (confirmation that you've successfully listed an item for sale)

note

You can't opt *not* to receive end-of-auction notices.

FIGURE 18.1

Configuring your email notification preferences.

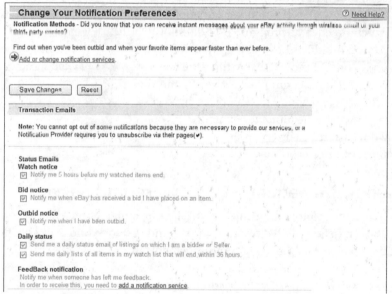

Using My eBay

eBay's Daily Status Report is a nice auction management tool—especially because eBay does all the work and emails you the results once a day. But what if you want to check the current status of your auctions in the middle of the afternoon, or late at night? If you want the latest auction information, you need a tool that accesses current auction information at any hour of the day.

One way to gather this live information is to perform a search on your user name. eBay will display all your open auctions as the results of this search.

But typing in your user information every time you want to check your auctions is unnecessarily time-consuming. Better to go to a single page that automatically displays all your auction info.

You can find such a page in My eBay. As you'll learn in Chapter 25, "Creating a Home Base with My eBay," My eBay displays key information about all your eBay activities—including items you're selling, watching, and bidding on, as well as recent feedback you've received.

When you click the My eBay link on eBay's Navigation Bar, you're taken to your My eBay page. To view all the items you're currently selling, click the All Selling link to display the All Selling page. The Items I'm Selling section of this page displays the item number, title, current price, number of bids, and time left for each of your open auctions—as well as the number of people watching each auction and any questions potential bidders have asked. By default, this page sorts your auctions by the time left, with the items ending first shown first in the list. You can change the sort order by clicking any item heading; for example, if you want to sort by current high bid, click the Current Price heading.

tip

Display the latest up-to-the-second bid information by clicking the Refresh or Reload button in your Web browser.

Using Auction Management Software and Services

If you're a high-volume individual seller or a merchant selling a ton of items on eBay, it gets really tedious really fast handling each and every auction—the listing, the ad creation, the auction management, the email notifications—one auction at a time. Automating some of your auction-management tasks would make the process easier.

Many users choose to outsource their auction management to an outside service, or utilize dedicated software programs to do the management for them. These programs and services not only track the progress of in-process auctions, but also manage all manner of post-auction activity.

One of the most popular of these auction-management services is eBay's very own eBay Selling Manager (pages.ebay.com/selling_manager/). For just $4.99 per month, Selling Manager will

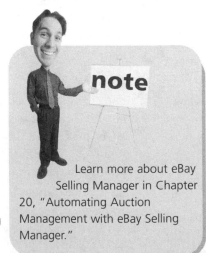

note

Learn more about eBay Selling Manager in Chapter 20, "Automating Auction Management with eBay Selling Manager."

let you manage your pending listings, monitor buyer activity for in-process auctions, track post-auction activity, send email to your buyers, print invoices and shipping labels, and leave user feedback—all from a special tab on your My eBay page. It's one of eBay's best features, and definitely worth checking out.

For higher-volume sellers, you can use eBay's Selling Manager Pro or any number of third-party solutions, such as those by ándale (www.andale.com), SpareDollar (www.sparedollar.com), and Vendio (www.vendio.com). You can find a complete list of these auction management programs in Chapter 28, "Using Auction Software and Services."

Editing In-Process Auctions

Sometimes you have to do more than just track your auctions. Sometimes you actually have to change an item listing.

Updating Your Auction Listing

Maybe you've received additional information about the item you're selling. Maybe a bidder has asked a question and you feel that question (and your answer) should be part of your item listing. Maybe you flat out made a mistake in your original listing and want to offer a correction in the item listing.

Whatever your reason might be, eBay makes it relatively easy to update your item listing.

If your listing hasn't received any bids yet (and there's more than 12 hours left in your auction), you can actually edit the original listing. eBay lets you edit your title, description, and pictures—as long as no one has yet placed a bid. To edit your listing, follow these steps:

1. Navigate to the item listing page.
2. Click the Revise Item link (located at the top of your listing, just below the item title).
3. Follow the onscreen instructions to access the listing editing screen.
4. Make the appropriate changes to your listing and then click the Submit button.

What do you do if you need to update your listing and you've already received a bid or two on the item? In this instance, eBay won't let you revise your item description or details; instead, when you go to revise your item, all you can do is add supplemental text below your existing item description—which is better than nothing.

Deleting Unwelcome Bidders

What do you do if a known deadbeat bidder makes a bid in one of your auctions? Although you could just sit back and pray that the deadbeat gets outbid, a better approach is to cancel that user's bid—and block that user from ever bidding in one of your auctions again.

Here's what to do:

1. Start by canceling the bid in question. Go to the Site Map page and click the Cancel Bids on My Item link. When the Bid Cancellation page appears, cancel that user's bid.

2. Now you want to block the bidder from any of your future auctions. Go to the Site Map page and click the Blocked Bidder/Buyer List link. When the Bidder/Buyer Management page appears, scroll to the Blocked Bidder/Buyer List section and click Continue.

note

You can ferret out deadbeat bidders by examining the feedback rating and comments for the high bidders in each of your auctions.

3. When the Blocked Bidder/Buyer List page appears, add the buyer's user name to the list; separate multiple names with commas.

4. Click the Submit button when done.

Now you don't have to worry about that questionable bid, and the deadbeat bidder won't be able to bother you again.

Canceling an Auction

One last little bit of auction maintenance: What do you do if you need to cancel an auction completely?

It happens, you know. Maybe you have an unexpected trip come up, so you won't be home when your auction ends (and when the item will need to ship). Maybe you discover you really don't have the item you thought you have. Maybe you drop the item and break it into a zillion pieces. Or maybe someone comes along with a better offer and you decide to sell the item outside of eBay.

caution

Frequent early cancellations may cause eBay to revoke your membership.

In any case, if you need to cancel an auction, eBay will accommodate you—as long as you have a good excuse, and don't make a habit of it.

To cancel an auction in progress, go to eBay's Site Map page and click the End My Listing link. When the next page appears, enter the item number of the auction you want to end. You'll then be prompted to cancel all current bids on the auction and end your auction early. (You also have the option of selling to the high bidder early, if you want to do this.) It's pretty easy.

Answering Bidder Questions

Over the course of a popular auction, chances are that a few potential bidders will ask questions about your item or your auction. eBay lets bidders email sellers during the course of an auction, so don't be surprised if you get a few emails from strangers asking unusual questions.

These questions will come to the email account you specified when you became an eBay member. Bidders can send these emails by clicking the Ask Seller a Question link on the item listing page.

When you receive a question from a potential bidder, answer that question promptly, courteously, and accurately. It's in your best interest to make the questioner happy; after all, that person could turn out to be your high bidder.

note

When you answer a bidder's question, you have the option of displaying the question and answer on the listing page, or of not doing so. If you think the question might be relevant to other potential bidders, choose to display the question and answer; it might save you from answering similar questions in the future!

Promoting Your Auctions

Here's something else you can do after you've started your auction: Tell people about it!

Yes, it's allowable (and encouraged) to promote your auction outside of eBay. You can drop notes about the item you're selling in newsgroups, message boards, and mailing lists; you can email your friends and family and colleagues and let them know about your auction; you can even include links to your auctions on your own personal web page.

tip

An easier way to obtain the link to your auction is to navigate to the item listing page and copy the URL from the address box in your web browser.

Linking to Specific Item Listings

When you mention your auction, be sure to include the URL for the specific item listing page. It should look like this:

cgi.ebay.com/ws/eBayISAPI.dll?ViewItem&item=*xx*

All you have to do is replace *xx* with the actual auction item number for your particular item, and you've created a direct link to your auction page.

Linking to All Your Auction Listings

To create a permanent link to *all* your eBay auctions, go to the Link Your Site to eBay Page (pages.ebay.com/services/buyandsell/link-buttons.html) and follow the instructions to add a My Listings with eBay button to your website.

Alternatively, you can add a link to your About Me page (discussed in Chapter 26, "Creating Your Personal About Me Page"). Just link to the following URL: members.ebay.com/aboutme/*userid*/. Be sure to replace *userid* with your own eBay user ID.

THE ABSOLUTE MINIMUM

Here are the key points to remember from this chapter:

- Configure eBay so that you receive a daily status report for your open auctions in each morning's email.

- You can use My eBay for up-to-the-minute tracking of all your open auctions.

- Some users prefer to use a third-party program or service to manage their in-process auctions and post-auction activity.

- When a potential bidder asks you a question about your auction, answer it—promptly and accurately.

- If you need to, you can update or append your item listing in the middle of an auction, as well as cancel individual bids, block unwanted bidders, and cancel the entire auction.

- Promote your auctions by linking to the URL of your item listing pages on your personal web page, in email correspondence, and in newsgroups, message boards, and mailing lists.

19

After the Auction: Concluding Your Business

You've waited the requisite 7 (or 1 or 3 or 5 or 10) days, and your auction has finally ended. What comes next?

The post-auction process involves more work, in most cases, than the listing process. You have to contact the buyer, arrange payment, receive payment, pack the item, ship the item, and leave feedback. And that's if everything goes smoothly!

The post-auction process can also be a long one, depending on how the buyer pays. If the buyer pays by PayPal (or other credit card method) as soon as the auction ends, the post-auction process can be over that day or the next—as soon as you pack and ship the item. If, on the other hand, the buyer pays by check—and is a little slow in putting the check in the mail—the post-auction process can last two or three weeks.

That means, of course, that you need to remember this potential time lag when you're planning your auction activity. For example, if you're planning to go on vacation in two weeks, now is not the best time to list an item for auction. You need to allocate a full month, from beginning to end, when you're planning your auction listings. If your buyers help you complete the process faster, that's great. But there will always be that one last buyer who hasn't sent the check yet—and there goes your schedule!

The Post-Auction Process

What happens during the post-auction process is actually rather cut and dried. Put simply, you contact the winning bidder with a final price; he or she sends payment to you; you pocket the payment; you package and ship the item; the buyer receives the item; and you both leave feedback for each other.

In checklist form, here's what you have to look forward to:

Checklist: After the Auction

☐ Receive an end-of-auction email from eBay

☐ If the buyer doesn't pay immediately via PayPal, send an email to the high bidder (containing final price and payment information)

☐ Receive payment from the buyer—and wait for payment to clear, if necessary

☐ Package the item

☐ Ship the item to the high bidder

☐ Leave feedback for the buyer

Communicating with the Winning Bidder

Minutes after the conclusion of your auction, eBay will notify you by email that your auction has ended. This email message, like the one shown in Figure 19.1, will include the user ID and email address of the item's high bidder.

Several things can now happen:

■ If you accept payment via PayPal and if the buyers opts to pay via credit card or bank debit, the buyer can initiate payment from the end-of-auction email he receives. If the buyer pays immediately like this, you'll receive a second email informing you of the completed payment.

■ If the buyer doesn't pay via PayPal, he can still go through eBay's checkout process, which then sends you an email notifying you of the buyer's intention to pay via check or money order or whatever, and providing you with the buyer's shipping address and other relevant information.

■ If the buyer doesn't pay or checkout immediately, you can send the buyer an invoice. Just click the Create and Send an Invoice link in the end-of-auction email you received (or the Send Invoice link on the closed auction page, or on your My eBay page) to display the Send Invoice to Buyer page, shown in Figure 19.2. Edit the payment information and instructions as necessary, and then click the Send Invoice button to email the thing.

■ Alternately, you can choose to send your own personal end-of-auction notice directly to the buyer. If you opt for this method, include your name and address (so the buyer will know where to send the payment); your email address (so the buyer can contact you with any questions or issues); the total amount the buyer owes you (the final auction price plus shipping/handling); and your preferred method(s) of payment.

note

eBay lets you combine multiple auctions into a single invoice, for those occasions where one buyer has made multiple purchases. The auctions are grouped by buyer, so all you have to do is select all the auctions from a single buyer to create a combined invoice. You can even manipulate the shipping/handling costs for the combined auctions, in order to offer a discount for multiple orders.

■ You can also use various auction-management tools to handle all this post-auction messaging and processing for you. One of the most popular tools is eBay Selling Manager; learn more in Chapter 20, "Automating Auction Management with eBay Selling Manager."

If the buyer doesn't pay immediately, he should at least respond to your invoice or end-of-auction email. If you haven't heard back from the buyer in a day or two, send another email. If, after three days, you still haven't been able to contact the buyer, you can consider that person a *deadbeat bidder*. See Chapter 22, "Dealing with Deadbeat Bidders," to learn how to deal with this situation.

FIGURE 19.1

A typical eBay email notifying you of the end of your auction.

FIGURE 19.2

Sending an invoice to the winning bidder.

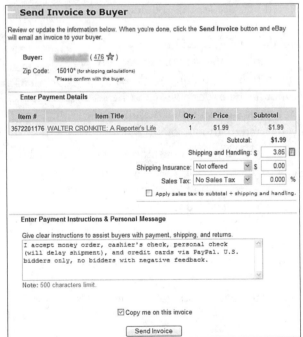

Accepting Payment

Now it's time to get paid. As recommended in Chapter 12, "Deciding on Your Payment Methods—And Using PayPal," you've presumably determined how you want to get paid, and indicated so in your item listing. You need to repeat your preferred payment methods in your post-auction email to the high bidder, and then wait for that user to make the payment.

Whatever you do, do *not* ship the item before you've received payment! Wait until you've received a cashier's check or money order in the mail, or been notified by PayPal that a payment has been made, and *then* prepare to ship the item.

When you receive payment, it's good business practice to email the buyer and let him or her know that the payment has been received. If you know when you'll be shipping the item, include that information in the email, as well.

And if the buyer never sends payment? Turn to Chapter 22 for my detailed advice.

caution

Remember, if you receive a payment via personal check, wait at least 10 working days for that payment to clear before you ship the item.

Packing and Shipping

One of the most crucial parts of the post-auction process is packing the item you've just sold. This process is so important, and so complicated, that I've devoted an entire chapter to it. So when you're ready to pack, turn to Chapter 21, "Shipping It Out—Cheaply and Safely," for more information.

Finishing Things Up and Leaving Feedback

As you ship the sold item, there are two more things you need to do:

- First, send an email to the buyer, letting him or her know that the item is on its way. (You should note in your message when and by which method the item was shipped—and if you have a tracking or confirmation number, pass it along.)

- Second, you need to leave feedback about the buyer. Whether it was a good transaction or a bad transaction, you need to let your fellow eBay members know how things turned out.

To leave feedback for the buyer, follow these instructions:

1. Go to the listing page for the item you just sold and click the Leave Feedback link.

2. When the Leave Feedback page appears, indicate whether you're leaving Positive, Negative, or Neutral feedback, and then enter your comments (80 characters, maximum) in the Comment box.

3. Make sure you really want to leave the comments you've written, and then click the Leave Feedback button. Your feedback will be registered and added into the buyer's other feedback comments.

See Chapter 27, "Understanding and Using Feedback," for more information about the type of feedback to leave in different situations.

Handling Buyer Complaints and Problems

Not all auctions go smoothly. Maybe the item arrived damaged. Maybe it didn't arrive at all. Maybe it wasn't exactly what the buyer thought he was getting. Maybe the buyer is a loud, complaining, major-league son of a rutabaga.

In any case, if you have a complaining customer, you need to do something about it. Here are some of your options:

- Ignore them. If you specified "all sales are final" in your item listing, you don't technically have to do anything else at this point. Of course, complaining customers tend to leave negative feedback, and might even complain to eBay about you; this is not the option I'd recommend.

- If the item never arrived, put a trace on the shipment, if you can.

- If the item was insured, you can initiate a claim for the lost or damaged item. (See Chapter 21 for more information on filing insurance claims.)

- Negotiate a lower price for a damaged or disappointing item, and refund the difference to the buyer.

- Offer to refund the purchase price if the item is returned to you.

- Offer a full refund on the item, no questions asked, no further action necessary. (With this option, the buyer doesn't have to bother with shipping it back to you; this is the way Nordstrom would take care of it.)

"Mike Sez"

There are really no hard and fast rules for handling post-auction problems. You have to play it by ear and resolve each complaint to the best of your ability. Most eBay users are easy to deal with and just want to be treated fairly. Others won't be satisfied no matter what you offer them. You have to use your own best judgment on how to handle individual situations.

Most important are those complaints that escalate to the eBay level, via eBay's Item Not Received or Significantly Not as Described process. Under this process (described in Chapter 7, "Dealing with Fraudulent Sellers"), a buyer can file a complaint if he doesn't receive his merchandise within ten days of the end of the auction. The problem here is that many transactions will fall outside this arbitrary waiting period.

For example, if a buyer pays by personal check and you hold the check for 10 business days before shipping, the buyer hasn't received his merchandise in 10 days and can technically file a complaint.

Fortunately, nothing major happens if the buyer files a claim at the 10-day mark. Once the buyer files a claim, eBay notifies you (the seller) of the claim and asks for a response; no formal action is taken until 30 days after the end of the listing. If, at that time, the buyer hasn't received the item (or the two of you haven't communicated and worked something out), the buyer has the option of escalating the complaint into eBay's Standard Purchase Protection Program.

At that point eBay can get involved and refund the buyer's money (up to $200) and take action against you as a seller. That action could result in a formal warning, a temporary suspension, or an indefinite suspension. Of course, it's also possible that eBay could evaluate the situation and take no action against you. The outcome depends on the situation.

Obviously, if you're doing your job right, no complaint should escalate into the Standard Purchase Protection Program. If you do get an Item Not Received complaint, make sure you respond and inform the buyer why he or she hasn't received the item yet. The key here is communication—especially when you're dealing with inexperienced buyers.

What If You Don't Sell Your Item?

Not every item up for auction on eBay sells. (eBay's "close rate" is right around 50%—which means that half the items listed at any given time don't sell.) If you reach the end of the auction and you haven't received any bids—or you haven't received high-enough bids in a reserve auction—you need to drop back ten and punt, and figure out what to do next.

Perhaps the easiest thing to do if your item didn't sell is to try again—by relisting your item. eBay makes this easy for you, by including a Relist Your Item link right on the original item listing page. Click this link to create a new item listing, based on the old item listing.

When you relist an item that didn't sell the first time, eBay still charges you a listing fee for the second listing. However, eBay will refund this second listing fee if your item sells the second time

> **" Mike Sez "**
>
> If you choose to relist your item, realize that there was probably something about the first listing that kept the item from selling. Maybe the starting price was too high; maybe the headline stank; maybe you didn't include a picture; maybe the description was too brief. (And maybe you just have an item that nobody wants to buy!) You need to figure out what was wrong with the first listing and change it on the relist—otherwise, you're probably doomed to another unsuccessful auction.

around. (But not if it doesn't.) You will, of course, have to pay the normal end-of-auction fee if the item sells the second time around.

What If the Buyer Doesn't Pay?

To an eBay seller, the worst thing in the world is a high bidder who disappears from the face of the earth. When you never receive payment for an auction item, you're dealing with a *deadbeat bidder*—and you're pretty much hosed. Still, you can report the bum to eBay, ask for a refund of your final value fee, and maybe offer the item in question to the second-highest bidder.

To learn more about how to handle a nonpaying buyer situation, turn to Chapter 22.

THE ABSOLUTE MINIMUM

Here are the key points to remember from this chapter:

- When the auction ends, eBay will contact you (and the high bidder) with end-of-auction information.

- You should then contact the high bidder with your final price and payment information.

- After you receive payment, pack and ship the item—and leave feedback for the high bidder.

- If an item doesn't sell, relist it—and if it sells the second time around, eBay will refund the second listing fee.

- If the high bidder is somehow dissatisfied or complains to eBay, try to work out a mutually agreeable solution.

IN THIS CHAPTER

- Introducing eBay Selling Manager
- Sending Buyer Emails
- Receiving Payment
- Printing Invoices and Shipping Labels
- After the Item Is Shipped

20

AUTOMATING AUCTION MANAGEMENT WITH EBAY SELLING MANAGER

In the preceding chapter you learned how important it is to manage all your post-auction activity—sending out invoices to winning bidders, keeping track of who has paid and who hasn't, preparing items for shipping, leaving feedback, and the like. If you run only a few auctions at a time, you can probably manage this activity by hand. But if you're running a half-dozen or more auctions simultaneously, it gets tough to keep track of everything you need to do.

When your number of active auctions increases, you should think about using some sort of auction management tool to help you keep things in control. Although various third-party auction management services are available (which you'll learn about in Chapter 28, "Using Auction Software and Services"), for many users the best tool is available from eBay itself. It's called eBay Selling Manager, and it's both easy to use and affordable.

Introducing eBay Selling Manager

eBay Selling Manager is one of eBay's official auction management tools. It's available in both basic and Pro versions; we'll discuss Selling Manager Pro later in this chapter.

The basic Selling Manager lets you keep track of current and pending auctions, as well as all your closed auctions; you can use Selling Manager to send emails to winning bidders, print invoices and shipping labels, and even leave feedback. Everything you need to do is accessed over the Web, on the eBay site, through your normal web browser. When you subscribe to Selling Manager, the All Selling page in My eBay is transformed into a Selling Manager page. From here, Selling Manager lets you manage all your post-auction activity.

To subscribe to eBay Selling Manager, go to pages.ebay.com/selling_manager/. The subscription cost for the basic version is $4.99 per month.

How Selling Manager Works

To use Selling Manager, all you have to do is go to your My eBay page and click the new Selling Manager link. As you can see in Figure 20.1, the main Selling Manager page provides an overview of all your active and closed auctions.

FIGURE 20.1

Access eBay Selling Manager from your My eBay page.

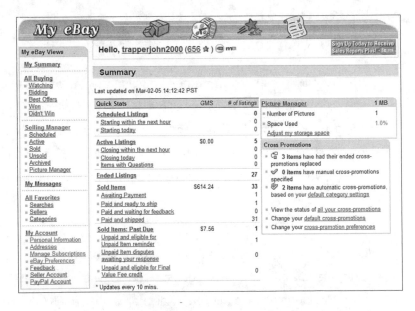

The Summary page divides your auctions into five major categories:

- **Scheduled Listings.** These are auctions you've scheduled to launch later. Selling Manager lists separately those auctions starting within the next hour and those starting sometime today.

- **Active Listings.** These are your current auctions—those that have already started but not yet ended. Selling Manager lists separately those auctions closing within the next hour and those closing sometime today, as well as those auctions with questions from bidders. The total value of current bids on these auctions is listed to the side of this section.

- **Ended Listings**. These are auctions that have ended—successfully or not—in the recent past.

- **Sold Listings.** These are recent auctions that have closed successfully. Selling Manager lists separately those items that are awaiting payment, paid and ready to ship, paid and waiting for feedback, and paid and shipped.

- **Sold Items: Past Due.** This final section lists those unpaid items that are eligible for an Unpaid Item Dispute and final value fee credit.

The most useful aspect of Selling Manager comes after the close of an auction. When you display any of the Sold Listings pages, like the one in Figure 20.2, you see a list of closed auctions, with the customer status indicated by a series of icons. You can select an individual auction to mark it paid or shipped, or to send it to your personal archive. You can also send various email messages to the winners of your auctions, as well as print invoices and leave feedback for multiple users in bulk.

"Mike Sez"

I find eBay Selling Manager an extremely useful tool if I have a moderate number of auctions running simultaneously. Running just a few auctions makes Selling Manager cost-prohibitive on a per-auction basis—and if I'm managing several dozen auctions, I come to curse its lack of batch email features. Still, for many sellers, Selling Manager does a fine job—and is a lot better than trying to manage post-auction activity manually.

FIGURE 20.2

Displaying a list of your closed auctions.

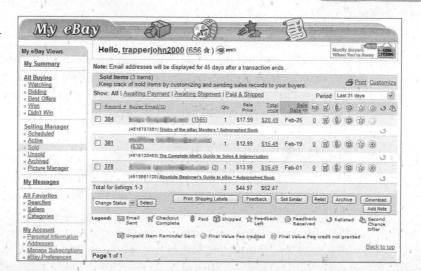

For Higher-Volume Sellers: eBay Selling Manager Pro

Selling Manager isn't perfect. One of its biggest problems is that you pretty much have to manage one auction at a time—it lacks features that let you effectively manage large numbers of auctions in bulk. If you're a high-volume seller, a better solution is eBay's higher-end Selling Manager Pro, which offers better bulk management and inventory management features. For $15.99 per month, Selling Manager Pro does everything the basic Selling Manager does, plus more:

- Manages individual inventory items, and issues restock alerts
- Offers free Listing Designer templates
- Generates a monthly profit and loss report, including all eBay fees and cost of goods sold

As you can see, this is a more complete auction management tool meant to compete directly with the offerings from ándale, Vendio, and other third parties. You can learn more about—and subscribe to—Selling Manager Pro at pages.ebay.com/selling_manager_pro/.

Sending Buyer Emails

Probably the most useful feature of Selling Manager is the capability to send various end-of-auction email messages to winning bidders.

Selling Manager includes six boilerplate messages, all of which you can customize:

- Winning buyer notification
- Payment reminder
- Request shipping address
- Payment received
- Item shipped
- Feedback reminder

You typically send a winning buyer notification at the close of an auction, a payment reminder if the buyer hasn't paid within a week or so, a payment-received message when you get paid, and an item shipped message when you ship the item. The other messages are used only when necessary.

Sending a Standard Email Message

To send an email to a winning bidder, follow these steps:

1. Go to any of Selling Manager's Sold Listings pages.
2. Click a specific Buyer Email link.
3. When the Email Buyer page (shown in Figure 20.3) appears, select the type of message you want to send from the Template list.

FIGURE 20.3

Sending a post-auction email.

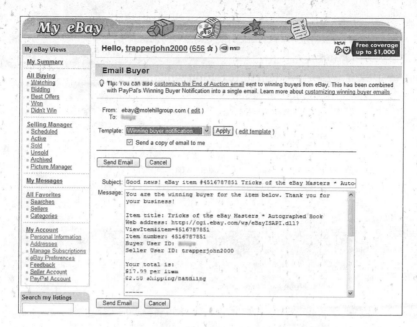

4. If you want, edit the subject of the message in the Subject box.

5. If you want, edit the text of the message in the Message box.

6. If you want to receive a copy of this message, select the Send a Copy of Email to Me option.

7. Click Send Email to send the message.

Editing an Email Template

Don't like Selling Manager's prepared email templates? Then customize them! Here's how:

1. From the Email Buyer page, click the Edit Template link.

2. When the Edit Email Templates page (shown in Figure 20.4) appears, select the template you want to edit from the Template list.

3. Edit the text in the Subject and Message boxes, as desired.

4. Insert automated text (buyer name, buyer item number, and so on) into the message by selecting text from the Autotext list and then clicking the Insert button. The automated text (surrounded by curly brackets) now appears at the

tip

To view a list of emails you've sent to a specific buyer, click the number link in the email column next to the record # on the Sold Listings page. This opens an Email Log dialog box that lists all messages sent to that buyer.

bottom of your message; cut and paste this text into its correct position within the message.

5. Click the Save Template button when you are done.

note

You can revert to the original template at any time by clicking the Reset to Default button.

FIGURE 20.4

Customizing a Selling Manager email template.

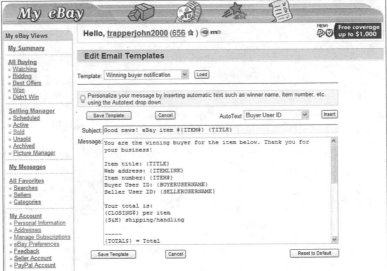

Receiving Payment

When you receive payment from a buyer, you want to update Selling Manager to reflect the payment, and to enter the buyer's shipping information. You do this from the individual Sales Record page, as described here:

1. On the Sold Listings page, click the Record # link for this specific auction.

2. When the Sales Record page appears, as shown in Figure 20.5, enter the buyer's name and address into the appropriate blanks.

3. Scroll to the Sales Status & Notes section, shown in Figure 20.6, and check the Paid On box. The current date will be automatically inserted; you can edit the date if necessary.

4. Enter any other pertinent information, and then click the Save & Finish button.

At this time you should also send the buyer a payment-received message. You can access the Email Buyer page by clicking the Email Buyer button on the Sales Record page.

tip

If the buyer has paid with PayPal or used eBay's Checkout system, this information will be automatically entered for you. You can also cut and paste the buyer's address from an email message into the Instantly Fill In Buyer Address box, and then click the Add button to add the data into the Sales Record.

FIGURE 20.5

Working with the buyer's Sales Record.

FIGURE 20.6

Marking an auction item paid.

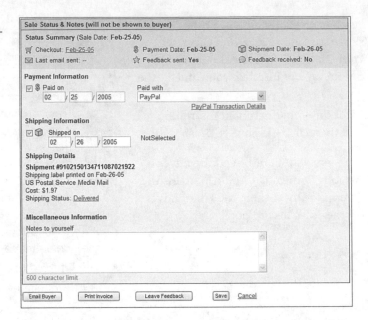

Printing Invoices and Shipping Labels

When you're ready to ship an item, you can use Selling Manager to print an invoice and shipping label. Follow these instructions:

1. On the Sold Listings page, click the Record # link for this specific auction.

2. When the Sales Record page appears, click the Print Invoice button.

3. When the Print page appears, select to print one of the following:

   ■ US Postal Service postage or UPS shipping label

   ■ Shipping labels and invoice/packing slip combo

   ■ Invoice/packing slip

   ■ Invoice for your own records

   ■ Store promotional flyer (if you have an eBay Store)

4. Click the Continue button to initiate printing.

tip

If you want to edit the information on the invoice, click the Edit Invoice Template link. This lets you edit your address or add a picture or additional text to the invoice.

At this time you should mark the item as shipped, and send the buyer an item-shipped message. You can do both of these from the Sales Record page.

After the Item Is Shipped

After you've shipped an item, you have some cleanup activities to do. In particular, you need to leave feedback about the buyer, and move the item listing into Selling Manager's archive.

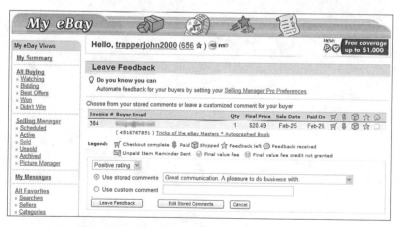

Leaving Feedback

You can use Selling Manager to leave semi-automated feedback about a buyer. Just follow these steps:

1. On the Sold Listings page, click the Record # link for this specific auction.

2. When the Sales Record page appears, click the Leave Feedback button.

3. When the Leave Feedback page appears, as shown in Figure 20.7, pull down the rating list and select positive, neutral, or negative ratings.

4. You now have the choice of using a stored comment or writing a custom comment. To use a stored comment, select the Use Stored Comments option and make a choice from the pull-down list. To enter a new comment, select the Use Custom Comment option and enter the comment into the adjacent box.

5. Click the Leave Feedback button to register your rating and comment.

> **note**
>
> Learn more about feedback in Chapter 27, "Understanding and Using Feedback."

FIGURE 20.7

Leaving feedback about a buyer.

Archiving Completed Listings

After you've shipped the item and left feedback, you don't want this old listing cluttering up your Selling Manager page. Instead, you can store all completed auctions in the Selling Manager archive, where they're out of the way but you can still access them (if you ever need to). Just follow these steps:

1. On the Sold Listings page, select those auctions you want to archive.

2. Click the Archive button.

3. When prompted, confirm the archive action.

That's it. You're all done with this auction—thanks to eBay Selling Manager!

THE ABSOLUTE MINIMUM

Here are the key points to remember from this chapter:

- eBay Selling Manager is a Web-based tool that helps you manage your in-process and closed auctions; it costs $4.99 per month.

- When you subscribe to Selling Manager, the All Selling page in My eBay is changed to a Selling Manager page.

- Selling Manager lets you send end-of-auction emails, print invoices and shipping labels, and leave feedback for winning bidders.

- If Selling Manager won't handle your auction volume, check out Selling Manager Pro; for $15.99 per month, it offers automated bulk management tools.

21

SHIPPING IT OUT—
CHEAPLY AND SAFELY

The auction's over, you've received payment from the high bidder, and now it's time to pack your item and ship it off. If you don't have much experience in shipping items cross-country, this might seem a bit daunting at first. Don't worry, though; if you've ever wrapped a Christmas present or mailed a letter, you have all the skills you need to ship just about anything anywhere in the world.

Packing 101

Before you ship, you have to pack—which doesn't sound too terribly difficult. However, if you pick the wrong container, don't cushion the contents properly, don't seal it securely, or mislabel the whole thing, you could risk damaging the contents during shipping—or, even worse, sending it to the wrong recipient. Even if you think you know how to pack and ship, you still probably want to read the following sections. You never know; you might pick up a few useful tips!

Essential Packing Supplies

Before you do any packing, you need to have some basic supplies on hand. I'm not just talking boxes here; I'm talking about the stuff you stuff inside the boxes, and seal them up with.

Any halfway busy eBay seller needs to have these basic packing supplies on hand so that they're not constantly running off to the office supply store every time one of their auctions closes. These items should always be available and easily accessed.

Okay, so what supplies do you need to have at hand? Take a look at this checklist:

Checklist: Packing Supplies

- ☐ Packing tape, clear
- ☐ Bubble wrap
- ☐ Styrofoam peanuts *or* old newspapers
- ☐ Scissors
- ☐ Box cutter or similar kind of knife
- ☐ Postal scale
- ☐ Black magic marker
- ☐ Large shipping labels
- ☐ Return address labels
- ☐ Other necessary labels: Fragile, This End Up, and so on
- ☐ Labels or forms provided by your shipping service of choice

Now for some explanations. I recommend clear tape over the normal brown because you can use it not just to seal the box but also to tape over the address label and make it somewhat waterproof. (That said, brown tape can be used to tape over labels and logos when you reuse an old box.) I also prefer peanuts to newspapers because peanuts don't leave ink stains, and because of the weight factor; using newspapers as filler can substantially increase your package weight, and thus your shipping costs. (Of course, newspapers are free and peanuts aren't—but peanuts are cheaper than the added shipping costs you'll incur with newspapers. And you can reuse all those peanuts that come in the items you purchase online!)

The other materials are somewhat self-explanatory—although you might ask why you need a knife when you're packing. I find myself using the knife primarily to slice off old shipping labels from boxes I reuse for my eBay shipping. Although some old labels tear off rather easily, most don't; to remove them, you have to cut (shallowly) around the label and then lift off the outermost layer of the cardboard box.

66 **Mike Sez** 99

I like to keep all my packing materials in a single, easy-to-access place—kind of like a ready-to-use packing station. For me, an otherwise-unused kitchen counter does the job; other users clear out a portion of their garage or home office for the same purpose.

Where to Find Boxes and Packing Materials

So where do you find all these packing materials and shipping containers? Lots of places.

First, some boxes are free. If you're shipping via the U.S. Postal Service, you can get free Priority Mail and Express Mail boxes, envelopes, and tubes. (Figure 21.1 shows some of the free boxes available for Priority Mail shipping.) Some post offices carry these free containers, or you can order in bulk (but still free) from the United States Postal Service (USPS) website at shop.usps.com.

FIGURE 21.1
Free shipping containers for USPS Priority Mail.

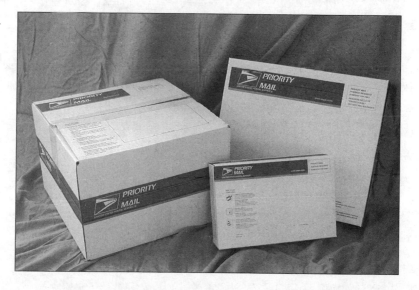

Most post-office locations also sell various types of boxes, padded mailers, mailing tubes, and other packing materials, although their prices tend to be a little on the high side. (They must figure you're a captive customer at that point.) You can find better prices and a much bigger selection at any major office supply superstore (Office Depot, Office Max, Staples, and so on) or at specialty box and shipping stores.

Another good source of shipping supplies is eBay itself—or, more accurately, retailers who sell on the eBay service. There are several eBay Store sellers who specialize in packing supplies for other eBay sellers; go to www.stores.ebay.com and do a search for "shipping supplies" or "boxes."

Many eBay sellers also do a good job recycling old boxes. That's right, you can reuse boxes that were shipped to you, either from other eBay users or from online or direct mail retailers. (I'm a big fan of Amazon.com's boxes; they recycle quite nicely!)

You'd be amazed how many times a box can be reused. As long as the box is still structurally sound—and sturdy enough for whatever you're shipping—it can be pressed back into service. Just be sure to remove or cross out any old shipping labels and confirm that the box is in good shape, with no weak spots or cracks—and reinforce the box with new tape, as necessary.

Finally, don't forget your local merchants. These stores receive a lot of merchandise daily, and all those goods are packed in *something*. All those shipping boxes come into the store, and end up in the trash or recycling bin.

note

Other carriers might or might not offer their own free shipping containers. FedEx, for example, offers certain sizes of envelopes and boxes for your (free) use. It's best to ask first—before you go buying an expensive new box.

tip

Many of these eBay Stores operate their own websites as well; in particular, check out BubbleFAST (www.bubblefast.com), eSupplyStore.com (www.esupplystore.com), and ShippingSupply.com (www.shippingsupply.com).

What a retailer calls trash you might call reusable packing materials. Short of dumpster diving (which many eBay sellers are masters of), try making a deal with a local retailer to help dispose of those excess boxes and Styrofoam peanuts. You'll get free packing supplies, and the retailer gets a little less stuff to throw away.

Picking the Right Shipping Container

After you have all your shipping supplies assembled, all you need to do is put your item in a box and seal it up. Easy, right? Not really—and the consequences of choosing the wrong container can be both disastrous and unnecessarily expensive.

First, you have to decide whether to use a box or an envelope. If you have a very large item to ship, the choice is easy. But what if you have something smaller and flatter, such as a laser disc or a coin? Your choice should be determined by the fragility of your item. If the item can bend or break, choose a box; if not, an envelope is probably a safe choice.

Whichever you choose, pick a container that's large enough to hold your item without the need to force it in or bend it in an inappropriate fashion. Also, make sure that the box has enough extra room to insert cushioning material.

On the other hand, the container shouldn't be so big as to leave room for the item to bounce around. Also, you pay for size and for weight; you don't want to pay to ship anything bigger or heavier than it needs to be.

If you're shipping in an envelope, consider using a bubble-pack envelope or reinforcing the envelope with pieces of cardboard. This is especially vital if your item shouldn't be bent or folded.

If you're shipping in a box, make sure that it's made of heavy, corrugated cardboard and has its flaps intact. Thinner boxes—such as shoe boxes or gift boxes—simply aren't strong enough for shipping. When packing a box, never exceed the maximum gross weight for the box, which is usually printed on the bottom flap.

Although a bunch of different-sized boxes are available, sometimes you need something somewhere in between this size and that size box. When you face this situation, you have two choices.

First, you can take a larger box and cut it down. That means cutting through each corner of the box to make it shorter, and then cutting off the ends of the flaps accordingly. Sometimes it's difficult to fold unscored flaps, so you may want to make your own scores by slicing a knife (shallowly) where you want to bend the box closed.

Second, you can combine two smaller boxes. If your box is 16 inches long and your item is 20 inches, just take two boxes and insert the open end of one inside the open end of the other. You'll need to use sufficient packing tape to keep the boxes from sliding apart, but you'll have created a box custom-sized for the item you're shipping.

caution

Use the combination box technique judiciously, because it can significantly increase the weight of the package—and thus your shipping costs.

How to Pack

Here's what you don't do: Drop your item in an empty box and then seal it up. A loose item in a big box will bounce around and get damaged, guaranteed. (Imagine your box being tossed around by a bunch of gorillas in a parking lot, and you get an accurate picture of what most packages endure in the shipping process.) No, you need to carefully pack your item to minimize any potential damage from dropping and rough handling—and from various weather conditions, including rain, snow, and heat.

How do you pack your box? Professional shippers use Styrofoam peanuts, and lots of them; amateurs tend to use crumpled-up newspapers and other materials found around the house. Here's where you can learn something from the pros—peanuts are *much* lighter than newspaper. Weight is a factor in how much you'll pay for shipping, so anything you can do to lighten the weight of your package is important. Because peanuts cost...well, *peanuts*, they've become my preferred cushioning material. (And I used to be a crumpled-up newspaper kind of guy, until the latest increase in Priority Mail rates.)

As you might expect, packing needs vary for different types of items. You can use these packing tips when it's time to ship your next item:

- If you have the item's original box or packaging, use it! Nothing ships better than the original shipping container.

- If you're shipping a common item—DVDs, videotapes, books, and so on— look for item-specific shipping containers. For example, most office supply stores stock boxes and padded mailers specifically designed for CDs and DVDs. These containers typically do what they're advertised to do.

- Always cushion your package contents, using some combination of shredded or crumpled newspapers, bubble wrap, or Styrofoam peanuts. (For example, when I ship a CD or DVD, I wrap it in bubble wrap and cushion it with peanuts.)

- Whatever cushioning material you use, don't skimp on it. Pack your items tightly to avoid shifting of contents during transit, and make sure that the cushioning material covers all sides of the item.

tip

You can also use plain (unbuttered!) air-popped popcorn for cushioning; it's inexpensive and environmentally friendly—and tastes good when you're watching a movie!

- Position the item toward the center of the box, away from the bottom, sides, and top. (This means placing peanuts *under* the item as well as on top of it.)

- If you're shipping several items in the same box, wrap each one separately (in separate smaller boxes, if you can), and provide enough cushioning to prevent movement and to keep the items from rubbing against each other.

- Not only should items be separated from each other in the box, but they also should be separated from the corners and sides of the box to prevent damage if the box is bumped or dropped.

- The preceding point argues for another technique: double-boxing items that are especially fragile, such as glass or ceramic items. That means packing the item tightly in a smaller, form-fitting box, and then placing that box inside a slightly larger, shock-absorbing box—with at least 3 inches of cushioning material between the boxes.

- If your item has any protruding parts, cover them with extra padding or cardboard.

- Be careful with the bubble wrap. Although it's great to wrap around objects with flat sides, it can actually damage more fragile figurines or items with lots of little pieces and parts sticking out. If the bubble wrap is too tight, it can snap off any appendages during rough handling.

- Stuff glassware and other fragile hollow items, such as vases, with newspaper or other packing material. This provides an extra level of cushioning in case of rough handling.

- When shipping jars and other items with lids, either separate the lid from the base with several layers of bubble wrap or tissue paper or (better still) pack the lid in a separate small box.

- When shipping framed photographs or artwork, take the glass out of the frame and wrap it separately. Do not let artwork come in direct contact with paper or cardboard.

- Wrap paper items (photographs, books, magazines, and so on) in some sort of plastic bag or wrap, to protect against wetness in shipment.

- When shipping electronic items (including toys and consumer electronics devices), remove the batteries before you ship. Wrap and place the batteries next to the items in the shipping container.

- When shipping computer parts—circuit boards, video cards, memory chips, and so on—pad the item well and pack it in an Electro Static Discharge (ESD) bag to prevent damaging static buildup. And *don't* use peanuts for filler—all that Styrofoam can carry a damaging static charge.

After you think you're done packing, gently shake the box. If nothing moves, it's ready to be sealed. If you can hear or feel things rattling around inside, however, it's time to add more cushioning material. (If you can shake it, they can break it!)

Packing for International Customers

Packing for international customers shouldn't be any different from packing for domestic customers—as long as you do it right. Foreign shipments are likely to get even rougher treatment than usual, so make sure that the package is packed as securely as possible—with more than enough cushioning to survive the trip to Japan or Europe or wherever it happens to be going.

What *is* different about shipping internationally is the paperwork—and the shipping costs. I cover all this in Chapter 29, "Going International," so turn there if you have a non-U.S. buyer to deal with.

> ## " Mike Sez "
>
> When you're packing an item, watch the weight. I make it a point to have a postal scale at my packing station, and to weigh the item—shipping container and all—during the packing process. When I'm using Priority Mail, the difference between shipping a one-pound package and a one-pound, one-ounce package is as much as $1.90, depending on where it's going. Finding some way to cut that extra ounce of packing material can save almost two bucks in shipping costs—which is why I want to know the weight before I seal the package.

How to Seal the Package

After your box is packed, it's time to seal it. A strong seal is essential, so always use tape that is designed for shipping. Be sure to securely seal the center seams at both the top and the bottom of the box. Cover all other seams with tape, and be sure not to leave any open areas that could snag on machinery.

What kind of sealing materials should you use?

- ■ **Do** use tape that is designed for shipping, such as pressure-sensitive tape, nylon-reinforced kraft paper tape, glass-reinforced pressure-sensitive tape, or water-activated paper tape. Whichever tape you use, the wider and heavier, the better. Reinforced is always better than non-reinforced.
- ■ **Don't** use wrapping paper, string, masking tape, or cellophane tape.

One last thing: If you plan to insure your package, leave an untaped area on the cardboard where your postal clerk can stamp "Insured." (Ink doesn't adhere well to tape.)

Labeling 101

You've packed the box. You've sealed the box. Now it's time for the label.

Buying the Right Kinds of Labels

For most purposes, you can't beat the standard 4-inch×6-inch blank white label. Anything smaller is tough to work with, and anything larger just leaves a lot of wasted space. Stick with 4-inch×6-inch and you'll be happy. You can purchase these labels at any office supply store, or even get free versions (for Priority Mail shipping) at your local post office.

If you want to splurge, you can even purchase labels with your name and return address preprinted at the top. This is a good idea if you do a lot of shipping (a dozen or more items a week); otherwise, it's probably not cost-efficient.

You can also purchase or create your own return address labels, to use in conjunction with your main shipping labels. It's easy enough to print a full page of smallish labels in Microsoft Word; most printing firms (such as FedEx Kinko's) can also do up a roll of address labels for a nominal charge.

If you use computer-generated labels, you can program your label-making program to include your return address when it prints the label. This is a good (and lower-cost) alternative to using preprinted labels.

tip

If you're unsure what label to use, go with Avery; just about every software program out there supports Avery labels. Plus, Avery offers its own label-making software and templates, downloadable for free from www.avery.com.

How to Create an Idiot-Proof Label

The best-packed box won't go anywhere if you get the label wrong. For fast and efficient delivery, keep these points in mind when addressing your package:

note

If you don't use a preprinted label, you'll want to hand-print your return address on the shipping container, or use some sort of return address label.

- Write, type, or print the complete address neatly.

- Always use complete address information, such as the suffixes Dr., Ave., St., and Blvd.

- Include the recipient's apartment or suite number, if applicable.

- Always use correct directions, such as N, S, E, W, or SW.

- Use the correct ZIP Code—and, when possible, use the four-digit add-on, ZIP+4 (example: 46032-1434). Be sure to hyphenate the ZIP+4.

- Always use the proper two-letter state abbreviation.

- When addressing to a P.O. Box or rural route destination, include the recipient's telephone number on the label.
- When shipping outside the U.S., include a contact name, telephone number, and postal code on the label—and don't forget to include the country name!
- Always include your return address information.
- If you're using any special services of the U.S. Postal Service (Priority Mail, First Class Mail, insurance, and so on), note this above the destination address and below and to the right of the return address.
- Place the delivery label on the top (not the side) of the box. To avoid confusion, place only one address label on the box. If using a packing slip, place it on the same surface of the box as the address label.
- Do not place the label over a seam or closure or on top of sealing tape.
- To avoid ink smudges and rain smears, place a strip of clear packing tape over the address label. (Notable exception: do *not* tape over any bar codes on a label with pre-paid postage; bar code readers have trouble reading through tape.)
- If you're reusing a box for shipping, remove or block out all old address labels or markings on a used box.

And here's one last tip. Make a duplicate of your shipping label and stick it *inside* the box, before you seal it. This way if the original shipping label gets torn off or destroyed, anyone opening the box can read the duplicate label and figure out where the box is supposed to go.

> **tip**
>
> Don't know the ZIP code for the address you're shipping to? Then look it up at the U.S. Postal Service's ZIP Code Lookup at www.usps.com/zip4/.

Printing Labels and Postage on Your Own Computer

Here's a real time-saver. If you're shipping via the U.S. Postal Service, you can print labels on your home printer—including labels with prepaid postage. When you print your own prepaid postage, you don't have to make a trip to the post office. Just print the label—including postage—on your own printer, attach the label to your package, and hand it to your postman. No more standing in line at the post office!

You can print these labels directly from eBay, and pay for them using your PayPal account. Here's how to do it:

1. Go to your closed item listing page and click the Print Shipping Label button.
2. You're now taken to a Print Your Label page on the PayPal site, as shown in Figure 21.2. You can choose to ship your item via Priority Mail, Express Mail,

Parcel Post, Media Mail, or First Class Mail; you can even choose to purchase insurance with your order.

3. Fill in the appropriate information and click the Continue button.

4. View the information on the confirmation page and authorize payment from your PayPal account.

5. Follow the onscreen instructions to print the label on your own printer.

6. The label prints on half of a sheet of paper. Cut off the label side of the paper (shown in Figure 21.3) and affix it to your package.

FIGURE 21.2

Pay for postage from your PayPal account.

> **U.S. Postal Service - Print Your Label** [See Demo]
>
> Create, purchase and print U.S. Postal Service® shipping labels from your PayPal account. Enjoy the affordable Postal Service rates without having to leave your desk.
>
> Shipping tools with U.S. Postal Service are currently only available for transactions where both the sender's and recipient's addresses are in the United States.
>
> **Address Information**
>
> **Ship From:** Michael Miller
> Edit this Address
> Carmel, IN 46032
> United States
>
> **Ship To:** don morrison
> Edit this Address
> holly lake ranch, TX 75755
> United States
> **Status:** Confirmed address
>
> **Shipment Options**   ? Shipment Options FAQ
>
> **Service Type:** Priority Mail®   Choose a different shipper
>
> **Package Size:** Package/Thick Envelope   Learn More About Package Sizes
>
> **Mailing Date:** 12/19/2004
> **Weight:** 1 lbs. 12 oz.
> **Label Printer:** Laser/Ink Jet Printer Edit Printer Settings
> **Delivery Confirmation:** FREE
> **Label Processing Fee:** FREE
> **Signature Confirmation:** ○ Yes ($1.30 USD) ● No
> Note: Signature of receipt is available upon request for Express Mail.
> **Display Postage Value on Label:** ☐
> **Email message to Buyer: (optional)**

Once you've affixed the label, your work is done. You can drop your package in the mail, or hand it to your local postal worker when he makes his daily rounds. There's no need to visit the post office—or if you do, you can bypass the long lines and drop the pre-paid package off at the nearest counter.

note

One plus to printing your own USPS labels is you get Delivery Confirmation included, at no charge.

FIGURE 21.3

Printing prepaid
postage labels
from PayPal.

Shipping 101

How often do you frequent your local post office? When was the last time you visited a UPS shipping center? Do you even know where your local FedEx branch is located?

If these questions make you nervous, you're not alone. For many users, the scariest part of the entire auction process is shipping the item. Not packing, not labeling, but actually taking the box to the shipping center and sending it on its way.

That's because when it comes to shipping, there are so many choices involved. Which carrier do you use? Which specific service offered by a carrier should you choose—the fastest one or the cheapest one? And what about all those extras, such as insurance and delivery confirmation? With all those choices, how do you avoid making the wrong decisions?

If shipping is somewhat foreign to you, don't worry. It isn't quite as difficult as it seems, and it will become old hat after just a few trips to the shipping center.

Examining the Major Shipping Services

You have several choices when it comes to shipping your package. You can use the various services offered by the U.S. Postal Service (regular mail, Priority Mail, Express Mail, Media Mail, and so on) or any of the services offered by competing carriers, such as UPS or Federal Express. You can deal directly with any shipping service or use a local shipping store to handle the shipping (and even the packing)—but at a cost.

As you've no doubt gathered, there are some significant differences in shipping costs from one shipping service to another. The cost differential is typically based on a combination of weight and distance; the heavier an item is and the farther it has to go (and the faster you need to get it to where it's going), the more it costs. As an example, the costs of shipping a two-pound box from New York to Los Angeles run from under two bucks to over $30. For this reason, it's a good idea to "shop" the major shipping services for the best shipping rates for the types of items you normally sell on eBay.

Of course, cost isn't the only factor you want to consider. You also want to compare how long it takes the package to arrive, what kind of track record the shipping service has, and how convenient it is for you to use. If you have to drive 20 miles to get to a UPS office, and you have a post office just down the street, that might offset a slightly higher cost for Priority Mail.

All that said, which shipping service should you use? That's a good question, but not always an easy one to answer. Ultimately, you have to strike a compromise between cost, convenience, and speed.

> **"Mike Sez"**
>
> Which shipping services do I use? For small items, I default to USPS Priority Mail; it's inexpensive and relatively fast, plus I get free packing materials from my local post office. For CDs, DVDs, and books, I use USPS Media Mail, which is cheaper and almost as fast. For really big items (over 10 pounds or so), I go with UPS. But I find that, 9 times out of 10, Priority Mail or Media Mail does the job for me.

Using the U.S. Postal Service

The USPS offers several shipping options:

- **Priority Mail.** This is the preferred shipping method for many experienced auction sellers, if only for its relative convenience. Although Priority Mail used to be predictably low-cost (with flat fees based on weight, not distance), recent price increases have left the service less competitive than before. (You also have to factor distance into the pricing equation, for packages over one pound.) There's also the advantage of getting a flat rate on small packages shipped in one of their flat-rate envelopes—just $3.85 to go anywhere in the U.S. Service is typically in the one-to-three–day range, and the postal service has lots of free Priority Mail boxes you can use. And you can print out Priority Mail shipping labels and postage on your own PC, direct from eBay/PayPal, as we discussed previously.

- **Express Mail.** This is the USPS's fastest service, offering guaranteed next-day delivery 365 days a year, including weekends and holidays. Merchandise is automatically insured up to $100. Express Mail is considerably more expensive than Priority Mail.

- **First Class Mail.** This is an option if your item fits into an envelope or small package. It also provides the benefit of shipping directly from your mailbox, without necessitating a trip to the post office—assuming that you can figure out the correct postage. Delivery is similar to Priority Mail, typically three days or less.

- **Parcel Post.** This used to be known as the "slow" USPS service for larger packages, but it has gotten faster of late—and it's priced lower than Priority Mail. Still, shipping something Parcel Post from coast to coast might take seven to nine days, as opposed to Priority Mail's two (or three) days.

- **Media Mail.** This is what USPS used to call "book rate"; it can be used to ship books, DVDs, videotapes, compact discs, and other printed and prerecorded "media." The rates are much cheaper than those for Priority Mail, although delivery is typically in the Parcel Post range—seven to nine days. Still, this is a good, low-cost way to ship many popular items; the cost for shipping a CD across the country is less than two bucks, compared to $3.85 for Priority Mail.

caution

Media Mail is reserved for publications without advertising—so you can't use it to ship magazines, newspapers, or comic books.

You can find out more about USPS shipping at the USPS website, located at www.usps.gov. This site includes a postage calculator (postcalc.usps.gov) for all levels of service.

Using UPS

UPS is a good option for shipping larger or heavier packages but can be a little costly for smaller items. UPS offers various shipping options, including standard UPS Ground, Next Day Air, Next Day Air Saver, and 2nd Day Air.

You can find out more about UPS shipping—and access a rate calculator—at the UPS website, located at www.ups.com.

Using FedEx

FedEx is probably the fastest shipping service, but it can also be the most costly. FedEx tends to target the business market (which can afford its higher rates), so it isn't widely used for auction or retail shipping—with one significant exception: FedEx Ground.

FedEx Ground is a terrific choice when you're shipping out larger items. It's designed for bigger and/or heavier packages, and its rates are well below similar services offered by the Postal Service and UPS. I use FedEx Ground to ship DVD players and various audio equipment, and it's extremely cost effective. For example, FedEx charges almost $5 less than Priority Mail to ship a five-pound item from coast to coast. That's a big savings!

FedEx is also a convenient choice for many sellers, especially since you can now ship from any Kinkos location. (The stores are now called FedEx Kinkos, by the way.) You can find out more about FedEx shipping at its website, located at www.fedex.com, and can access the company's rate finder directly at www.fedex.com/us/rates/.

Using Other Shipping Companies

USPS, UPS, and FedEx are the three most popular shipping services in the United States; they're not the only services available, however. Among the other services available are DHL (www.dhl.com) and Purolator Courier (www.purolator.com).

Using a Professional Packing and Shipping Service

If you're new to this packing and shipping thing, you might want to do your packing and shipping through a professional shipping store. These stores—such as The UPS Store (www.theupsstore.com) or FedEx Kinkos (www.fedexkinkos.com)—will handle the entire process for you. Just bring them the item you want to ship, and they'll find the right-sized box, pack it up for you, and fill out all the shipping paperwork.

Of course, all this work comes at a cost. Make sure you find out how much you'll have to pay for this service, and add that cost to your shipping/handling charges in your auction item listing.

How to Reduce Shipping Weight—And Shipping Costs

Because weight is an important part of the shipping equation, here are a few tips for bringing down the weight of the items you ship:

- Use peanuts instead of paper for cushioning; peanuts are *much* lighter—and don't leave ink stains on the merchandise.
- Even better, use air instead of peanuts—in the form of those air-filled bags that Amazon.com uses to cushion their packages.
- Use less heavy-duty boxes, if you can. (This is generally an option only when you're shipping light objects.) You'd be surprised at the difference in weight between similarly sized boxes, based on the thickness of the cardboard.
- Don't use oversized boxes. If the box is too large, either trim down the unused portion of the flaps or move to a smaller box.

Finally, be sure to include the weight of the box and the cushioning material when you weigh your item for shipment. A big box with lots of crumpled paper can easily add a half-pound or more to your item's weight—excess weight you'll have to pay for.

Shipping Large or Heavy Items

Some items are just too big to ship via conventional means. Suppose you just sold an old pinball machine, or a roll-top desk, or a waterbed. How do you deal with items that big?

Assuming that the item is too big even for UPS, you have to turn to traditional trucking services. Some of these services will pack or crate the item for you (for a fee); others require you to do all the crating. In addition, some of these firms require you to deliver the item to their shipping terminal, and for the buyer to pick it up from their dock. (Other firms offer door-to-door service—again, sometimes for a higher fee.) In any case, it helps to make a few calls and ask for specifics before you decide on a shipper.

> **caution**
>
> Most of the standard shipping services I mentioned earlier in this chapter, such as the U.S. Postal Service, won't handle packages that weigh more than 70 pounds, or have a combined length and girth of more than 130 inches.

For shipping oversized items, here are some of the trucking services that other eBay sellers have used. Check with each firm for information on fees and shipping policies.

- AAA Cooper Transportation (www.aaacooper.com)
- Forward Air (www.forwardair.com)
- Vintage Transport Services (www.vintagetransport.com)
- Yellow Freight (www.yellowfreight.com)

In addition, eBay itself offers a Freight Resource Center (ebay.freightquote.com) for shipping large items; you can obtain freight quotes and initiate shipping directly from this page. You can also contact Freightquote.com via phone, at 888-875-7822.

How to Price Shipping and Handling for Your Item Listings

Let's think back to the start of the auction process. You probably remember that I recommended you include your shipping and handling charges up front so that bidders know what to expect.

But how do you figure shipping costs before you know where the item is going?

Working with Flat Fees

The solution is easy if you're shipping something that weighs (packaging included) less than a pound. For these lightweight items, you can use USPS Priority Mail, which ships one-pound packages anywhere in the U.S. for a single price ($3.85 at the time of writing). Because you can also use free boxes (provided by the postal

service), you know that your cost to package
and ship a one-pound item will be $3.85. Easy.

If you're shipping books, CDs, or videos, you
also have it easy—if you choose to ship via
USPS Media Mail. These rates are so cheap that
you can do some creative rounding of numbers
and say that any item weighing two pounds or
less can ship anywhere in the U.S. for $2.00.
The actual Media Mail rate might be $1.42 or
$1.84 or whatever, but $2.00 makes a convenient number to state up front; the gap between
actual and projected shipping can go toward
the purchase of an appropriate box or envelope.

tip

When you're shipping light
items, such as a single CD,
check with your post office
for the best rate. Sometimes
First Class can be cheaper
than Media Mail!

Working with Variable Fees

When you're shipping items that weigh more than a pound, the calculation gets much
more complex. The fact is that if you're selling an item that weighs, let's say, four
pounds, the actual shipping costs (via Priority Mail) can range from $5.30 to $10.35,
depending on where you are and where the buyer is. That's because Priority Mail
rates—most shipping rates, actually—vary by distance. So there's no way to quote an
exact shipping cost until the auction is over and you get the buyer's ZIP Code.

That said, there are three ways you can deal with this situation in your auction
listings.

First, you can calculate an *average* shipping cost for your item, figuring a cost halfway
between the minimum and the maximum possible costs. Using our four-pound example, the minimum cost for Priority Mail shipping is $5.30 and the maximum is $10.35,
so you would charge the buyer the average of these two numbers, or $7.83. (Or maybe
you would round up to $8.00.) The theory here is that you lose money on some ship-
ments and make it back on others, so over the long term it's a wash. Of course, nearby
buyers might complain that they're paying too much (which they are, because they're
in fact subsidizing sellers who live farther away). You'll have to decide whether you
can live with the occasional complaint—or refund the difference if it's too large.

Next, you can simply state that buyers will pay actual shipping cost based on location,
which will be calculated at the conclusion of the auction, and not include a flat shipping and handling charge in your listing. If you take this approach, you have to
request the buyer's ZIP Code at the end of the auction, refer to various rate charts to
figure the shipping cost, and then relay that cost to your buyer. It's a bit of work, but it
gets the job done. (It's also made easier by the fact that eBay is now including the
buyer's ZIP Code—when available—in its end-of-auction notification emails.)

Using eBay's Shipping Calculator

Finally, and this is my new preferred method, you can choose to include eBay's Shipping Calculator in your item listings. The Shipping Calculator, shown in Figure 21.4, is a great tool; it lets buyers enter their ZIP Code on the auction listing page, and then calculates the actual shipping cost, based on the shipping service you selected. (You can also choose to have the Shipping Calculator add a predetermined *handling charge* for each shipment, which we'll discuss in a minute.) When buyers use eBay Checkout at the end of an auction, or choose to pay via PayPal, they can also use the Shipping Calculator to automatically add shipping and handling fees to their total.

FIGURE 21.4

Add eBay's Shipping Calculator to your item listings so that buyers can automatically determine shipping and handling fees.

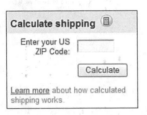

You can activate the Shipping Calculator when you're creating a new item listing on the Sell Your Item page. Just follow these steps:

1. Select the Calculated Shipping Rates tab to open the Shipping Calculator section, shown in Figure 21.5.

2. Enter the package weight, in pounds and ounces. (Round up any fractional ounces.)

3. Select a package size from the pull-down list.

4. Select which shipping service you plan to use, from the pull-down list.

5. Enter your ZIP Code.

6. Enter any handling fee you want to charge (over and above the actual shipping rate) into the Packaging & Handling Fee box.

tip

If you have multiple items for sale, there is every possibility that a single buyer will purchase more than one item. If that happens, you don't need to pack two or more separate boxes for that buyer; you can easily pack all the items purchased in a single box, which will reduce shipping costs. You should pass on that savings to your customer, in the form of a combined shipping and handling fee for all items purchased. If you're inflexible in adjusting your shipping and handling for multiple purchases, you're ripping people off—and will lose customers for it.

7. Select whether you want to offer shipping insurance.

8. Select whether you charge sales tax, and enter the sales tax rate.

Because the Shipping Calculator can be added to your item listings free of charge, there's no reason not to use it—especially because it greatly simplifies the task of calculating exact shipping charges to your customers.

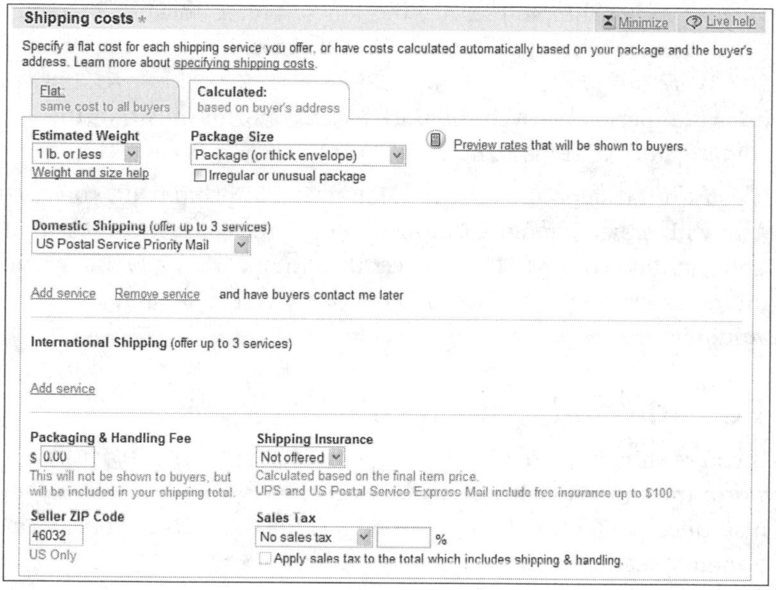

FIGURE 21.5

Activating eBay's Shipping Calculator from the Sell Your Item page.

Determining the Handling Charge

Aside from the pure shipping costs, you should consider adding a handling charge to the shipping fees your customers pay. After all, you need to be sure that you're compensated for any special materials you have to purchase to package the item. That doesn't mean you charge one buyer for an entire roll of tape, but maybe you add a few pennies to your shipping charge for these sorts of packaging consumables. And if you have to purchase a special box or envelope to ship an item, you should definitely include that cost in your shipping charge. (This argues for planning your shipping before placing your item listing—which is always a good idea.)

So you should have no compunction against "padding" your shipping fees with an additional handling charge. In fact, eBay's Shipping Calculator lets you add a separate handling charge to its calculations. It's an accepted part of doing business online.

> **" Mike Sez "**
>
> When I'm supplying quality packaging for a shipment, I find that a handling charge of $1 meets with little or no objection from my customers. If I'm using free Priority Mail packaging, I charge less.

How to Track Your Shipment

If you think the package might be lost in transit (it's taking too long to arrive), you can always avail yourself of the tracking services provided by UPS, FedEx, and other major carriers. These services typically provide tracking numbers for all packages shipped. In most cases, you can track your package by entering the package's tracking number into the carrier's website.

The one major shipping service that doesn't offer tracking (by default) is the U.S. Postal Service. What you can get from the postal service (at a cost of from $0.45 to $0.55) is delivery confirmation. USPS confirmation, however, does not confirm that an actual person received the package; it confirms only that the mail carrier delivered it. (Stuck it in the mailbox, that is.)

If you want a signature confirmation on a USPS shipment, you need to send your item with either Signature Confirmation or the certified mail option. Signature Confirmation costs $1.80, while certified mail costs $2.30. Both require the recipient to sign on delivery, and are good options if you're shipping something extremely valuable.

When to Recommend Insurance

If you're shipping a moderately expensive item (over $50, let's say), it might be worth the expense to insure it. You can always give the buyer the option of buying insurance—or just do it yourself and include the costs in your normal shipping and handling fee.

As to cost, the U.S. Postal Service charges $1.30 to insure items up to $50, or $2.20 for items between $50 and $100. UPS includes $100 worth of insurance in its basic rates; additional insurance can be purchased for additional cost.

What to Do When Things Go Wrong

If the package never arrives—or arrives damaged—you have some work to do. If you insured the package, you have to file a claim with the carrier. Information for claim filing appears on most of the shipping services' websites, but you might have to visit your carrier's local office to obtain the proper claim forms.

Note, however, that the procedure for filing a claim can be long and involved. Take the example of the U.S. Postal Service. The process starts with the buyer, who must take the package (merchandise, box, peanuts, and all) to their local post office to fill in half of a claim form (PS 1000). After this form is processed, the post office sends you (the seller) the half-filled-out form, via the mail. You then fill out the rest of the form and take it (along with your original insurance receipt) to *your* local post office for processing. When enough time goes by the USPS will (or won't, if you filled in something wrong) send a check for the insured amount directly to the buyer.

Other shipping services work differently, and some even send the insurance check to you instead of to the buyer. However it works, you need to communicate with the buyer while you're waiting for the claim to be paid so that both of you are in the loop about what's going on. If you receive the insurance check, you'll then need to refund the buyer's money; if the buyer receives the check, he should notify you when he's been paid.

> **tip**
>
> You can speed up this process by obtaining the claim form yourself, filling in your part, and then sending the claim form and the original insurance receipt to the buyer—and let him deal with the post office through the rest of the process.

Tips for Less-Painful Shipping

To wrap things up, here are some additional tips you can use to take some of the hassle out of shipping your eBay items:

- When you're using the U.S. Postal Service for shipping, try to time your visits to avoid long lines. That means avoiding lunch hour and the last half hour or so before closing; avoiding Mondays; and avoiding peak shipping periods around major holidays, such as Christmas and Valentine's Day. Early morning and mid-afternoon are typically low-volume times.

- Don't feel obligated to ship every single day of the week. Save up your shipments and go to the post office just one or two days a week.

> **caution**
>
> If you didn't insure your package—or if the carrier didn't offer automatic insurance—then you have a situation. eBay protocol has it that the seller is responsible for any losses in shipment, so you might end up refunding the buyer's money out of your own pocket.

- When you have a lot of packages to ship, don't go to the post office by yourself. Take a helper—and, if large shipments are common, invest in a small hand truck to help you cart all those boxes to the counter.

- If you're a heavy shipper, consider setting up an account with a single shipper and arranging daily pickups from your home. Pickup service will cost you a little more but can be more than worth it in time savings. (Most carriers will also pick up single items if you arrange so in advance—but at a much higher fee.)

- You may need to factor weather conditions into which type of shipping you choose. If it's summertime and you're shipping something that might melt in extreme heat (like an old vinyl LP), pick the fastest shipping method possible.

THE ABSOLUTE MINIMUM

Here are the key points to remember from this chapter:

- Pack your item so that it doesn't rattle when you shake it.
- Pack your item so that the package is as light as possible.
- Calculate shipping costs based on the weight of the item being shipped and the packaging—including the box and cushioning material.
- Get free boxes for Priority Mail shipping from the post office, or from the USPS website.
- Don't be afraid to reuse boxes you receive from other sources—as long as they're still in serviceable shape and you remove all previous labels.
- Make sure that your label is neatly printed and includes a full address and ZIP Code.
- You can print U.S. Postal Service labels with pre-paid postage direct from the eBay site, on your own computer and printer.
- Place a layer of clear tape over the delivery label (but not over any bar codes) so that it doesn't get smeared in transit.
- For most packages, the U.S. Postal Service is a good shipping option, either via Priority Mail, Media Mail, or Parcel Post.

22

Dealing with Deadbeat Bidders

A *deadbeat bidder* is someone who wins an auction but never follows through with the transaction. Not only should you leave negative feedback about these deadbeats, but you also should request a credit from eBay for your final value fee.

What do you do when you have a deadbeat bidder in one of your auctions? Fortunately, you still have the merchandise, which you can relist and (hopefully) sell again. You are out some eBay fees, however—although you can probably get them refunded when you report the deadbeat to eBay.

When eBay receives what it calls a Non-Paying Bidder Alert, the service automatically sends a warning to the user in question. If the buyer is found at fault, he receives an Unpaid Item strike against his account. After three such strikes, he's indefinitely suspended from the eBay service.

So there!

How to Handle Bum Bidders

If you are unfortunate enough to get stuck with a deadbeat bidder, there is a set procedure to follow, as you can see in the following checklist:

Checklist: Dealing with Deadbeat Bidders

- ☐ Contact the nonpaying bidder
- ☐ File an Unpaid Item Dispute
- ☐ Close out the dispute to receive a final value fee credit
- ☐ Leave negative feedback on the deadbeat bidder
- ☐ Offer the item in question to the second-highest bidder

    or

- ☐ Relist the item

Contacting an Unresponsive Bidder

It's on your shoulders to go to whatever lengths possible to contact the high bidder in your eBay auctions. This should start with the standard post-auction email, of course. If the buyer hasn't responded within three days, resend your original email with an "URGENT" added to the subject line. You should also amend the message to give the buyer a deadline (two days is good) for his response.

If another two days go by without a response, send a new message informing the buyer that if you don't receive a response within two days, you'll be forced to cancel his high bid and report him to eBay.

If a full week goes by and you still haven't heard from the buyer, you can assume the worst. Which means it's time to let eBay know about the bum.

Filing an Unpaid Item Dispute

The way you notify eBay about a deadbeat bidder is to file an Unpaid Item Dispute. You have to file this form (and wait the requisite amount of time) before you can request a final value fee credit on the auction in question.

An Unpaid Item Dispute must be filed between 7 and 45 days after your auction ends. You file the dispute by going to eBay's Security & Resolution Center (pages.ebay.com/securitycenter/), shown in Figure 22.1. Check the Unpaid Item option, and then click the Report Problem button. When the Report an Unpaid Item Dispute page appears, enter the auction's item number, click the Continue button, and follow the onscreen instructions.

FIGURE 22.1

Begin the dispute
process in eBay's
Security &
Resolution
Center.

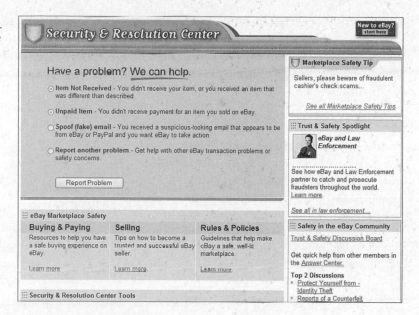

Asking eBay to Refund Your Fees

After an Unpaid Item Dispute has been filed, eBay sends a message to the bidder
requesting that the two of you work things out. (It's not a very strong message, in my
humble opinion, but it's what it is.) You then have to wait 7 days before you can
request a refund of your final value fee. You have to make the request no later than 60
days after the end of your auction, and your claim has to meet one of the following
criteria:

- The high bidder did not respond to your emails or backed out and did not buy
  the item.

- The high bidder's check bounced or a stop payment was
  placed on it.

- The high bidder returned the item and you
  issued a refund.

- The high bidder backed out, but you sold
  the item to another bidder at a lower
  price.

- One or more of the bidders in a Dutch
  auction backed out of the sale.

If your situation fits, you're entitled to a full
refund of eBay's final value fee—but you must
request it. To request a refund, go to your My
eBay page, click the My Account link, and then

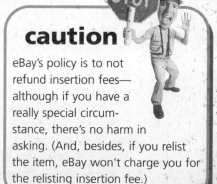

caution

eBay's policy is to not
refund insertion fees—
although if you have a
really special circum-
stance, there's no harm in
asking. (And, besides, if you relist
the item, eBay won't charge you for
the relisting insertion fee.)

click the Dispute Console link. When the Dispute Console page appears, click through to the item in dispute and select the I No Longer Wish to Communicate With or Wait For the Buyer option. eBay then issues a final value fee credit, and your item is eligible for relisting.

Leaving Negative Feedback

Naturally, you want to alert other eBay members to the weasel among them. You do this by leaving negative feedback, along with a description of just what went wrong—no contact, no payment, whatever. Be descriptive but professional; there's no reason to resort to insults and name-calling. Just state the facts, and you'll be fine.

To leave negative feedback, go to the item listing page, click the Leave Feedback to Bidder link, and when the Leave Feedback About an eBay User page appears, check Negative and enter your comments. Click the Leave Feedback button when done.

note

Learn more about feedback in Chapter 27, "Understanding and Using Feedback."

Giving Other Bidders a Second Chance

When a bidder backs out of an auction, you're stuck with the merchandise you thought you had sold. Assuming that you still want to sell the item, what do you do?

eBay offers the opportunity for you to make what it calls a Second Chance Offer to other bidders in your failed auction. This lets you try to sell your item to someone else who was definitely interested in what you had to sell.

You can make a Second Chance Offer to any of the under-bidders in your original auction. The offer can be made immediately at the end of the auction, and up to 60 days afterward.

To make a Second Chance Offer, return to your original item listing page and click the Second Chance Offer link. When the Second Chance Offer page appears, follow the onscreen instructions to fill out the form and make the offer.

tip

Second Chance Offers can also be used, in a successful auction, to offer duplicate items to nonwinning bidders.

Note that when a bidder accepts your Second Chance Offer, eBay charges you a final value fee. You are not charged a listing fee. Buyers accepting Second Chance Offers are eligible for eBay's normal buyer protection services.

Relisting Your Item

If you don't have any takers on your Second Chance Offer, you can always try to sell the item again by relisting the item. See Chapter 19, "After the Auction: Concluding Your Business," for more details.

THE ABSOLUTE MINIMUM

Here are the key points to remember from this chapter:

- If 7 days go by with no contact from the high bidder in your auction, you probably have a deadbeat on your hands.
- After you've made all reasonable effort to contact the buyer, file an Unpaid Item Dispute with eBay.
- Wait another 7 days, and then close out the dispute to receive a final value fee credit from eBay.
- You can try to sell the item in question by making a Second Chance Offer to other bidders, or by relisting the item in a new auction.

23

OTHER WAYS TO SELL ON EBAY

Most users buy and sell on eBay via the traditional online auction format. Granted, the auction format can vary a little (reserve price, Dutch auctions, Buy It Now, and so on), but most listings still use the same old bidding format.

That doesn't mean you *have* to sell your items via the online auction format. eBay offers several different ways for you to sell online, without doing the whole auction thing. Read on to learn more.

Fixed-Price Selling on Half.com

eBay isn't just eBay. The eBay corporation also owns a site called Half.com (half.ebay.com), which lets anyone sell certain types of merchandise in a fixed-price format. List your items for sale, wait for someone to buy them, and then collect the money. In this respect Half.com works a lot like the Amazon Marketplace—which, by the way, is another viable place for you to sell your stuff.

As you can see in Figure 23.1, Half.com special-izes in specific types of merchandise: books, CDs, DVDs, videotapes, video games, computers and software, and general consumer electronics (cell phones, digital cameras, MP3 players, home audio, televisions, and the like). Buyers can purchase items from multiple sellers, and have all their purchases consolidated into a sin-gle shopping cart and checkout. They make one payment, and then eBay deposits funds into each seller's account individually.

note

Learn more about Half.com from a buyer's perspective in Chapter 8, "Other Ways to Buy on eBay."

FIGURE 23.1

Items for sale on Half.com.

To sell on Half.com, all you have to do is click the Sell Your Stuff link in the left-hand column. When the Sell Your Items page appears, as shown in Figure 23.2, select a category and click the Continue button. You list each item by using the item's UPC or ISBN code. Half.com then inserts pre-filled item information from a massive product database. (It's the same database that feeds eBay's pre-filled information in the same categories.) There are no listing fees, but you do have to pay Half.com a commission when an item sells. You'll pay a 15% commission on items under $50, and lower commissions as the price rises. Instead of a buyer paying you directly, Half.com collects the payment; the site sends you your payment every two weeks.

FIGURE 23.2
Getting ready to sell on Half.com.

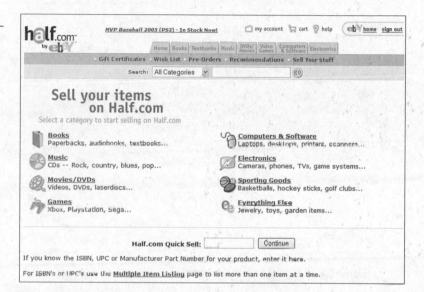

Finding Buyers with Want It Now

Another way to bypass the auction process is to go directly to buyers who want to buy what you have for sale. You can do this with eBay's new Want It Now feature, where buyers create "wish lists" of specific items. You search the Want It Now listings, and when you find a match, you offer the item for sale to the interested buyer. (eBay still takes their normal cut, of course.)

Start by clicking the Want It Now link on eBay's home page. When the Want It Now page appears, as shown in Figure 23.3, you can browse through the listings by category, or use the Sellers search box to search for specific items that might be listed in the database. Click a particular listing for more detail from the interested buyer, like that shown in Figure 23.4.

To respond to a request, click the Respond button to display the Respond to a Post with a Listing page, shown in Figure 23.5. If you already have an item listed, enter the item number and click the Respond to a Post button. If you haven't yet listed the item, click the Sell Your Item button, create an item listing, and then return to the Respond to a Post with a Listing page to enter the listing's item number.

FIGURE 23.3

Looking for prospective buyers with Want It Now.

FIGURE 23.4

A hopeful buyer's Want It Now ad.

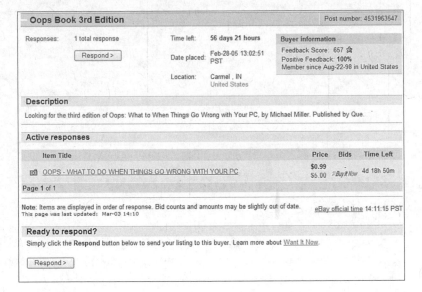

FIGURE 23.5

Responding to a Want It Now request.

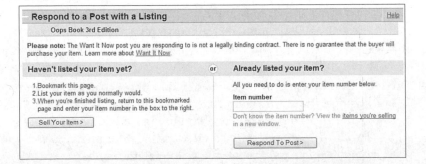

The interested buyer is now emailed a message containing a link to your item listing. To place a bid on your item, all the recipient has to do is click a button.

Letting Someone Else Sell It for You

Maybe you find the whole eBay process a little intimidating. You have some things you'd like to sell, but don't want to bother with the online auction process. What do you do?

If you don't want to sell your own stuff on eBay, you can let someone else sell it for you. In essence, you let another seller sell your goods on consignment. If the items sell, you pay the consignment seller a percentage of the final price. The consignment seller handles all the eBay stuff for you—taking photographs, creating item listings, managing the auctions, collecting payments, and packing and shipping the items. All you have to do is deliver the merchandise to the seller, and let him do all the work for you.

eBay calls this type of consignment seller an eBay Trading Assistant, and there are lots of them. Many individual sellers operate as Trading Assistants; there are also numerous local and national businesses that operate eBay consignment stores.

To search for a Trading Assistant near you, go to eBay's Trading Assistant Directory (pages.ebay.com/tradingassistants.html), shown in Figure 23.6. Enter your ZIP code and select a category (for what you want to sell) from the pull-down list, and then click the Search button. This returns a list of Trading Assistants in your area; click the link to view the Trading Assistant's profile, like the one in Figure 23.7. If you like what you see, click the Contact Assistant button to send a message and get the process going.

> **tip**
>
> If you'd like to become a Trading Assistant yourself, go to the Trading Assistants Directory page and click the Create/Edit Your Profile link. To become a Trading Assistant, you must have sold at least four items in the past 30 days, have a feedback rating of at least 50, and have a positive feedback percentage of at least 97%.

Not all Trading Assistants are individual sellers. eBay consignment selling has become a big business, with lots of stores opening their doors in communities all across America. Locally-owned consignment stores can be found in your local Yellow Pages. The two largest national chains are iSold It (www.i-soldit.com) and QuikDrop (www.quikdropfranchise.com); visit their websites to find a location near you.

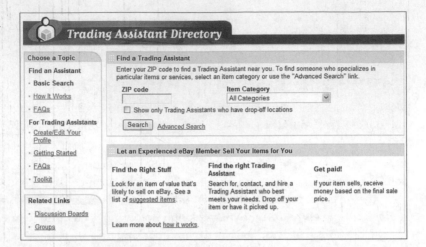

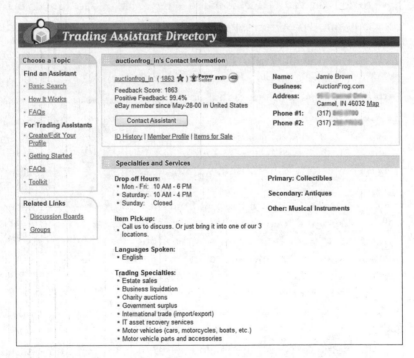

Listing Your Real Estate on eBay

If you have a house or other type of real estate to sell, you can list it for auction on
the eBay Real Estate site (pages.ebay.com/realestate/), shown in Figure 23.8. Or if
you don't quite trust the auction format for something this expensive, you can use
eBay to create a traditional real estate listing, like the kind a realtor might make in
your local paper. The difference is that an eBay real estate listing is browsable by
all of eBay's 125 million users—a pretty big audience when you have a house
to sell.

FIGURE 23.8

List your home with eBay Real Estate.

When you click the Sell link at the top of the eBay Real Estate page, you're offered a choice of three selling formats. You can choose to sell your property at a traditional auction, sell at a fixed price, or to create a traditional real estate listing, like the one in Figure 23.9. From there, you enter the specifics of your property—number of bedrooms, number of bathrooms, type of property, square footage, lot size, year built, and so on. You can also choose to run a 1-, 3-, 5-, 7-, 10-, or 30-day auction, or a 30- or 90-day non-auction listing.

FIGURE 23.9

A typical eBay Real Estate listing.

eBay Real Estate charges both listing and final value fees. The charge for a 1-, 3-, 5-, 7-, or 10-day auction listing is $100; a 30-day auction listing costs $150. If you prefer to create a non-auction listing, you'll pay $150 for a 30-day listing, or $300 for a 90-day listing. (Fees for timeshares and land are slightly lower.) The final value fee for timeshares and land is $35; there is no final value fee on residential and commercial real estate.

THE ABSOLUTE MINIMUM

Here are the key points to remember from this chapter:

- Half.com is an eBay site that lets anyone sell books, CDs, DVDs, and the like at fixed prices.

- You can use eBay's Want It Now feature to search for buyers who've expressed an interest in specific items.

- If you'd rather not bother with the auction process, find a Trading Assistant to sell your merchandise for you, on consignment.

- You can create traditional real estate listings on eBay Real Estate—or sell your property via the online auction format.

24

SECRETS OF SUCCESSFUL SELLERS

You have things to sell. You want to make sure that you actually sell them and that you get the highest price possible. But you're also competing with millions of other items up for auction at the same time. How do you stand out from the crowd, attract a bunch of bidders, and goose up the high bids?

If you're looking for extra-special selling secrets, this chapter is for you. Discover the secrets and strategies that will help you be a successful online auction seller!

Forty Sure-Fire Tips for Closing More Auctions—And Increasing Your Revenues

tip

Want even more advice? Then check out my companion book, *Tricks of the eBay Masters* (Que, 2004). It's filled with 600 tricks and tips that any eBay seller can use!

All eBay sellers want to sell more stuff and for higher prices. Fortunately, the tricks of the trade aren't limited to the guys who list 100 auctions a week. Here are 40 tips that can help anyone be a more profitable seller at any online auction.

Tip #1: Research Your Price

Don't sell without doing your homework first; make sure you know the true value of an item before you put it up for auction. Before you price your item, search for similar items in eBay's closed auctions. What was the starting bid price? What was the final selling price? You should also research the price of similar items offline; sometimes you can get a feel for relative value if you compare your item to a newer version of the same. Be informed, and you won't set the price too high or too low; you'll set it just right.

Tip #2: Make Your Listing Stand Out

Do everything in your power to make your item listings stand out from all the other listings currently online. Work on both the title and the description, and consider using a listing-creation tool (or using HTML formatting) to create a more dynamic ad.

note

See Chapter 16, "Creating a Great-Looking Listing," for more ideas about creating eye-catching item listings.

Learn more about Turbo Lister in Chapter 17, "Automating Item Listing with eBay Turbo Lister."

Tip #3: Use Turbo Lister to Create Your Listings

If you list a lot of items for auction, take advantage of eBay's free bulk-listing tool. Turbo Lister is great for listing multiple items at one time, but also makes it easier to create great-looking listings for just an item or two. Besides, there's no reason *not* to use it—it's free!

Tip #4: Get All the Buzzwords in the Title

Make sure you have the right words and phrases in the title of your item listing. If your audience looks for "compact discs," say compact disc; if they look for "CDs," say CD. If they look for both, use both. Use all possible words (up to your auction's character limit) to hit all possible keywords your potential bidders might be searching for—even if some of the words are redundant.

note

See Chapter 14, "Writing a Listing That Sells," for more ideas for effective listing descriptions.

Tip #5: A Picture Says a Thousand Words

Nothing increases your chances of selling an item like including a picture of it in your listing. Take a photo of your item, scan it in, upload it, and include it with your listing—even if it's just a plain text listing. (And when you take your picture, make sure that it's a good one—there's no point in posting a picture if the item is too small and out of focus.)

Tip #6: Be Descriptive

Include as much descriptive text about your item as you can. The better you describe your item, the fewer mid-auction emails you'll get asking about it and the greater the chance that your ultimate buyer won't get any unpleasant surprises. In addition, you never know when that single "unimportant" detail is just the thing a specific bidder is looking for—so don't overlook any detail, no matter how small.

Tip #7: Reuse Text That Sells

After you find a winning formula, reuse it! This is especially so if you sell a lot of similar items. Cut and paste descriptive text from your successful listings into additional listings, or use eBay's Relist Similar Item function so you're not always starting from scratch. If nothing else, this gives you a head start when creating new item listings!

Tip #8: Include Shipping and Payment Details

Don't forget to include all the details about shipping and handling (how much and who pays), payment methods, and the like. (That means estimating shipping and handling up front, if you can.) Don't leave anything open to interpretation.

Tip #9: Be Honest

Be honest in your description of the item. If the item has a few flaws, mention them. If there's damage or the item is otherwise imperfect, make note of it. Misleading a buyer will only cause you grief.

Tip #10: Promote Yourself with Your About Me Page

eBay's About Me page is the perfect way to provide more background information about you as a seller, and to drive potential bidders to your other live auctions. Be sure to create an About Me page—and use it to help "sell" yourself and your other items.

Learn more about eBay's About Me pages in Chapter 26, "Creating Your Own Personal About Me Page."

Tip #11: Make the Buyer Pay

Stipulate in your listing that the buyer pays all shipping and handling costs (and you might even want to detail these costs ahead of time in your listing). Also, make sure that the buyer pays for any "extras" that might be added after the sale. If the buyer wants insurance, the buyer pays for it. If the buyer wants to use an escrow service, the buyer pays for it. If the buyer wants expedited shipping, the buyer pays for it. See the trend?

Tip #12: Go Long...

When it comes time to choose the length for your auction, go for the 7- or 10-day option. The longer your item is up for auction, the more potential bidders who will see it—and the more potential bidders, the better your chances of selling the item for a higher price. Don't cheat yourself out of potential sales by choosing a shorter auction.

Tip #13: ...Or Create a Short-Term Frenzy

On the other hand, if you have something really hot, create a bidding frenzy by choosing a very short auction length. If you do this, play it up in your item's title: 3 Days Only! works pretty well.

Tip #14: There's No Reason to Reserve

I don't know of a single bidder who likes reserve price auctions. Why use something that scares some bidders away? (Remember, many beginning users don't understand reserve price auctions, and thus don't bid in them.) Set a realistic minimum, and get on with it.

Tip #15: Single Items Are Best...

If you're looking for the highest total dollar, don't group items together. Multiple-item lots seldom bring as much money as multiple items sold individually.

Tip #16: …Although You Can Unload Some Dogs in a Pack

On the other hand, if you have a lot of things to sell, selling in lots can reduce your personal overhead, as well as help you unload some less attractive items that you probably couldn't sell individually. (Plus, you get hit for only a single insertion fee!)

Tip #17: Don't Compete Against Yourself

If five people are looking to buy footstools today, don't give them five choices all from one person (you). If you have five footstools to sell, don't sell them all at once. Sell one this week, one next week, and one the week after that. Spread it out to create an illusion of scarcity, and you'll generate more total revenue.

Tip #18: Start and End in Prime Time

When you *start* your auction is important—because that affects when your auction *ends*. If you start a seven-day auction at 6:00 p.m. on a Saturday, it will end exactly seven days later, at 6:00 p.m. the following Saturday.

Why is it important when your auction ends? Because some of the most intense bidding takes place in the final few minutes of your auction, from snipers trying to steal the high bid at the last possible moment. To take advantage of last-minute bidders, your auction needs to end when the most possible bidders are online.

If you end your auction at 3:00 in the morning, everyone will be asleep and you'll lose out on any last-minute bids. Instead, try to end your auction during early evening hours, when the most users are online.

Remember, though, that you're dealing with a three-hour time-zone gap between the East and the West coasts. So, if you time your auction to end at 7:00 p.m. EST, you're ending at 4:00 p.m. PST—when most potential bidders are still at work. Conversely, if you choose to end at 9:00 p.m. PST, you just hit midnight in New York—and many potential bidders are already fast asleep.

The best times to end—and thus to *start*—your auction are between 9:00 p.m. and 11:00 p.m. EST, or between 6:00 p.m. and 8:00 p.m. PST. (Figure the in-between time zones yourself!) That way you'll catch the most potential bidders online for the final minutes of your auction—and possibly generate a bidding frenzy that will garner a higher price for your merchandise!

Note, however, that the best time to end an auction can be influenced by the type of item you're

note

eBay operates on Pacific (West Coast) time. If you're in another time zone, be sure to do the math to determine the proper time for your area.

selling. For example, if you're selling an item that appeals to grade-school or high-school kids, try ending your auction in the late afternoon, after the kids get home from school and before they head off for dinner. Items with appeal to housewives do well with a late morning or early afternoon end time. And business items sell best when they end during normal business hours.

Tip #19: End on a Sunday

When you end your auction on a Sunday, you get one full Saturday and *two* Sundays (the starting Sunday and the ending one) for a seven-day item listing. Sunday is a great day to end auctions because almost everybody is home—no one is out partying, or stuck at work or in school. End your auction on a Sunday evening, and you're likely to get more bids—and higher prices.

There are exceptions, however.

As with the time you end your auction, your ending day might also be influenced by the type of item you're selling. If you're selling an item of interest to college students, for example, you might be better ending on a night during the week, because a lot of students travel home for the weekend; you'll catch them in the dorms on a Wednesday or Thursday night. Items targeted at churchgoers might also be better ending during the week so that you don't catch bidders when they're at Sunday evening church services.

Tip #20: Don't End on a Friday or Saturday Night

If Sunday is normally the best night of the week to end your auction, what's the worst night?

Friday and Saturday are probably the worst nights to end most auctions, because a lot of eBay users are out partying on these non-school nights. End an auction for any item (especially youth-oriented items) on a Friday or Saturday night, and you eliminate a large number of potential buyers.

You should also try not to end your auction right in the middle of a hit television series or any blockbuster sporting events or award shows—some potential bidders might find it difficult to tear themselves away from the old boob tube.

Tip #21: Slow Down in the Summer

For whatever reason, eBay traffic slows way down in the summertime. (Lots of potential buyers are on vacation, and even more are outside enjoying the sunshine.) If you want to maximize your bids, you'll get a higher price when fall and winter come along.

Tip #22: Promote Your Auctions

Let people outside eBay know about your auction. Mention your auction in relevant newsgroups and mailing lists, feature it on your personal website, and send emails about it to all your friends. Include your item listing's URL in everything you do so that anyone interested can click the link to view your auction. Do anything you can think of to draw traffic to your listing—and thus increase your chances of selling it.

Tip #23: Use My eBay to Track Your Auctions

Don't let your auction activity get away from you. Use My eBay to look at all your auctions daily, or use auction management software to track your auctions automatically.

You can also use My eBay to track your favorite auction categories, as well as your feedback ratings and account status. Personalize your My eBay page the way you like and then bookmark it; it's a great home page for the heavy auction trader.

Learn more about My eBay in Chapter 25, "Creating a Home Base with My eBay."

Learn more about Selling Manager in Chapter 20, "Automating Listing Management with eBay Selling Manager."

Tip #24: If You Sell a Lot, Use eBay Selling Manager

My eBay is great for tracking your auctions, but when it comes to managing your end-of-auction activities, consider subscribing to eBay Selling Manager. For just $4.99 per month you get assistance in sending emails, printing invoices and packing slips, and leaving feedback. It's great if you run a lot of auctions simultaneously.

Tip #25: Avoid Premature Cancellation

Know that many bidders wait until the very last minute to place a bid. (It's called sniping, and it really works.) If you cancel an auction early, you'll miss out on the bulk of the potential bids. So don't cancel!

Tip #26: Avoid Deadbeats

You don't have to sell to just anybody. You can stipulate that you won't sell to bidders with negative feedback or with feedback ratings below a certain level. If you receive bids from these potential deadbeats, cancel them. If the deadbeats continue to bid (after being warned off via email by you), block their bids. You want to sell to someone who will actually consummate the transaction and send you payment; bidders with negative feedback are more likely to leave you high and dry.

Tip #27: Include All Your Shipping Costs

When figuring your shipping and handling costs, be sure to factor in all your costs—not just the shipping itself, but also the cost of the packaging, the labels, and the packing tape. Don't gouge your buyer (this isn't meant to be a profit center), but don't cheat yourself, either. If actual shipping costs are $3.50, think about charging the buyer $4 to cover your additional costs.

And, when you're figuring the item's shipping weight, remember that you don't just ship the item—you also ship the box and all cushioning materials. These items have weight and must be included when you're weighing your item for shipment. (Those free Priority Mail boxes are especially heavy—and can easily increase your cost of shipping.)

Tip #28: Use a Middleman for Expensive Items

If you're selling a high-priced item, consider offering the buyer the option of using an escrow service. It's a good deal for you; the buyer pays for the service (in the neighborhood of 5%, typically), it provides a level of peace of mind for the buyer, and it lets you accept credit card payments that you might otherwise not accept.

Tip #29: Document Everything

In case something goes south, it helps to have good records of all aspects of your transaction. Print copies of the confirmation email, plus all email between you and the buyer. Be sure to write down the buyer's user ID, email address, and physical address. If the transaction is ever disputed, you'll have all the backup you need to plead your case.

Tip #30: Communicate Quickly—And Clearly

When your auction ends, get in touch with the high bidder *immediately*. Don't wait until the next day; send your post-auction email within minutes of the auction close. Remember, the faster you notify the high bidder, the faster you'll get paid.

And here's something the best sellers do. Email the buyer again when you receive payment and once more when you're ready to ship the item. The more everyone knows, the fewer surprises there are.

Also, remember that not everyone reads his or her email daily, so don't expect an immediate response. Still, if you don't receive a response, send another email. If you're at all concerned at any point, get the buyer's phone number or physical address from the auction site and call or write him. A good phone conversation can clear up a wealth of misunderstandings.

Tip #31: Be Nice

Remember that you're dealing with another human being, someone who has feelings that can be hurt. A little bit of common courtesy goes a long way. Say please and thank you, be understanding and tolerant, and treat your trading partner in the same way you'd like to be treated. Follow the golden rule; do unto other auction traders as you would have them do unto you.

Tip #32: Ship Promptly

Ship promptly after you've received payment (and after the check has cleared). Nobody likes to wait too long for something they've paid for—and you don't want to gain a reputation as a slow shipper.

Tip #33: If Nobody Buys, Relist—With a Different Description

If you didn't sell your item the first time, try it again. eBay lets you relist unsold items at no additional listing charge; even if you have to pay again, you still want to sell the item, right? But remember that if it didn't sell the first time, there was probably a reason why. Was your asking price too high? Was your description too vague? Was the title too boring? Should you have included a picture or used HTML to spice up the listing? Whatever you change, change something to increase your chances of selling your item the second time around.

Tip #34: If You Get Stiffed, Ask for a Refund

When your high bidder does a vanishing act, file an Unpaid Item Dispute and request a refund of the auction's final value fee. There's no sense paying eBay for something you didn't get paid for!

Tip #35: Don't Forget About Number Two

If you run up against a nonpaying bidder, you can try to sell the now-unsold item to the next highest bidder, if he or she is still interested. It never hurts to ask, in any case; just use eBay's Second Chance Offer feature and see whether the bidder bites.

caution

If you do offer a refund, don't send the money until you've received and examined the item in dispute. Some smarmy buyers might try to dupe you by sending back a different item than the one you shipped!

Tip #36: The Customer Is Always Right...

Although many sellers take a hardball attitude and refuse any discussion of refunds, I recommend a more customer-friendly approach. When I have a dissatisfied buyer, I offer a full refund.

Yeah, some buyers might try to take advantage of you, but most are honest. So if you have a buyer with a complaint, you can generally assume that it's a legitimate beef. You'll get better feedback—and sleep easier at night—if you have the customer return the item and refund the purchase price. It's the right thing to do!

Tip #37: ...Or All Sales Are Final

If you choose *not* to offer a "satisfaction guaranteed" policy, be sure to state that "all sales are final" in your item listing. (Alternatively, you can say that your item is "sold as-is" or that there are "no returns.")

Tip #38: Accept Credit Cards—Via PayPal

One of the easiest ways to increase the number of bids in your auction is to accept payment via credit card. Unless you're a real business with a merchant bank account, this means signing up for PayPal—which is extremely easy to do.

Tip #39: Wait for the Check to Clear

The reality is that many buyers prefer to pay by check. That's okay, as long as you wait a good 10 business days for the check to clear. Don't be stupid and ship an item before the check proves good—you're bound to get burned!

Tip #40: If It's a Business, You Pay Taxes

This book isn't meant to offer tax advice (and you'd be foolish to consult me for such!), but larger eBay sellers need to be aware of the tax issue. In general, if you're an individual who classifies as a casual eBay seller, you probably don't have to worry about collecting sales taxes or reporting taxable income. However, if you're a business or an individual at the power seller level, the Internal Revenue Service will want their share. The best advice here is that no matter what level your eBay sales, you should consult your accountant or a similar tax expert—and never, never try to fool Uncle Sam.

Learn more about running a full-fledged eBay business (and paying taxes!) in my companion book, *Making a Living from Your eBay Business* (Que, 2005).

One Extra Tip: Join the eBay Community

Here's a tip of value to both sellers and buyers. When you have questions or problems with your eBay auctions, You can get *tons* of help from other eBay users, via eBay's community discussion boards. Just click the Community link on the eBay

Navigation Bar (or go directly to hub.ebay.com/community), and you'll see eBay's Community hub, as shown in Figure 24.1. Click the Discussion Boards link to see all the different boards available.

FIGURE 24.1

Get help and support from other members of the eBay community.

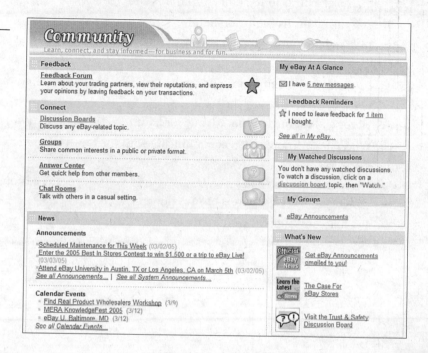

eBay offers discussion boards for individual product categories, as well as more general boards for buying, selling, and creating auction listings. The users who frequent these boards are extraordinarily helpful, and can answer just about any question you pose.

caution

As helpful as the board members are, they probably can't answer all the questions you might have. In particular, don't expect these users to reveal their personal buying/selling secrets, merchandise suppliers, or other proprietary information. So be realistic about the help you can get—and make sure you thank those who answer your questions!

THE ABSOLUTE MINIMUM

Here are the key points to remember from this chapter:

- Research your listing beforehand.
- Take the time and effort to create an attractive and descriptive auction listing.
- For best results, time your auction to end on a Sunday evening in prime time.
- Never end an auction on a Friday or Saturday night, or on a holiday.
- When the auction's over, communicate with the buyer—the more often, the better.
- Treat your auction sales as a business, and your buyers as customers; and remember, the customer is always right!
- Get help and support from other eBay users, in eBay's discussion boards.

PART IV

USING EBAY'S ADVANCED FEATURES

CREATING A HOME BASE WITH MY EBAY

Whether you're a buyer or a seller, if you're active at all on eBay, it's likely you'll have more than one auction going at any one time. Just how do you keep track of all this auction activity?

The best way to monitor all the auctions you're participating in is to use eBay's self-professed "best-kept secret": *My eBay*. My eBay is a page—actually, a set of pages—that you can personalize to track your bidding and selling activity in your own way. I highly recommend that you avail yourself of this useful feature.

Accessing and Using My eBay

You access My eBay from any eBay page by clicking the My eBay link on the Navigation Bar. This opens My eBay in the My Summary view, which (as we'll discuss in a moment) presents a general overview of all your current auction activity. My eBay actually offers several different pages, which you access by clicking the appropriate links contained in the navigation panel along the left side of the page. We'll look at each of these pages individually.

My Summary View

The My Summary view, shown in Figure 25.1, is the default view when you access My eBay. It consists of several distinct sections:

- **My Messages**, which contains important messages from eBay or from other sellers and buyers.

- **Buying Reminders**, which prompts you about actions you need to take regarding those items you've recently purchased.

- **Selling Reminders**, which prompts you about actions you need to take regarding those items you've recently sold.

- **General eBay Announcements**, which includes links to the most recent eBay system news.

- **Items I'm Watching**, which lists those auction items you've placed on your watch list.

- **Buying Totals**, which summarizes those items you're bidding on and those you've won.

- **Items I'm Bidding On**, which lists all items you're currently bidding on.

- **Item's I've Made Best Offers On**, which lists those items you've made a best offer on, for those auctions that utilize this feature.

- **Items I've Won**, which lists recent auctions in which you were the high bidder.

- **Items I Didn't Win**, which lists recent auction in which you were outbid.

- **Selling Totals**, which summarizes those items you currently have for sale or have recently sold.

- **Items I'm Selling**, which lists all items you currently have for sale.

- **Items I've Sold**, which lists all items you've recently sold.

> **tip**
>
> One other nice thing about the My Summary view is that you can customize it to display as much—or as little—information as you wish. Just click the Customize Summary link near the top of the page to remove sections you don't use often.

FIGURE 25.1

The My eBay My Summary page.

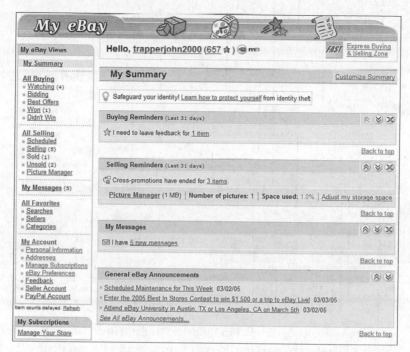

I use My Summary as my "home page" for all my eBay activities. It presents a great visual overview of all your important eBay activity, and lets you link directly to individual activities.

All Buying Page

You use the All Buying view, shown in Figure 25.2, to keep track of all items you're either bidding on or watching—or have won or lost. The page contains the following sections:

- Buying Reminders
- Items I'm Watching
- Buying Totals
- Items I'm Bidding On
- Items I've Won
- Items I Didn't Win

The Items I've Won list is worth an extra glance. Not only does it list those auctions in which you're the winning bidder, but it also includes an Action column that lets you know what you need to do next for each item—leave feedback, view payment status, and so on. Click the link in the Action column to perform that action.

FIGURE 25.2

The My eBay All Buying page.

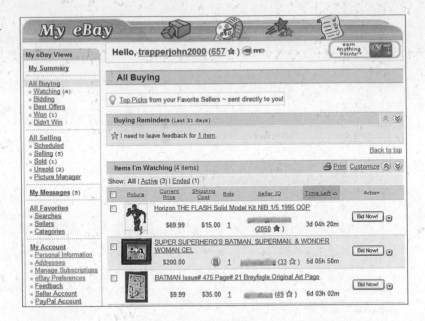

Also interesting is the Items I'm Bidding On list, which presents all your current bidding activity—even those auctions in which you've been outbid. All auctions you're currently winning are in green; all auctions you're currently losing are in red. And, at the bottom of the page, you'll find a set of links to various buying-related services on the eBay site.

All Selling Page

You use the All Selling Page, shown in Figure 25.3, to keep track of all the items you're currently selling or have recently sold. The page contains several lists of use to sellers:

- Selling Reminders
- Scheduled Items
- Selling Totals
- Items I'm Selling
- Items I've Sold
- Unsold Items

One of the things I like about the Items I'm Selling section is the column for # of Watchers. This lists how many potential bidders have placed your item on their watch lists; it's a good indication of total demand, and a predictor of last-minute sniping.

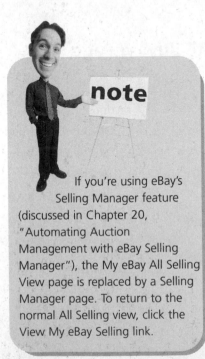

note

If you're using eBay's Selling Manager feature (discussed in Chapter 20, "Automating Auction Management with eBay Selling Manager"), the My eBay All Selling View page is replaced by a Selling Manager page. To return to the normal All Selling view, click the View My eBay Selling link.

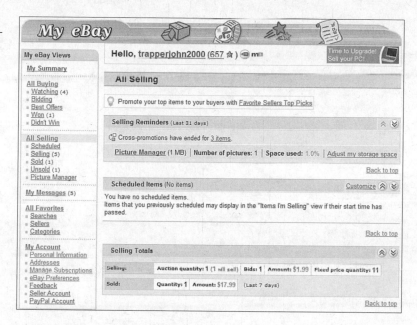

Like the Items I've Won list on the All Buying page, the Items I've Sold list is especially useful. The Action column lists the next action you need to take for every one of your closed auctions; click the link to perform the appropriate action.

Also useful is the Items I'm Selling list, which lets you see, in a single glance, the status of everything you're currently selling on eBay. All items that currently have a bid higher than your minimum or reserve price are listed in green; all items that haven't yet reached the minimum bid level are listed in red. And, at the bottom of the page, you'll find a set of links to various selling-related services on the eBay site.

My Messages Page

The My Messages page, shown in Figure 25.4, lists all recent messages and announcements from eBay. Click a message title to read the complete message.

All Favorites Page

The All Favorites page, shown in Figure 25.5, is where you can access your most-used categories, searches, and sellers. There are three lists on this page:

- My Favorite Searches
- My Favorite Sellers
- My Favorite Categories

You can add items to your favorites by clicking the Add links to the right of each list—Add New Search, Add New Seller or Store, and Add New Category. From there, follow the onscreen instructions to add the items you want to appear on the All Favorites page in the future.

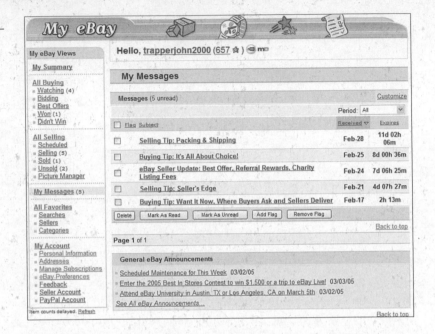

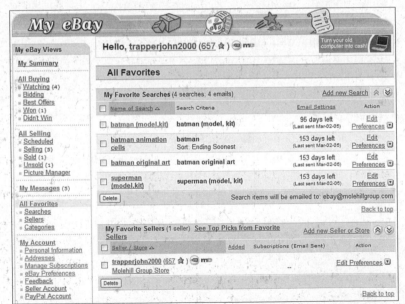

My Account Page

The My Account page, shown in Figure 25.6, is where you can manage your eBay seller's account and leave feedback about specific transactions.

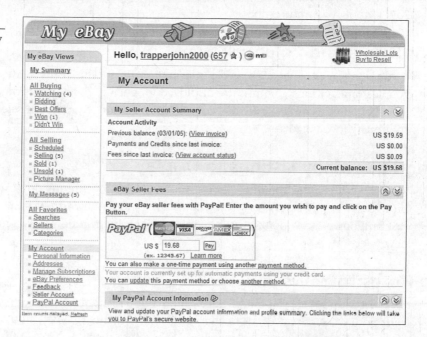

The My Account Summary list, at the top of the page, displays your last eBay invoice total, any payments and credits made since your last invoice, and any fees accessed since your last invoice. There's also a section that lets you pay your eBay fees via PayPal.

Managing and Personalizing My eBay

Each of the My eBay views can be personalized according to your personal tastes. Let's take a quick look at these common view management features.

Sorting and Filtering

The information in any My eBay list (what eBay calls an *information table*) can be sorted by any individual column. Just click the column header to sort by that column.

tip

The My Account page is particularly useful because it contains direct links to some of eBay's normally well-hidden customer service features, including fees and credits, payment terms, credit card setup, credit requests, and refunds. It's easier to click these services here than to hunt them down on eBay's Site Map page.

You can also filter the listings presented in most tables to cut down on information overload. At the top of each information table is a series of Show links; click a link to filter the information accordingly. For example, in the Items I've Won table (in the All Buying view), you can choose to show All items, or just those items Awaiting Payment or Awaiting Feedback.

Hiding or Displaying Columns

If you don't need to see all possible information for specific listings, My eBay lets you customize which columns are displayed for each individual information table. Just click the Customize link above the information table, and then select which columns you want to see.

Changing How Many Listings to Display

For most My eBay information tables, you can select how many days' worth of listings you want to display; you can display up to 60 days' worth of items if you want. Just pull down the Period list at the top of a given information table and make a new selection.

Leaving Notes to Yourself

Every now and then you might have an auction that requires additional action on your part, or somehow needs further annotation. Fortunately, My eBay lets you add electronic "sticky notes" to any auction listing. Just check the option box next to a particular listing and then click the Add Note button; add your comments into the resulting text box.

Printing Key Information

The information presented in My eBay looks great onscreen but can be a little much if you need a hard copy. Fortunately, My eBay lets you print a simplified, printer-friendly version of any information table. All you have to do is click the Print link next to any section of any view page. For example, to print a list of auctions you've won, go to the All Buying view and click the Print link at the top of the Items I've Won section.

" Mike Sez "

My eBay is such a useful tool that I make it my primary gateway to the entire eBay site. I never use eBay's home page—I use My eBay instead. It's the very first bookmark in my web browser!

THE ABSOLUTE MINIMUM

Here are the key points to remember from this chapter:

- My eBay lets you track all your eBay activities and information in one place.

- My eBay includes separate pages for tracking items you're bidding on or watching, items you're selling, your favorite searches and categories, and your eBay account.

- You can customize My eBay for your own personal preferences—including how you like your lists sorted, and how many days' worth of items you want to display.

26

CREATING YOUR OWN PERSONAL ABOUT ME PAGE

If you buy or sell a lot of items on eBay, wouldn't it be nice to have a web page you could show to other users? You know, a page that would tell all those buyers and sellers you deal with all about yourself—and the items you have for sale?

Well, eBay lets you create such a page. It's called *About Me*.

Introducing the About Me Page

eBay's About Me page is a personal web page just for you. It's a great way to personalize the eBay experience, tell a little about yourself, and inspire bidder trust. It's also easy to do—no HTML coding necessary. (My personal About Me page is shown in Figure 26.1.)

FIGURE 26.1
About *Me*, your author!

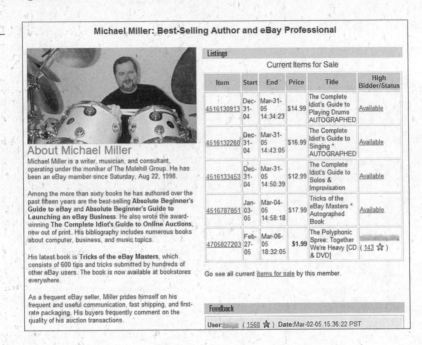

You can view any user's About Me page by clicking the Me icon next to his or her user name on any item listing page. (If no icon is displayed, that user doesn't have an About Me page.) You can also search for other users' About Me pages by clicking the Advanced Search link at the top of eBay's home page and using the Find a Member search option.

Creating Your Own About Me Page

As I said, you don't have to be a web programmer to create your own About Me page. All you have to do is click a few options and fill in some blanks, and you're ready to go.

Follow these steps:

1. On any eBay page, click the Services link (above the Navigation Bar), and then click About Me.

2. When the main About Me page appears, as shown in Figure 26.2, click the Create Your Page button.

FIGURE 26.2

Your About Me page starts here!

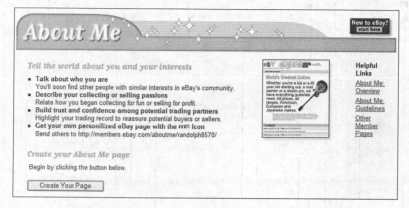

3. When the Choose Your Editing Options page appears, check the Use Our Easy Step-by-Step Process option, and then click the Continue button.

4. When the Enter Page Content page appears, as shown in Figure 26.3, start by entering a title for your About Me page.

5. On the same page, you can now enter two paragraphs of information, using the supplied formatting controls or (by clicking the Enter Your Own HTML link) with HTML codes.

6. Still on the same page, enter a link to any picture you want to include on your page, as well as an optional title for the picture.

note

If you're an HTML wizard and want to code your own About Me page, select the Enter Your Own HTML Code option instead.

7. In the Show Your eBay Activity section, choose how many feedback comments and current auction listings you want to display.

8. If you want to include any links to external web pages, enter them in the Add Links section.

9. When you're done entering all this information on the Enter Page Content page, click the Continue button.

10. When the Preview and Submit page appears, as shown in Figure 26.4, choose a layout for your page, and then click the Submit button.

FIGURE 26.3

Enter all the information you want to include on your About Me page.

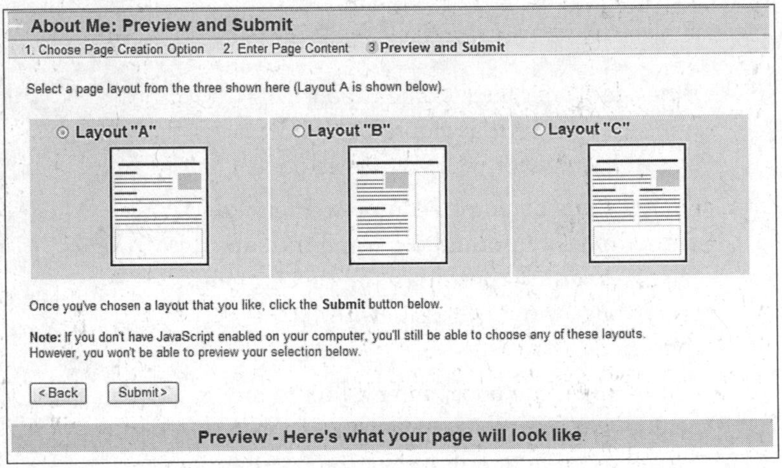

FIGURE 26.4

Choose a layout for your About Me page.

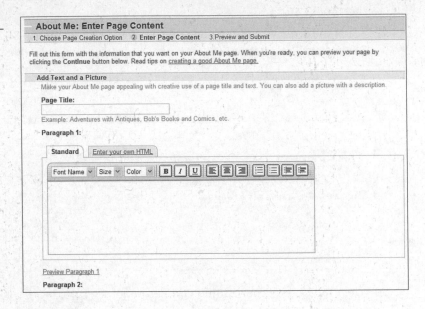

You'll now see a confirmation page, which includes a link to your new About Me page. Click this link to view your new page.

Publicizing Your eBay Auctions with About Me

The great thing about the About Me page is that it's a page with an unchanging URL that always lists your current auctions. When you want to direct other users to your eBay auctions, it's easier to direct them to your About Me page than it is to enter the individual URLs for all your item listing pages.

The address for your About Me page is shown in the address box of your web browser. The address is typically in the form of members.ebay.com/aboutme/*userid*/; just replace *userid* with your own user ID and you should have the URL. (As mentioned previously, my eBay ID is trapperjohn2000, so my About Me address is members.ebay.com/ aboutme/trapperjohn2000/.)

You can then insert this URL into your personal web page, your email signature, or any other item you can think of. It's a great way to publicize your ongoing eBay activity!

tip

You can edit your About Me page at any time by repeating the above steps.

"Mike Sez"

The About Me page is also a good way for other eBay users to get to know you—especially those who are bidding in your auctions, or hosting auctions in which you're bidding. Be sure to include text that positions you as a reputable eBay citizen—and not some goofball flake who's likely to cause trouble.

THE ABSOLUTE MINIMUM

Here are the key points to remember from this chapter:

- The About Me page is your personal page on the eBay site—you can create it in less than five minutes, no HTML coding necessary.

- Your About Me page can include descriptive text, a photo, links to your favorite sites, a list of your current auctions, and a list of your most recent feedback comments.

- You can use your About Me page to publicize your eBay activities outside of the eBay site.

27

UNDERSTANDING AND USING FEEDBACK

eBay regards its feedback function as the best protection against fraudulent transactions. I certainly recommend that, whether a transaction went swell or went south, you leave feedback about your partner in every transaction. I know that I check the feedback rating of every seller I choose to deal with; it really is a good way to judge the quality of the other party in your eBay transactions.

What Do All Those Stars and Numbers Mean?

Next to every buyer and seller's name on eBay are a number and (more often than not) a colored star. (Figure 27.1 shows my personal star and feedback number.) This number and star represent that user's feedback rating. The larger the number, the better the feedback (and the more transactions that user has participated in).

FIGURE 27.1

Check the feedback rating next to a member's name.

Seller information
trapperjohn2000
(657 ☆) m☰
Feedback Score: 657
Positive Feedback:
100%
Member since Aug-22-
98 in United States

How are feedback ratings calculated?

First, every new user starts with 0 points. (A clean slate!) For every positive feedback received, eBay adds 1 point to your feedback rating. For every negative feedback received, eBay subtracts 1 point. Neutral comments add 0 points to your rating.

Let's say you're a new user, starting with a 0 rating. On the first two items you buy, the sellers like the fact that you paid quickly and give you positive feedback. On the third transaction, however, you forgot to mail the check for a few weeks, and the seller left you negative feedback. After these three transactions, your feedback rating would be 1. (That's $0 + 1 + 1 - 1 = 1$.)

If you build up a lot of positive feedback, you qualify for a star next to your name. Different colored stars represent different levels of positive feedback, as noted in Table 27.1.

TABLE 27.1 eBay Feedback Ratings

Color/Type	Points
Yellow star	10–49
Blue star	50–99
Turquoise star	100–499
Purple star	500–999
Red star	1,000–4,999
Green star	5,000–9,999
Yellow shooting star	10,000–24,999
Turquoise shooting star	25,000–49,999
Purple shooting star	50,000–99,999
Red shooting star	100,000 or more

Obviously, heavy users can build up positive feedback faster than occasional users. If you're dealing with a shooting-star user (of any color), you know you're dealing with a trustworthy—and extremely busy!—eBay pro.

Reading Feedback Comments—And Contacting Other Users

You can also read the individual comments left by other users by going to the user's Member Profile page. To access this page, just click the user's name or feedback number.

The Member Profile page, like the one shown in Figure 27.2, includes a lot of information you can use to judge the trustworthiness of other users. At the top of the page is the user's Feedback Score, followed by the Positive Feedback percentage. You'll also see the raw numbers—the number of members who left positive feedback, and the number who left negative feedback. Recent feedback ratings are summarized in the Recent Ratings table.

> **tip**
>
> You can also use the Member Profile page to read feedback comments about you—just click your own member name on any page. (Even more convenient: Go to your My eBay Feedback page.)

FIGURE 27.2

A typical Member Profile page; hey, people like this guy!

Member Profile: trapperjohn2000 (657 ⭐)				

Feedback Score: 657
Positive Feedback: 100%

Members who left a positive: 658
Members who left a negative: 0
All positive feedback received: 830

Learn about what these numbers mean.

Recent Ratings:	Past Month	Past 6 Months	Past 12 Months
positive	12	53	122
neutral	0	0	0
negative	0	0	0

Bid Retractions (Past 6 months): 0

Member since: Aug-22-98
Location: United States
- ID History
- Items for Sale
- Visit my Store
- Add to Favorite Sellers
- Learn more About Me

[Contact Member]

Feedback Received | From Buyers | From Sellers | Left for Others

830 feedback received by trapperjohn2000 (0 mutually withdrawn) Page 1 of 34

Comment	From	Date / Time	Item #
The day I bought this book, I sold $700 in my eBay store! All right!!!	Buyer ___ (1568 ⭐)	Mar-02-05 15:36	4516787851
Fast shipping, very nice book and personalized too! Thank you!	Buyer ___ (632 ⭐)	Mar-01-05 15:13	4516133453
Item arrived safe and sound. Thank You!	Buyer ___ (267 ⭐)	Feb-23-05 03:38	6360006184
Very Good, great item value, delivered quickly	Buyer ___ (241 ⭐)	Feb-20-05 19:46	7118703627
Most excellant transaction and very fast delivery! Thanks!!!	Buyer ___ (63 ⭐)	Feb-13-05 10:06	6362146073
quick delivery, as described. Thanks!	Buyer ___ (10 ⭐)	Feb-11-05 02:51	6362146078
dISK ARRIVED AS PROMISED QUICK SHIP. GREAT EBAYER	Buyer ___ (45 ⭐)	Feb-08-05 05:51	6359983623

To the right of the Recent Ratings Table are links you can use to find out even more about this user—his ID History, current Items for Sale, a link to his eBay Store (if he has one), and a similar link to his About Me page (again, if he has one). Below these links is a Contact Member button; click this to send an e-mail to this user.

Below the summary information is a list of all the feedback comments for this user. You can click a tab to view All Feedback Received, just those comments From Buyers or From Sellers, or comments that this user Left for Others.

How to Leave Feedback

You can leave feedback from any item listing page; just click the Leave Feedback link. When you see the Leave Feedback page, shown in Figure 27.3, you can choose to leave Positive, Negative, or Neutral feedback, along with a brief comment (80 characters maximum).

Make sure your feedback is accurate before you click the Leave Feedback button; you can't change your comments after they've been registered.

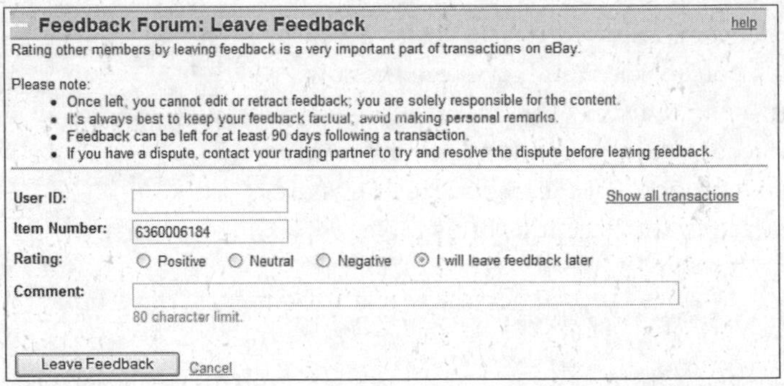

FIGURE 27.3

Leaving feedback comments for a transaction partner.

Feedback Forum: Leave Feedback   help

Rating other members by leaving feedback is a very important part of transactions on eBay.

Please note:
- Once left, you cannot edit or retract feedback; you are solely responsible for the content.
- It's always best to keep your feedback factual, avoid making personal remarks.
- Feedback can be left for at least 90 days following a transaction.
- If you have a dispute, contact your trading partner to try and resolve the dispute before leaving feedback.

User ID: Show all transactions

Item Number: 6360006184

Rating: ○ Positive   ○ Neutral   ○ Negative   ● I will leave feedback later

Comment:
              80 character limit.

[Leave Feedback]   Cancel

Figuring Out What Kind of Feedback to Leave

You should leave feedback at the end of every auction—whether it was a positive or a negative experience for you. Don't miss your chance to inform other eBay users about the quality of the person you just got done dealing with.

Table 27.2 offers some guidelines on when you should leave positive or negative feedback—and the types of comments you might use to embellish your feedback.

TABLE 27.2   Recommended eBay Feedback

Transaction	Feedback	Comments
Transaction transpires in a timely fashion.	Positive	"Great transaction. Fast payment/shipment. Recommended."
Transaction goes through, but buyer/seller is slow or you have to pester the other user to complete the transaction.	Positive	"Item received as described" or "Payment received," accompanied by "a little slow, but otherwise a good seller/buyer."
Transaction is very slow (over a month to completion).	Neutral	"Very slow payment/shipment;" if you're buying, follow by "item received as described."
Other user backs out of transaction, but with a good excuse.	Neutral	"Buyer/seller didn't follow through on sale but had a reasonable excuse."
Other user backs out of transaction without a good excuse, disappears off the face of the earth before paying/shipping, or bounces a check.	Negative	"Buyer/seller didn't complete transaction—avoid!"
Transaction goes through, but item isn't what you expected or was damaged in transit; seller refunds your money.	Positive	"Inaccurate description of item" or "Item was damaged in shipping," followed by "seller refunded money."
Transaction goes through, but item isn't what you expected; seller won't refund your money.	Negative	"Item not as described and seller ignored my complaint—avoid!"

As you can see, there's a proper feedback and response for every situation. Just be sure to think twice before leaving *any* feedback (particularly negative feedback). After you submit your feedback, you can't retract it.

Dealing with Negative Feedback

Many eBay users are zealous about their feedback ratings. Although it's a good thing to want to build up a high rating, some users get quite obsessive about it.

For that reason, you want to be very sure of yourself before you leave negative feedback about a

" **Mike Sez** "

Don't get too upset if you receive the occasional negative feedback; it happens to the best of us—especially those that run a *lot* of auctions. You can't please everyone all the time, and sometimes you make mistakes that justify a negative feedback response. Just try to work out as many issues with other users as you can, and don't let the occasional negative feedback get to you.

user. Some overly zealous users might retaliate by leaving negative feedback about you—even if it wasn't warranted.

Unfortunately, there's not much you can do if you receive negative feedback; under normal conditions, feedback comments cannot be retracted. (There have been some exceptions, when the feedback has been obscene or slanderous in nature.) What you *can* do is offer a response to the feedback, which you do by going to your My eBay Feedback page and clicking the Review and Respond to Feedback About Me link. When the feedback comments list appears, click the Respond link next to a particular comment and then enter your response. Your new comment is listed below the original feedback comment on the Feedback Profile page. Just try not to get defensive; the best response is one that is calm, clear, and well-reasoned.

note

If you and the other user work out your issues, you can agree to mutually withdraw any negative feedback. Complete the form at feedback. ebay.com/ws/eBayISAPI.dll?MFWRequest to initiate the removal process.

THE ABSOLUTE MINIMUM

Here are the key points to remember from this chapter:

- You can use feedback ratings and comments to judge the trustworthiness of other eBay users.

- For quick reference, different levels of feedback ratings are indicated by a different color and type of star.

- You can view other users' feedback by clicking on the feedback rating numbers next to their user names.

- At the end of every auction, you should take the time to leave feedback about the other user—although you should be cautious about leaving negative feedback.

PART V

Becoming a Power Seller

28

USING AUCTION SOFTWARE AND SERVICES

Throughout this book I've mentioned several third-party software programs and services you can use to automate various parts of the online auction process. This chapter is where you get the complete list of products and services, along with some personal comments and recommendations about which are the best to use.

So if you want to make bidding and selling in eBay auctions a little easier—particularly important if you're a high-volume power seller—this chapter is for you!

Listing and Auction Management

If you're running a lot of auctions at one time, you need some way to keep track of which auctions are still open, which have closed, which need emails sent to high bidders, which need to be shipped out, and so on. It also helps if you can somehow automate the listing process itself, and create great-looking HTML-based listings to boot.

Making life easier for eBay power sellers has become somewhat of a cottage industry. There are a large number of software programs and web-based services that handle some or all of the eBay selling process—from ad creation to post-auction management.

The tools listed here are the most popular of what's currently available. Although many perform similar functions, there are a lot of important differences, so pay attention. And know that most of these programs and websites cost real money to use—in some cases, the kind of serious bucks that only big-volume sellers can afford.

All My Auctions

All My Auctions (www.rajeware.com/auction/) is a basic auction management software program. It includes template-based listing creation, live auction management (including the capability to track competitors' auctions), end-of-auction email notification, and report generation. The price is $39.95 for a one-year license.

Ándale

Ándale (www.andale.com) is a site that offers various services for eBay sellers. In fact, it's the only site that offers the full range of tools from pre-auction research to post-auction management.

Ándale's auction tools are first-rate, and they're extremely easy to use. Here's a short list of what's available:

note

In case you're wondering, Ándale is pronounced *on-de-lay*, not *an-dale*.

- Ándale Checkout—Provides one-stop customer checkout, as well as automatic end-of-auction emails
- Ándale Counters—Free traffic counters for your item listings
- Ándale Email Manager—Enables you to mine your customer list for additional sales
- Ándale Gallery—Displays other items you have for sale
- Ándale Images—Image hosting
- Ándale Lister—Bulk listing creation with predesigned templates
- Ándale Lister Pro{md]Offline bulk listing creation
- Ándale Research Tools, including the What's Hot, Price Finder, Suppliers, How to Sell, and Sales Analyzer reports
- Ándale Suppliers—Identify and contact suppliers for specified types of merchandise
- Ándale Store—Your own branded fixed-price online storefront

You have the option of using—and paying for—each of these tools separately; you're not locked into the complete toolkit, unless that's what you want. Although some of these tools can be used free of charge, most carry either a per-month or a per-transaction charge. The individual fees might seem reasonable, but they can add up very quickly. In fact, the thing I like least about Ándale is the cost; depending on which services you subscribe to, you could end up spending more money here than at any other site.

Auction Hawk

Auction Hawk (www.auctionhawk.com) is a web-based service with affordable pricing. The site offers various tools in its main service, including image hosting, bulk listing creation, end-of-auction checkout with automated winning-bidder email, bulk feedback posting, and profit-and-loss reporting.

One nice aspect of Auction Hawk's services is that it doesn't charge any per-transaction or final value fees. In addition, all its services are included in a single price, so you're not nickel-and-dimed to death with a la carte pricing. The full-service monthly plans range in price from $12.99 (for 110 listings) to $89.99 (unlimited listings). At these prices, it's worth checking out.

Auction Lizard

Auction Lizard (www.auction-lizard.com) is an easy-to-use listing-creation software program. It creates great-looking HTML-based listings using forms and templates. Auction Lizard is shareware, with a $29 registration fee.

Auction Wizard 2000

Auction Wizard 2000 (www.auctionwizard2000.com)—that's *wizard*, not *lizard*—is an auction management software program that includes an image editor, a listing creator, a report generator, an FTP manager, and an auction database. Auction Wizard 2000 costs $75 for the first year (and $50 for each subsequent year) with no monthly subscription fees.

AuctionHelper

AuctionHelper (www.auctionhelper.com) offers various auction management tools, including image hosting, customer tracking and invoicing, and inventory management. The site also offers several auction reporting tools.

AuctionHelper charges no monthly fees. (It does, however, have a $10 monthly minimum, which you'll need to plan for.) Instead, the site charges 1.95% of gross merchandise sales, with a minimum $0.15 and a maximum $1.25 charge per auction. It also adds a flat $0.02 fee to each transaction.

AuctionSage

AuctionSage (www.auctionsagesoftware.com) is a software program that lets you post and manage your eBay auction transactions. It also includes email and bulk feedback functions. Cost is $29.95 for 3 months, $49.95 for 6 months, or $79.95 for a year.

AuctionTamer

AuctionTamer (www.auctiontamer.com) is an all-in-one auction management software program for both sellers and bidders. For sellers, it lets you create auction listings, schedule delayed auction listings, manage your live auctions, send post-auction emails, and print shipping labels. Cost is $12.95 per month or $99.95 for a year.

Auctiva

Auctiva (www.auctiva.com) offers a variety of different services, including bulk listing, image hosting, auction tracking and management, and a showcase photo gallery. Several pricing plans are available, starting from $9.95/month (50 listings) all the way up to $109.95/month (unlimited listings).

Auctiva also offers eBud, an interesting auction management tool that tracks all your current and closed auctions in a separate software program that looks and works pretty much like an Excel spreadsheet. Each auction is displayed in a row in the spreadsheet; auction details are displayed in columns. You can use eBud not only to track your auctions, but also to send post-auction emails, print invoices and shipping labels, and generate various eBay sales reports. Auctiva charges $11.95 for eBud subscriptions.

ChannelAdvisor

ChannelAdvisor (www.channeladvisor.com) is the latest incarnation of GoTo.com and Auction Rover, two third-party sites from the early days of the online auction business. The site offers a fairly affordable suite of auction management tools—as well as services for bigger online merchants. The service you want to look at is ChannelAdvisor Pro, which is actually HammerTap Manager in disguise. This service is a surprisingly easy-to-use collection of auction management tools, quite reasonably priced at a flat fee of just $29.95 per month. If you're doing more than 50 auctions a month, it's definitely worth considering—even more so if you're a heavier lister.

eBay Seller's Assistant

Although Turbo Lister is eBay's recommended listing creation software, the site still offers an older program called eBay Seller's Assistant. Seller's Assistant is available in two different versions: Basic and Pro.

Seller's Assistant Basic (pages.ebay.com/sellers_assistant/basic.html) is best for casual users, offering HTML-based listing creation (using forms and templates), auction tracking, and basic post-auction management (including automatic email notification and feedback generation). The software is available on a per-month subscription; you'll pay $9.99 each month, no matter how many listings you create.

Seller's Assistant Pro (pages.ebay.com/sellers_assistant/pro.html) is a more powerful software-based tool for high-volume sellers. This program is essentially SA Basic on steroids, with many more post-auction management features. In particular, you get inventory management, sales management and reporting, bulk feedback posting, and the ability to print invoices and shipping labels—in addition to the standard bulk listing creation and end-of-auction emails. The program costs $24.99 per month, and comes with a free subscription to eBay Selling Manager Pro. Use it with eBay's standard checkout feature, and you're in business.

eBay Selling Manager

As you learned in Chapter 20, "Automating Auction Management with eBay Selling Manager," Selling Manager (pages.ebay.com/selling_manager/) lets you manage your pending, in-process, and closed auctions right from within My eBay. It's a fairly complete service, equal to that offered by many third-party providers. It includes predefined email templates and automatic feedback forms, automatically tracks buyer checkout and payment, and lets you print shipping labels, invoices, and reports. At

$4.99 per month, it's a pretty good deal—definitely worth checking out if you have a lot of auctions to manage.

eBay Selling Manager Pro

The more robust Selling Manager Pro (pages.ebay.com/selling_manager_pro/) adds features of value to power sellers, including bulk listing and relisting, bulk email, inventory management, report generation, and the capability to create and print shipping labels. The subscription fee is $15.99 per month.

eBay Turbo Lister

eBay Turbo Lister (pages.ebay.com/turbo_lister/) is eBay's official software program for the bulk uploading of multiple auctions. Although Turbo Lister doesn't offer any auction tracking features, it excels at bulk uploading—and it's free! Many sellers use Turbo Lister to create their listings and Selling Manager to manage their auctions; it's a good combination.

Learn more about eBay Turbo Lister in Chapter 17, "Automating Item Listing with eBay Turbo Lister."

HammerTap

HammerTap (www.hammertap.com) offers various auction management software and services, all priced separately. These tools include the following:

- HammerTap Manager—web-based auction posting and management
- Auction Informant—Software that sends you email alerts when your items receive bids
- BayCheck and BayCheck Pro—Software for background checks of eBay users
- BayMail and BayMail Pro—Software for sending emails to eBay users
- BidderBlock—Software for managing blocked bidder lists
- DeepAnalysis—Auction research tool
- FeeFinder—Software for calculating eBay, PayPal, and shipping fees

HammerTap Manager is the same service as ChannelAdvisor Pro, just under a different name.

Each of these tools is priced separately, so you can pick and choose among those you actually need. The basic HammerTap Manager service runs a flat $29.95 per month.

inkFrog

inkFrog (www.inkfrog.com) is a cute name for some heavy-duty web-based auction management services. inkFrog offers auction listing, tracking, and management, along with image hosting and listing creation and design. Various plans are offered, starting at $7.95 per month.

ManageAuctions

ManageAuctions (www.manageauctions.com) offers web-based listing creation, auction tracking, email notification, shipping label printing, feedback generation, and other post-auction management. Pricing is on an a la carte basis; listings cost $0.05 each and post-sale management is $0.05 per auction. There's a minimum monthly charge of $4.95, and a maximum of $24.95; image hosting is extra.

Marketworks

Marketworks (www.marketworks.com), formerly known as Auctionworks, is one of the oldest and most established third-party auction management services. The site offers various professional auction tools, including inventory management, a bulk listing creator, traffic counters, image hosting, automatic end-of-auction emails, a checkout system, reciprocal feedback posting, web-based storefronts, and customizable reports.

Marketworks charges no monthly fees for its service, instead opting for a 2% fee on each successful transaction, with a $0.20 minimum and $3.00 maximum fee per transaction. The site caters to high-volume sellers, however; their minimum monthly fee is $29.95.

Shooting Star

Shooting Star (www.foodogsoftware.com) is a software program designed to manage the end-of-auction process. It uses what it calls a "workflow system" to move you through various post-auction operations, including email notification. Price is a one-time $49.95.

SpareDollar

SpareDollar (www.sparedollar.com) is low-priced auction service, ideal for small or occasional sellers. It's extremely affordable, with everything offered for a flat $4.95 per month price.

SpareDollar's auction tools include the following:

- sdCounter—Traffic counters for your item listings
- sdGallery—Photo gallery of all your auction items
- sdImage—50MB of image hosting
- sdLister—Bulk listing creation with predesigned templates
- sdTracker—Post-auction tracking and emails

While SpareDollar is attractively priced, its services might prove too limited for really high-volume sellers. That said, many high-volume sellers do use SpareDollar, and are quite happy with the results. Give it a try to see if it fits your particular eBay business.

Vendio

Vendio (www.vendio.com), formerly known as Auctionwatch, is one of the top two auction management services. Vendio claims 125,000 sellers use its services, which makes it a very popular site.

Vendio Sales Manager is a powerful set of listing creation and auction management tools. You can use Sales Manager not only to create new item listings, but also to manage all of your current and post-auction activity. Sales Manager will automatically generate end-of-auction emails, print invoices and packing slips, and upload customer feedback to eBay.

Vendio offers Sales Manager in both Inventory and Merchandising Editions; the mix of features is a little different between the two, but the pricing is the same. The company tries to appeal to different types of sellers by offering a mix of fixed and variable priced monthly subscriptions.

For example, the Sales Manager Pay as You Go Plan carries no fixed fee, although you'll pay $0.10 per transaction and a 1% final value fee. On the other hand, the Sales Manager Variable Rate Power Plan costs $29.95 a month, but with no listing fee and a 1.25% final value fee; and the Flat Rate Power Plan costs $39.95 a month, with a $0.10 per-transaction charge but no final value fee. Confusing? You bet—but it does let you choose the type of payment (flat versus variable versus per-transaction) that best suits your needs.

I like Vendio's tools almost as much as Ándale's—although the range of tools isn't quite as wide. (No research, for example.) The variable-rate pricing is actually a little more

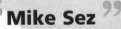

" Mike Sez "

Of all these auction management tools, I still like the combination of eBay Turbo Lister/Selling Manager, especially for small sellers. For more active eBay sellers, I like either Ándale, SpareDollar, or Vendio, all of which offer a wide variety of very professional tools.

attractive to me, especially because my sales volume varies from month to month. And I like the fact that Vendio doesn't nickel-and-dime me to death. All in all, a service definitely worth your consideration.

Sniping and Bidding Tools

Just as there are a lot of third-party tools for eBay sellers, there also are various software and services designed for serious eBay buyers. Most of these programs and websites help you track auctions you're interested in, and then perform automated last-minute bidding—otherwise known as sniping. (If you don't remember sniping, refer to Chapter 9, "Secrets of Successful Bidders.")

Auction Sentry

Auction Sentry (www.auction-sentry.com) is a software program for auction tracking, bidding, and sniping. You can use Auction Sentry just to watch auctions you're interested in, to alert you when someone else makes a bid on an item, to place instant bids, or to make scheduled snipes. The Auction Sentry program costs $14.95.

Auction Sniper

Auction Sniper (www.auctionsniper.com) is a web-based sniping service with more than 70,000 registered users. You're charged 1% of the final value fee, with a minimum charge of $0.25 and a maximum of $5.

AuctionStealer

AuctionStealer (www.auctionstealer.com) is a web-based service that lets you track an unlimited number of auctions and perform unattended auction sniping. The site claims to have sniped more than 7 million auctions to date, and to have more than 300,000 active registered users. The site offers both a free service and a more fully featured priority service that costs $11.99 per month, $29.99 for 3 months, or $49.99 for 6 months.

AuctionTamer

We discussed AuctionTamer (www.auctiontamer.com) back in the "Listing and Auction Management" section, because it's a tool for both bidders and sellers. For bidders, it lets you search and track auctions across multiple auction sites, save and repeat your most popular item searches, automatically snipe auctions, and leave feedback on items you've won. You pay $2.95 per month (or $24.95 a year) for AuctionTamer's Buyer Access Plan; seller features are extra.

BidNapper

BidNapper (www.bidnapper.com) is a web-based subscription sniping service that costs $9.95 for 1 month, $16.95 for 3 months, $26.95 for 6 months, or $45.95 for 12 months. If you're an infrequent bidder, consider the "$19.95 for 10 winning snipes" package.

BidRobot

BidRobot (www.bidrobot.com) is a web-based sniping service with more than 70,000 users. Pricing is $19.95 for 6 months or $34.95 for 12 months.

BidSlammer

BidSlammer (www.bidslammer.com) is a web-based sniping service. Cost is $0.10 per losing bid or 1% of the winning bid price if you win—with a minimum charge of $0.25 and a maximum charge of $5.00.

Cricket Power Sniper

Cricket Power Sniper (www.cricketsniper.com) is a simple, easy-to-use eBay sniping program. It costs $19.99.

eSnipe

eSnipe (www.esnipe.com) is a web-based sniping tool that claims more than 100,000 users. The site charges $0.25 or 1% of the final value fee (up to a $10 maximum) for each successful snipe.

HammerSnipe

HammerSnipe (www.hammertap.com) is a web-based sniping service that comes with its own customized browser, called HammerSnipe PowerTool. The PowerTool software is free, as is the basic ad-supported service.

Vrane

Vrane's public sniping tool (www.vrane.com/snp.html) is a web-based service that lets you place one snipe at a time. To place more than one snipe, you can sign up for their Gold service, which

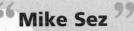
Mike Sez

I don't really have a favorite among these sniping programs and services. However, I do prefer the sniping sites over the software, because you don't have to bother with having your computer on and connected to the Internet for the sniping to take place. (It's important to note that the sniping sites typically charge a percentage of your winning bid—whereas the sniping programs have only a one-time purchase price.)

operates on a somewhat unusual credit basis. You can purchase 450 credits for $7.99, and use them as necessary.

THE ABSOLUTE MINIMUM

Here are the key points to remember from this chapter:

- Many big websites offer news, education, community, and auction management services for online auction users—particularly for power sellers.

- If you're a power seller (listing dozens of auctions every week), check out sites like Ándale or Vendio.

- If you're a smaller seller (listing a half-dozen or fewer auctions a week), eBay's combination of Turbo Lister and Selling Manager does a good job at an affordable price.

- If you're a serious eBay buyer, consider using a sniping service or software program to automate your last-second bids.

- Whichever programs or services you use, remember to factor the cost of the software/service into your overall auction costs.

29

GOING INTERNATIONAL

If you're a seller doing any amount of volume on eBay, you will sooner or later be faced with an interesting situation: someone from outside the United States bidding on one of your items. Becoming an international seller sounds exotic and glamorous, but the honor comes with an increase in paperwork and effort on your part. Although you might be able to increase the number of potential bidders by offering your merchandise outside the United States, you also increase your workload—and, more important, your risk.

Should you sell internationally? And if so, how do you handle payment and shipping and all those other niggling details? Read on to learn more about international sales via eBay—as well as hear my own opinion on the subject.

Pros and Cons of Selling Internationally

Let's start with the big question: Should you sell internationally? The answer to this isn't a simple one. It depends a lot on your tolerance for differences (in money, in language, in routine), and your ability to deal with unusual post-auction activity—especially in regard to payment and shipping.

The pros of opening your auctions to non-U.S. bidders include the following:

- You might be able to attract additional bidders—and thus sell more items at (presumably) higher prices.
- You can offset some of the seasonality of the U.S. market; when it's winter here, you can still be selling swim suits to the summer market in Australia.
- You establish a reputation as a hard-working global trader.
- It's fun (sometimes) to interact with people from different countries and cultures.

The cons of selling outside the Unites States include the following:

- You might run into difficulties communicating with bidders from outside the United States.
- You might have to deal with payment in non-U.S. funds, on non-U.S. banks.
- You'll have to put extra effort into the packing of an item to be shipped over great distances.
- You probably won't be able to use your standard shipping services—which means investigating new shipping services and options.
- Shipping costs will be higher than what you're used to—and will need to be passed on to the buyer.
- You'll need to deal with the appropriate paperwork for shipping outside the United States—including those pesky customs forms.
- If there are any problems or disputes with the item shipped, you have an international-sized incident on your hands.

Just looking at this list, it may appear that the cons outweigh the pros. That might not always be the case, however—especially if you're a real "people person." Many eBay sellers get great joy from interacting with people from different cultures, sometimes turning foreign buyers into lasting friends. I can vouch from my limited personal experience that most non-U.S. buyers I've dealt with are exceedingly polite and tolerant of the extra effort required to complete an international transaction.

If you decide to sell outside the United States, you'll want to state this in your auctions, along with a line indicating that "shipping and handling outside the United States is higher," "listed shipping charge is for United States only," or something to that effect. If, on the other hand, you decide *not* to sell internationally, state that in your ad also—with a "U.S. bidders only" type of notice.

Selling Outside the United States

If you decide to take the leap and open your auctions to an international audience, you need to be prepared for a new world of activities—no pun intended. Selling outside the United States—especially the shipping part of the process—is much different from selling to someone in New York or California. Although I can't prepare you for all the issues you might encounter, I will point out some of the bigger hassles to look out for.

Communicating with International Bidders

One of the joys—and challenges—of selling internationally is communicating with non-U.S. bidders. Although citizens of many countries speak English, not all do—or do so well. This means you're likely to receive emails in fractured English, or in some language that you might not be able to easily translate.

The solution to this problem isn't always easy. It's one thing to say you should send non-English-language emails back to the buyer, requesting communication in English. But if the buyer can't read or write English, how is he supposed to read your request? This problem is a tricky one.

> **" Mike Sez "**
>
> My personal opinions on international sales are sure to invite argument. No offense to non-U.S. users, but I don't ship internationally, period. I've done it in the past, and the hassle factor simply isn't worth it. Even if the transaction goes smoothly (and it often doesn't, all things considered), the big issue is that the procedures involved are just too different from what I have set up for my normal day-to-day auction activities. In other words, international auctions are unusual transactions that mess up my normal domestic auction production line. My apologies to buyers outside the United States—most of whom I've found to be wonderful people to deal with—but I can't let my normal activity be jeopardized by these high-maintenance shipments. (I do, however, make the occasional exception—primarily with small items shipping into Canada that can be handled without much additional paperwork or hassle.)

I have found, however, that communication goes more smoothly if you keep your written communications short and simple. Use straightforward wording, and avoid slang terms and abbreviations.

In addition, you have to deal with the time difference between the United States and many other countries. If you're dealing with a buyer in the Far East, you're sleeping while he's sending emails, and vice versa. This introduces an unavoidable lag into the communication that can sometimes be problematic.

The only advice I can give you here is to be aware of the time differences, and plan accordingly. Don't expect an immediate response from someone on a different continent, and try to avoid the kind of back-and-forth communications that can go on for days and days.

Accepting Foreign Payments

One of the issues with selling outside the United States is in dealing with foreign currency. First, you have to convert it to U.S. dollars. (How many lira to the dollar today?) Then you have to receive it in a form that is both secure and trusted. (Do you trust a personal check drawn on a small Spanish bank?) Then you have to find a way to deposit those funds—and convert them to U.S. dollars. (Does your bank handle foreign deposits?)

tip

When you need to convert foreign funds, use the Universal Currency Converter (www.xe.net/ucc/).

The currency issue is simplified somewhat when you specify bidding and payment in U.S. funds only. This puts the onus of currency conversion on the buyer, which is a plus.

The payment process can be further simplified when the buyer pays by credit card—or, even better, by PayPal. PayPal is now active in 45 countries (including the United States) and can handle all the payment, conversion, and deposit functions for you.

Another good method of payment for non-U.S. buyers is international money orders—in particular, via BidPay (www.bidpay.com), formerly known as Western Union Auction Payments. The buyers pay BidPay via credit card, and BidPay sends you a U.S. money order. Simplicity itself.

Shipping Across Borders—And Oceans

The biggest difficulty in selling to non-U.S. buyers is shipping the item. Not only are longer distances involved (which necessitates more secure packaging—and longer shipping times), but you also have to deal with different shipping options and all sorts of new paperwork.

Chances are your normal method of shipping won't work for your international shipments. For example, you can't use Priority Mail to ship outside the United States—not even to Canada or Mexico. This means you'll need to evaluate new shipping methods, and possibly new shipping services.

If you want to stick with the U.S. Postal Service, you can check out Global Priority Mail (reasonably fast and reasonably priced), Global Express Mail (fast but expensive), Airmail (almost as fast, not quite as expensive), or Surface/Parcel Post (slow but less expensive). In addition, UPS offers its Worldwide Express service, FedEx offers its FedEx Express service internationally, and DHL is always a good option for shipping outside the United States. Be sure to check out your options beforehand, and charge the buyer the actual costs incurred.

tip

Given the increased chances of loss or damage when shipping great distances, you should purchase insurance for all items shipping outside North America

You'll also have to deal with a bit of paperwork while you're preparing your shipment. All packages shipping outside U.S. borders must clear customs to enter the destination country—and require the completion of specific customs forms to make the trip. Depending on the type of item you're shipping and the weight of your package, you'll need either Form 2976 (green) or Form 2976-A (white). Both of these forms should be available at your local post office.

When you're filling out these forms, describe the item in terms that ordinary people can understand. That means using simple, generic terms. A "greatest hits CD compilation" becomes "compact disc." A "SimCity extension pack" becomes "video game." And so on.

You should also be honest about what you're shipping. Some buyers will try to talk you into describing the item as a gift so that they can save on duties or tax on their end. That's lying, and you shouldn't do it.

tip

eBay offers several pages of advice for international trading at pages.ebay.com/internationaltrading/.

In addition, there are certain items you can't ship to foreign countries—firearms, live animals and animal products, and so on. (There are also some technology items you can't ship, for security reasons.) You need to check the government's list of import and export restrictions to see what items you're prohibited from shipping outside U.S. borders. Check with your shipping service for more detailed information.

Finally, note that shipping across borders takes longer than shipping within the United States. This is especially true if an item is held up at customs. Make sure your international buyers know that shipping times will be longer than what you might state for domestic buyers.

eBay's International Marketplaces

To better participate in marketplaces outside the United States, eBay has established separate sites for 25 foreign countries. Each of these sites lists items in the country's native language, using the local currency. (You can see this in Figure 29.1, which shows the eBay Germany site.)

FIGURE 29.1

One of eBay's many international sites: eBay Germany.

The list of eBay's international sites includes the following:

- Argentina (www.mercadolibre.com.ar)
- Australia (www.ebay.com.au)
- Austria (www.ebay.at)
- Belgium (www.ebay.be)
- Brazil (www.mercadolivre.com.br)
- Canada (www.ebay.ca)
- China (www.ebay.com.cn)
- France (www.ebay.fr)
- Germany (www.ebay.de)
- Hong Kong (www.ebay.com.hk)
- India (www.baazee.com)
- Ireland (pages.ebay.com/ie/)

- Italy (www.ebay.it)
- Korea (www.auction.co.kr)
- Malaysia (www.ebay.com.my)
- Mexico (www.mercadolibre.com.mx)
- Netherlands (www.ebay.nl)
- New Zealand (pages.ebay.com/nz/)
- Philippines (www.ebay.ph)
- Singapore (www.ebay.com.sg)
- Spain (www.ebay.com.es)
- Sweden (www.ebaysweden.com/)
- Switzerland (www.ebay.ch)
- Taiwan (www.tw.ebay.com)
- United Kingdom (www.ebay.co.uk)

Although these sites were designed for trading within a specific country, there's nothing keeping you from searching them for items to buy—which will put you on the opposite side of the international buyer/seller argument!

THE ABSOLUTE MINIMUM

Here are the key points to remember from this chapter:

- When dealing with non-U.S. buyers, be sure to specify payment in U.S. funds—ideally via PayPal or an international money order.
- Shipping outside the United States requires the completion of customs forms (available at your local post office) and the use of special international shipping services.
- eBay offers 25 country-specific online auction sites (in addition to the main U.S. site), for trading within each local region.

30

MAKING A LIVING FROM EBAY

Chances are you're just starting out on your online auction adventures—learning how to buy and sell and take advantage of everything eBay has to offer. As you gain more experience, however, you may decide that you're pretty good at the whole thing, and start to wonder what it might take to ramp up your eBay activities. You might even dream about one day making your living from selling goods online.

For tens of thousands of eBay users, making a living from online auctions isn't a dream—it's reality. It's definitely possible to sell enough items to generate a livable income from eBay auctions. It takes a lot of hard work and it's as complex as running any other business; but it can be done.

Let me tell you how.

Becoming an eBay PowerSeller

One of the steps to running your own eBay business—although not a requirement, by any means—is to become an eBay PowerSeller. eBay's 100,000-plus PowerSellers generate enough business to warrant special attention from eBay, in the form of dedicated customer support, premier tools, and the occasional special offer. Plus they get to display that cool PowerSeller logo in all their auction listings.

To become a PowerSeller, you must meet the following qualifications:

- Maintain a consistently high level of eBay sales (see Table 30.1)
- Maintain a minimum of four average monthly total item listings for three straight months
- Have been an active eBay seller for at least 90 days
- Achieve and maintain a minimum feedback rating of 100, 98% positive
- Deliver post-auction messages to successful bidders within three business days of each auction close
- Be an eBay member in good standing and uphold eBay's "community values"—including honesty, timeliness, and mutual respect

The most important point is the first, because it's the most quantifiable. There are five levels in the PowerSeller program; qualification for each level is based on average gross monthly sales, calculated over the past three months of selling activity. Table 30.1 shows the qualifying requirements for each level.

Table 30.1 PowerSeller Requirements, by Level

Level	Requirement (average monthly sales)
Bronze	$1,000
Silver	$3,000
Gold	$10,000
Platinum	$25,000
Titanium	$150,000

note

That's right, there are some eBay sellers who average $150,000 or more a month. That's almost two million dollars a year in revenues from eBay auctions—no slight accomplishment!

Membership in eBay's PowerSellers program is free. However, you can't apply; PowerSeller status is by invitation only. Each month eBay

To keep your PowerSeller status, you have to *maintain* this sales rate. If your sales drop below these levels, eBay will give you 30 days to bring your account back into compliance; if you don't, your membership in the program will be revoked. (You're free to requalify at a later date, however.)

sends out invitations to sellers who meet the PowerSeller criteria. You become a member by (1) meeting the criteria; (2) receiving an invitation; and (3) responding positively to the invitation.

Want to see whether you qualify? Then go to the main PowerSeller's page (pages.ebay.com/services/buyandsell/welcome.html) and click the Check Here to See If I Qualify link. eBay will calculate your recent sales and tell you whether you qualify.

Turning Your Online Auctions into a Real Business

How easy is it to turn your online auction hobby into a profitable business? It's all a matter of volume—and good business planning and management.

Let's consider an example. Caitlin has found a source for iron-on transfers for T-shirts and sweatshirts. She can buy these transfers for $1 each and (based on her experience and research) can sell them on eBay for an average price of $5. That's four dollars profit for every transfer she sells.

Caitlin has huddled over her copy of Quicken and determined that she needs to generate $30,000 in profit (*not* in revenues!) to make her eBay business worthwhile. Assuming that she works 50 weeks a year (everyone needs a vacation), that means she needs to average $600 in profit each week. At $4 profit per item, she has to sell an average of 150 iron-on transfers a week—each and every week.

Because only about half of all eBay auctions end with a sale, Caitlin knows that to sell those 150 items she has to launch 300 auctions each week. That's a lot of work, as you can imagine.

Can Caitlin make a go of it? It depends. Can she physically manage 300 auctions a week? Can she pack and ship 150 items a week? And, more important, can she realistically *sell* 150 items a week—is the market big enough to support that sort of sales volume?

If Caitlin answers yes to all those questions, there's still more planning to be done. To begin with, this example greatly simplifies the costs involved. Caitlin will need to figure eBay's costs for all those auctions—the listing fees for 300 auctions, and the final value fees for 150 completions. If she accepts PayPal payments, she'll need to determine what percentage of her buyers will use PayPal, and what her fees for those transactions will amount to. Assuming that she uses a third-party website to help her launch and manage those auctions, she'll also need to figure those fees into her cost structure.

All totaled, these auction listing and management costs can add up to 5%–10% of her revenues. That means increasing her cost per item from $1.00 to $1.50 or more—which reduces her profit per item to just $3.50. With this reduced profit margin, she'll need to sell even more items to hit her profit dollar targets—an extra 20 or so successful auctions each week.

All this needs to be factored in—before Caitlin launches a single auction. And at these volume levels she's definitely running a business, which means reporting the income to the IRS and paying taxes. There's also the matter of *sales taxes*, which she'll need to collect on all sales made to buyers in her home state.

The takeaway here is that making a living from eBay sales is just like running a business, especially in its financial complexities. Anyone contemplating this type of endeavor should do some serious business planning, which should include consulting an accountant or another financial planner.

If the numbers work out, you need to answer one more question: Is this something you'll enjoy doing every day of the week, every week of the year? Even if you can make money at it, managing hundreds of auctions a week can wear down even the best of us. Make sure that you're up to it, and that you'll enjoy it, before you take the leap.

note

Turning your eBay sales into a real business is a major undertaking. If you're serious about making the leap from occasional seller to full-time merchant, check out my companion book, *Making a Living from Your eBay Business* (Que, 2005), available wherever business books are sold.

Maintaining Your Sales Inventory

If you need to be launching several hundred auctions a week, where do you find all those items to list? It's a simple fact that you can't become a power seller by listing onesies and twosies. Instead, you need to find an item you can buy in bulk, and then list multiples of that item week after week.

Although beginning eBayers can find items to sell by haunting flea markets and estate auctions, power sellers most likely won't find what they need in those venues. A better strategy is to approach local retailers or wholesalers and offer to buy 10 or 20 (or more) of a particular item. Buy whatever quantity earns you the best price break—as long as you think you can move them.

You can also buy bulk lots of merchandise from online wholesalers and liquidators. We discussed some of these sites in Chapter 11, "Determining What to Sell—And for How Much." Check out Liquidation.com (www.liquidation.com) and Wholesale411 (www.wholesale411.com) to see what's available, or use Ándale Suppliers (www.andale.com) to hook up with suppliers of specific types of merchandise.

If you're a serious collector, you might have your eBay business right there. When your comics collection numbers in the tens of thousands, or you have thousands of rare coins filed away in your basement, you're ready for power selling—and power buying. Just remember to buy low and sell high, and you'll be in business.

Finally, consider the selling price of the items you want to sell—and the profit you generate on each item. You have to sell a lot more of a $5 item than you do of a $50 item to make the same amount of profit. (Assuming both generate a similar profit percentage.) And, of course, the more items you sell, the more work you have to do. The most successful power sellers do it by selling higher-priced, higher-profit items, for which the revenues—and the profits—add up a lot quicker.

Automating Your Auction Activities

Managing hundreds of simultaneous auctions is hard work. Most power sellers end up working more than a standard 8-hour day, and more than five days a week. (eBay reports that most of their PowerSellers work anywhere from 10 to 16 hours a day on their auctions!) The time it takes to find new items to sell, photograph them, write detailed item descriptions, post the auctions, send post-auction emails, and pack and ship all those items quickly adds up.

note

See Chapter 28, "Using Auction Software and Services," to learn more about the services offered by these auction management sites.

The more auctions you list, the more it behooves you to automate as much of the auction process as possible. For most power sellers, that means signing up with one of the big websites that offer bulk listing and post-auction management, such as Ándale (www.andale.com), SpareDollar (www.sparedollar.com), or Vendio (www.vendio.com). Be sure to factor the site's fees into your cost structure, and let them help you manage all your auctions.

You should also try to automate your physical auction activity. That means creating some sort of auction "office" or workspace in your home. This workspace should include everything you need in order to create auction listings (including your digital camera and scanner) and to pack and ship your finished auction items. In addition, you'll need space to store all your excess auction inventory; this may be your basement or garage, or even a rented storage locker.

Automating your processes also means establishing some sort of auction-related schedule. Pick one or two days a week to launch all your auctions; pick one or two days to visit the post office. Stick to your schedule and you'll avoid running around like a chicken with your head cut off; after all, dead chickens aren't known for their business efficiency.

On the subject of shipping, you should try to simplify your packing and shipping activities as much as possible. This means limiting the types of items you sell to just a few so that you can standardize on packaging. It's much easier to stock just one or two different-sized boxes than it is to store a dozen or more sizes. If you sell a limited variety of merchandise, you'll also be able to better estimate your shipping costs ahead of time.

Using Caitlin's iron-on transfer business as an example, this is a great item to sell. She's dealing with a standard-size product that's both flat and light—ideal for shipping in an oversized envelope, at a flat rate. This means she can not only purchase shipping envelopes in bulk, but also purchase postage ahead of time—and eliminate those regular trips to the post office.

Tracking Revenues and Costs

Every business should keep detailed records, and your online auction business is no exception. Whether you use an auction management service that offers report generation, a financial-management program like Quicken, or your own homemade spreadsheet or database, you need to track what you're doing.

In particular, you want to track unit cost and final selling price for every auction you list. You should also track all your ancillary costs—shipping, PayPal fees, eBay listing and final value fees, and so on. By tracking all your costs and revenues, you can generate an accurate profit and loss statement, and thus determine how much money (if any) you're generating from your online auction activities.

It also helps to track information about the buyers of your auction items—name, shipping address, email address, and so on. The name and shipping address are necessary in case an item gets lost in transit; the email address is necessary not only for auction-related communication but also for promotional purposes—which we'll discuss next.

Promoting Your Online Auctions

If you're running a hundred or more auctions a week, you want to draw attention to your auctions. That might mean splurging for some of eBay's listing enhancements (boldface, gallery, and so on), although these extras typically aren't worth the extra cost. Better to promote your auctions on your personal website, via message board postings, and in all your emails.

Probably the most important type of promotion, however, is word of mouth—based on your good reputation. You want to encourage repeat bidders and drive buyers into your online store (if you have one) for additional sales. That means treating your buyers fairly and with respect, and going the extra mile to ensure their satisfaction. It also means sending previous buyers emails when you have items up for auction that they might be interested in. (Which argues, of course, for keeping comprehensive records of all your eBay auctions.)

Supplementing Your Auctions with an eBay Store

The final step in your creation of a successful eBay business is to set up your own online storefront to offer additional merchandise to your auction customers. If you're selling printer cartridges, direct your buyers to your online store selling paper and other printer supplies. If you're selling collectibles, direct your buyers to your online store selling non-auction collectibles. Or, in Caitlin's example, she can direct buyers of her iron-on transfers to her store selling T-shirts and sweatshirts—as well as additional transfers.

Setting up your own online storefront is surprisingly easy to do, thanks to a service called eBay Stores. An eBay Store is an online storefront where professional eBay merchants market fixed-price goods, in addition to their traditional auction items. If you're a heavy seller thinking of making the move into real honest-to-goodness retailing, eBay Stores is a relatively painless way to start.

You access the eBay Stores home page at www.stores.ebay.com.

> **tip**
>
> Another benefit of selling merchandise in an eBay Store is that eBay will automatically advertise items from your store on the Bid Confirmation and Checkout Confirmation pages it displays to bidders in your regular auctions. These "merchandising placements" help you cross-sell additional merchandise to your auction customers.

Do You Qualify?

Just about any seller can open an eBay Store. All you have to do is meet the following criteria:

- Be a registered eBay seller, with a credit card on file
- Have a feedback rating of 20 or more, or be ID verified
- Accept credit cards for all fixed-price sales

Given that accepting credit cards can mean using PayPal, you can see that you don't actually have to be a big traditional retailer to open an eBay Store. Any individual meeting the requirements can also open an eBay Store, thus making eBay Stores a great way for entrepreneurial types to get started in retailing.

Why would you want to open your own eBay Store? Well, it certainly isn't for casual sellers; you do have to set up your own web page, and keep the store filled with merchandise. But if you're a high-volume seller who specializes in a single category (or even a handful of categories), there are benefits to opening your own store. These include being able to sell more merchandise (through your store) than you can otherwise list in auctions; being able to display a special eBay Stores icon next to all of your auction lists; and being able to generate repeat business from future sales to current purchasers.

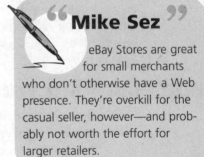

"Mike Sez"

eBay Stores are great for small merchants who don't otherwise have a Web presence. They're overkill for the casual seller, however—and probably not worth the effort for larger retailers.

The Costs of Running an eBay Store

Naturally, it costs money to open an eBay Store. (eBay isn't in this for the betterment of mankind, after all.) You pay a monthly fee to be an eBay Store merchant, and there are three subscription levels to choose from, as shown in Table 30.2.

TABLE 30.2 eBay Stores Subscription Levels

Subscription	Price	Description
Basic	$15.95/month	Store listed in every category directory where you have items listed; position based on number of items listed; receive monthly store reports; send 100 emails a month to buyers; create 5 customizable pages; free subscription to eBay Selling Manager

Subscription	Price	Description
Featured	$49.95/month	All features of Basic, plus store rotated through a special featured section on the eBay Stores home page; store receives priority placement in Related Stores section of search and listings pages; store featured within the top-level category pages where you have items listed; cross-sell products on view item pages; receive more detailed monthly reports; create 10 customizable pages; send 1,000 emails a month to buyers; and you get a free subscription to Selling Manager Pro and promotional dollars to spend on the eBay Keyword program
Anchor	$499.95/month	All features of Featured, plus premium placement in Related Stores section of search and listings pages; your store logo rotates through category directory pages (1 million impressions); send 4,000 emails a month to buyers; create 15 customizable pages; and you get dedicated 24-hour live customer support

You also have to pay eBay for each item you list and each item you sell—just as in a normal auction. The difference is you're not listing for a (relatively short) auction; you're listing for longer-term inventory.

Table 30.3 details the insertion fees that eBay charges for eBay Stores listings. Note that eBay allows listings of up to 120 days in length—although the longer listings carry an insertion fee surcharge.

> **tip**
>
> eBay also offers a Good 'Til Cancelled option, which automatically relists unsold items every 30 days. The cost is $0.02 for each 30-day period.

TABLE 30.3   eBay Stores Insertion Fees

Listing Length	Insertion Fee (Plus Surcharge)
30 days	$0.02
60 days	$0.02 + $0.02
90 days	$0.02 + $0.04
120 days	$0.02 + $0.06

For every item you sell in your eBay Store, eBay charges a final value fee. Table 30.4 lists the final value fees.

TABLE 30.4   eBay Stores Final Value Fees

Closing Value	Fee
$0.01–$25	8%
$25–$1,000	8% on first $25 *plus* 5% on remaining balance
$1,000 and up	8% on first $25 *plus* 5% on the part between $25.01 and $1,000 *plus* 3% on the remaining balance

eBay Stores also offers a full assortment of listing upgrades, just like the ones you can use in regular eBay auctions. These enhancements—gallery, bold, highlight, and so on—are priced according to the length of your listing. You can also offer multiples of the same item in Dutch auction format.

Setting Up Your eBay Store

Opening your own eBay store is as easy as clicking through eBay's setup pages. There's nothing overly complex involved; you'll need to create your store, customize your pages (otherwise known as your virtual storefront), and list the items you want to sell. Just follow the onscreen instructions, and you'll have your own store up and running in just a few minutes.

When you're ready to set up your store, go to the eBay Stores home page and click the Open a Store button. When you accept the user agreement, the store creation process begins. On seceding pages you'll be asked to choose a store theme, enter a store name and description, provide a logo (or choose from supplied clipart), and then choose a subscription level. On the last page you'll click the Start My Subscription Now button, and then eBay will create your store. It's that simple!

THE ABSOLUTE MINIMUM

Here are the key points to remember from this chapter:

- If you're selling more than $1,000 per month, you may be eligible for eBay's PowerSeller program.

- To turn your eBay hobby into a money-making profession, you need to start with some detailed business and financial planning.

- Most power sellers specialize in a specific type of item—and buy it in bulk.

- Successful eBay businesses keep detailed records and perform regular analyses of their auction activities.

- The more auctions you list, the more value you'll get from third-party auction management sites and services.

- Opening an eBay Store is a good way to sell various fixed-price merchandise through the eBay system.

- When you start making a living from your eBay auctions, be sure to engage the services of a qualified accountant—to manage your tax liabilities, if nothing else.

Index

G - H

I

symbols, titling item listings, 173

synchronizing bids (bidding tips), 112

T

taxes
  auction strategies, 290
  sales taxes, PowerSellers, 342

templates (item listings), 198-199

text
  auction strategies, 283
  format codes (HTML), 202
    bold text, 203
    centering text, 203
    first-level headlines, 203
    horizontal rule codes, 204
    italic text, 203
    line break codes, 204
    new paragraph codes, 204
    second-level headlines, 203
    third-level headlines, 203
    underline text, 203

third-level headline text format codes (HTML), 203

third-party listing-creation tools, 200

third-party Web hosts, loading image files to, 193-194

thrift stores, 145

timing auctions (auction strategies), 285-286

timing bids (bidding tips), 112

title searches, 99

titling item listings, 37, 172-173

"too good to be true" deals (bidding tips), 109

tracking
  auctions, tips and strategies, 113, 287
  bids, 49
  revenue/costs (PowerSellers), 344
  shipments, 264

tracking tools (auctions)
  Auction Sentry software, 327
  Auction Sniper website, 327
  AuctionStealer website, 327
  BidNapper website, 328
  BidRobot website, 328
  BidSlammer website, 328
  Cricket Power Sniper software, 328

Trading Assistant Directory website, 277

transactions
  backing out of, 90
  fees, 9
  intercepting, 90

trends, 144

tripods (digital cameras), 185

trucking services (shipping & handling), 260

"try again tomorrow" (bidding tips), 110-111

Turbo Lister, 199, 282
  auction management, 324
  configuring, 208-209
  Create a New Item screen, 209
  downloading, 208
  Enter Multiple Items screen, 213

Format Specifics screen, 212
item listings
  creating, 209-214
  uploading, 215-216

U

underline text format codes (HTML), 203

Unpaid Item Disputes, filing, 268

unwanted bidding, 90

UPC (Universal Product Codes), 99, 132

updating
  accounts, phishing scams, 27
  credit card information, 24
  item listings, 223
  seller accounts, 20
  user ID accounts, 20

upgrading item listings, 163
  Bold option, 165
  Border option, 165
  Featured Plus! option, 166
  Gallery Featured option, 165
  Gallery option, 164
  Gift icon option, 167
  Highlight option, 166
  Home Page Featured option, 167
  Listing Designer option, 167
  subtitle option, 163

uploading item listings, Turbo Lister, 215-216

UPS (United Parcel Service), 258-259

URL (Uniform Resource Locators), 309

used retailers, 145